This is the first English translation of Johann Friedrich Daube's *Musical Dilettante: A Treatise on Composition* (Vienna 1773). Written as a practical, comprehensive guide for aristocratic dilettantes wishing to compose instrumental chamber music for their social entertainment, the treatise covers genres from duets to double fugues, and includes the earliest instruction in string quartets and idiomatic orchestration of symphonies.

Daube's *Musical Dilettante* has long been overlooked due to his better-known *Thorough-Bass in Three Chords* (1756). Nevertheless, *Musical Dilettante* is the keystone of Daube's theoretical writing, and offers the most comprehensive view of *galant* composition available in a single volume. The signature of *Musical Dilettante* is its unique textural emphasis, and Daube's examples sparkle with *concertante* interplay, conversational part-writing and idiomatic instrumentation. These features combine to create a volume which is not only a theoretical treatise but a record of the aesthetic and musical values of the day. The volume includes an introduction to Daube's life and theoretical works and a bibliography.

CAMBRIDGE STUDIES IN MUSIC THEORY
AND ANALYSIS

GENERAL EDITOR: IAN BENT

THE MUSICAL DILETTANTE:
A TREATISE ON COMPOSITION BY J. F. DAUBE

TITLES IN THIS SERIES

THE MUSICAL DILETTANTE

A TREATISE ON COMPOSITION BY
J. F. DAUBE

Translated and edited by
Susan P. Snook-Luther

CAMBRIDGE
UNIVERSITY PRESS

Published by the Press Syndicate of the University of Cambridge
The Pitt Building, Trumpington Street, Cambridge CB2 IRP
40 West 20th Street, New York, NY 10011–4211, USA
10 Stamford Road, Oakleigh, Victoria 3166, Australia

First published 1992

Printed in Great Britain at the University Press, Cambridge

A catalogue record for this book is available from the British Library

Library of Congress cataloguing in publication data

Daube, J. F. (Johann Friedrich), 1730–1797.
[Musikalische Dilettant. English]
The Musical Dilettante: a Treatise on Composition / by J. F. Daube
translated and edited by Susan P. Snook–Luther.
p.   cm. – (Cambridge Studies in Music Theory and Analysis)
Translation of: Der musikalische Dilettant.
Includes bibliographical references (p.   ) and index.
ISBN 0 521 36564 3 (hardback)
1. Composition (Music) 2. Music – Theory – 18th century.
I. Snook-Luther, Susan P. (Susan Pauline), 1943–II. Title. III. Series.
MT40.D2313 1991
781.3 – dc20 90–25963 CIP MN

ISBN 0 521 36564 3 hardback

CONTENTS

FOREWORD BY IAN BENT

Theory and analysis are in one sense reciprocals: if analysis opens up a musical structure or style to inspection, inventorying its components, identifying its connective forces, providing a description adequate to some live experience, then theory generalizes from such data, predicting what the analyst will find in other cases within a given structural or stylistic orbit, devising systems by which other works – as yet unwritten – might be generated. Conversely, if theory intuits how musical systems operate, then analysis furnishes feedback to such imaginative intuitions, rendering them more insightful. In this sense, they are like two hemispheres that fit together to form a globe (or cerebrum!), functioning deductively as investigation and abstraction, inductively as hypothesis and verification, and in practice forming a chain of alternating activities.

Professionally, on the other hand, "theory" now denotes a whole subdiscipline of the general field of musicology. Analysis often appears to be a subordinate category within the larger activity of theory. After all, there is theory that does not require analysis. Theorists may engage in building systems or formulating strategies for use by composers; and these almost by definition have no use for analysis. Others may conduct experimental research into the sound-materials of music or the cognitive processes of the human mind, to which analysis may be wholly inappropriate. And on the other hand, historians habitually use analysis as a tool for understanding the classes of composition – repertories, "outputs," "periods," works, versions, sketches, and so forth – that they study. Professionally, then, our ideal image of twin hemispheres is replaced by an intersection: an area that exists in common between two subdisciplines. Seen from this viewpoint, analysis reciprocates in two directions: with certain kinds of theoretical enquiry, and with certain kinds of historical enquiry. In the former case, analysis has tended to be used in rather orthodox modes, in the latter in a more eclectic fashion; but that does not mean that analysis in the service of theory is necessarily more exact, more "scientific," than analysis in the service of history.

The above epistemological excursion is by no means irrelevant to the present series. Cambridge Studies in Music Theory and Analysis is intended to present the work of theorists and of analysts. It has been designed to include "pure" theory – that is, theoretical formulation with a minimum of analytical exemplification; "pure" analysis – that is, practical analysis with a minimum of theoretical underpinning; and writings that fall at points along the spectrum between the two extremes. In these capacities, it aims to illuminate music, as work and as process.

However, theory and analysis are not the exclusive preserves of the present day. As subjects in their own right, they are diachronic. The former is coeval with the very study of music itself, and extends far beyond the confines of Western culture; the latter, defined broadly, has several centuries of past practice. Moreover, they have been dynamic, not static fields throughout their histories. Consequently, studying earlier music through the eyes of its own contemporary theory helps us to escape (when we need to, not that we should make a dogma out of it) from the preconceptions of our own age. Studying earlier analyses does this too, and in a particularly sharply focused way; at the same time it gives us the opportunity to re-evaluate past analytical methods for present purposes, such as is happening currently, for example, with the long-despised methods of hermeneutic analysis of the late nineteenth century. The series thus includes editions and translations of major works of past theory, and also studies in the history of theory.

Heinrich Christoph Koch, nowadays more widely known than his older contemporary Johann Friedrich Daube, discusses in detail, in his *Versuch einer Anleitung zur Composition* of 1782–93, the principal instrumental forms of music, and quotes extensively from German orchestral and vocal music of the 1760s and 1770s, at times even in open score. Yet he displays no apparent sensitivity to the quality of sound that those pieces produced. He could quote 132 bars of the Andantino of Haydn's Symphony No. 42, he could give in score ten bars of a cantata by Scheinpflug using violin figuration alternating with oboes, he could quote the entire Grave section of a French overture, and show no consciousness of their sound-colours. By contrast, Daube's acute sensitivity to timbre, dynamic and attack, comes through right from the beginning. Thus, whereas Koch simply defines open-position chords, Daube advises that their effect is "good on the organ, harpsichord, or piano, but still better when played by two violins and a violoncello." Where Koch introduces the first-inversion chord purely in pitch terms, Daube shows it with the third played by cello *sfz* slurring to the root of the next chord. Whereas Koch's entire discussion of harmony and counterpoint is conducted in monochrome, Daube's is unfolded in the vivid sound-world of mid-eighteenth-century flutes and oboes, horns, and strings.

In short, his is an awareness of the sonic world of music that we do not associate with eighteenth-century writing about music. We find it rarely before Antoine Reicha's *Cours de composition musicale, ou Traité complet et raisonné d'harmonie pratique*, dating from *c*.1816–18, the last forty pages of which offer us a miniature instrumentation manual under the title "The Treatment of Harmony within the Orchestra"; and ultimately before Berlioz's celebrated *Grand traité d'instrumentation et d'orchestration modernes* of 1843.

In Daube's *Der musikalische Dilettant* of 1773 we find a down-to-earthness, an avoidance of abstraction, an immediacy, which is a delight to read. Daube adopts a "how-to-do-it" approach to composition that must have appealed to the readers of his time, and affords us today some real insight into the late eighteenth-century Kapellmeister at work. Of most particular interest is the chapter "Composition in five and more parts," in which we learn how to employ sustained and moving lines simultaneously, how to fashion textures and distribute melodic motives, and how to blend strings with wind and brass, and how to deploy solo instruments.

TRANSLATOR'S PREFACE

In translating J. F. Daube's *The Musical Dilettante: A Treatise on Composition* (1773), my aim has been to provide an accurate rendering of the author's ideas, while preserving the clarity and fluency of his prose.

Daube occasionally describes procedures and styles without using technical labels, since many of the concepts presented antedate standardized terminology, i.e., quartet styles and fugal writing. This practice is reflected in the translation, although modern terms sometimes appear in square brackets and/or in footnotes for the sake of brevity and clarification. In the same vein, and partly to preserve the original connotative value, descriptive German terms are often expressed literally, rather than by a more common foreign equivalent, i.e., "der herrschende Akkord" as "the ruling chord" rather than "the tonic chord," and "der Endigungston" as "the ending tone" rather than "the final, finalis, or tonic note." (Also, Daube's use of "die Note" always carries a rhythmic connotation, and is therefore translated as "note," to distinguish it from the more commonly used "Ton," which usually refers primarily to pitch.)

For insight into eighteenth-century shades of meaning of German words and musical terms, I have consulted Sulzer's *Allgemeine Theorie* (1771, 1774), Koch's *Lexicon* (1802), and Adelung's *Wörterbuch* (1796), among others. In cases in which the meaning of an entire clause or section was ambiguous, I based my interpretation upon accompanying examples, or passages dealing with similar concepts in Daube's other theoretical works.

In keeping with its accessible nature, the original *Der Musikalische Dilettant* contained no Latin terms, with the exception of "feste Gesang (Cantus firmus)" in the penultimate paragraph of the book. Other foreign words were limited to Italian terms common in musical directives, i.e., "Allegro." Since the present work is intended specifically for English-speaking readers, I have translated all foreign language quotations that occur in the introduction and footnotes to the text, citing – but not necessarily quoting – published English translations.

In editing Daube's musical examples, the forms of clef signs, sharps, rests and repeat signs have been modernized and dynamic markings standardized to f and p, etc. Brackets and braces have been added where needed and obvious printing errors in clef placement and key signatures have been corrected without editorial comment.

Triplet markings, added only where necessary for consistency within an example or for clarity or rhythmic intention, are indicated as editorial. Ambiguously placed slur markings have been interpreted in the light of Daube's usage in other instances. However, with a few indicated exceptions, obvious or apparent omissions of articulation marks

in recurring figures have been left as authentic reminders of the difficulties and incon-
sistencies of eighteenth-century moveable type. Likewise the internal repeat signs used
for short passages – a frequent shorthand of eighteenth-century printers – have been
retained, thus preserving to some extent the appearance of the original examples.

It gives me great satisfaction to introduce Daube's *The Musical Dilettante* (1773) – an
elegant artistic representative of *galant* musical thought – to the English-speaking
audience. With Daube I would say that "at least we spared no time nor effort," and hope
that readers might find this work a "valuable and enjoyable" guide to "the purest pleasure
in music."

In publishing this work, I would like to express my appreciation to all the people
who have generously shared with me their knowledge and skills over the years; despite
the general nature of this acknowledgment, I am keenly aware of their individual
contributions.

Of those directly involved in this project, I am most indebted to Dr. Leonard G.
Ratner, Professor Emeritus of Music at Stanford University, for years of rewarding study,
for suggesting Daube's *Dilettante* as my dissertation topic, and for many thought-
provoking insights along the way.

I am also grateful to the late Dr. Imogene Horsley, formerly Associate Professor
of Music at Stanford University, for her careful reading of my commentary and
knowledgeable discussions of fugal theory; and to Dr. Kurt Mueller-Vollmer, Professor of
German Studies and Humanities at Stanford University, for his assistance with the translation and enlightening glimpses into German culture.

For facilitating my European research, thanks are offered to Dr. William Loran
Crosten, Professor Emeritus of Music and former Stanford University Music Department
Chairman; Dr. Lincoln Moses, former Dean of Graduate Studies at Stanford; Dr. Peter
Frank, Curator of Germanic Collections and Lecturer in German Studies at Stanford
University; Dr. Robert Rosenzweig, former Vice Provost of Stanford University;
Dr. Franz Steiniger, Director of the Department of Printed Books, Austrian National
Library, Vienna; Dr. Günter Brosche, Director of the Music Collection, Austrian
National Library, Vienna; and Dr. Robert Münster of the Music Division of the Bavarian
National Library, Munich.

I would also like to thank the staff of the Stanford University Libraries, especially
Mr. Edward E. Colby, Stanford Music Librarian (1949–78) and Lecturer in Music
(1951–79) at Stanford University, for his generous help and expertise in the location
of materials needed for this project; Drs. Katharina and Momme Mommsen, Professor
and Professor Emeritus of German Literature at Stanford University; Elfie Wiesendanger,
Assistant Curator of Germanic Collections at Stanford University; Elizabeth Green,
research librarian at Stanford University; the staff of the University of Wyoming Library,
particularly Joanna D. Orr, Dee Jewett, Elizabeth Latham, Paul B. Cors, Karen Lange and
Betsy Porter; Beth Bartlett, Music Librarian at the University of Mississippi; Marsha
M. Parsons, Head Librarian, Fine Arts Library at the University of Texas at Austin;
Dr. Raymond van De Moortell, Curator of the de Bellis Collection of the California State

University System at San Francisco State, and Colomba Ghigliotti, Library Assistant; and Dr. Karl Kroeger, Associate Professor and Head of the University of Colorado Music Library at Boulder.

I am also grateful to Dr. Deborah Hayes, Associate Professor of Music History at the University of Colorado at Boulder, for encouraging me to pursue the publication of this work, and for providing various bibliographic details; Mr. Howard O. Allen of my home-town of Saratoga, California for a solid grounding in the German language at Campbell Union High School and for reading my preliminary translation; Fr. Theodore J. Rynes, SJ, Assistant Professor of English at the University of Santa Clara, for his encouragement, perspective, and editorial advice; and Mrs. Jane Edwards of San Jose, California for a cheerful, efficient application of her typographical skills.

It has been a great pleasure to work with the editors at Cambridge University Press. I would especially like to thank Penny Souster and Ian Bent for bringing this work to publication and Ian Bent for his patient help and expert guidance during the process.

I would also like to thank my husband, Dr. David C. Snook-Luther, for sharing his computer skills, patiently extricating my Daube files from countless quagmires, and for his support of my musicological efforts.

It is with profound and lasting gratitude that I dedicate this book – "our book" – to my parents, Davis William Snook and Paulina Klaus Snook; only they can realize the magnitude of their contributions to its completion.

INTRODUCTION

DAUBE'S LIFE AND SURROUNDINGS

In 1773 Johann Friedrich Daube introduced to the musical society of Vienna a unique and timely work, *Der Musikalische Dilettant: eine Abhandlung der Komposition*. This treatise on *galant* chamber music composition constitutes the keystone of Daube's theoretical writing. Yet its significance as an enlightening reflection of *galant* tastes and techniques has not been widely recognized, due perhaps to the attention given his *General-Baß in drey Accorden* (1756), to confusion surrounding its identity as the second in a projected series of four *Dilettant* publications, and to the relative obscurity of its author in the history of music theory.[1]

Daube's awareness of the latest musical trends and his uniquely practical approach to composition in the current style stem from his experience as a performer on lute and flute in some of the foremost musical centers in the German-speaking lands – Berlin, Stuttgart-Ludwigsburg, Augsburg, and Vienna – where he worked among those who were influential in shaping musical styles and tastes.

The earliest document in which "ein Lautenist Taube" is mentioned, his official appointment in 1744 as chamber lutenist to Duke Karl Eugen von Württemburg (1728–93), establishes his former residence as Berlin, where Karl Eugen had been a pupil of C. P. E. Bach at the court of Frederick the Great. Although Daube's musical activities in Berlin remain undocumented, circumstantial evidence points toward some connection with the court,[2] where he may have performed at the royal opera house, or studied with Ernst Gottlieb Baron (1696–1760) and J. J. Quantz (1697–1773), eminent teachers of lute and flute respectively. Moreover, Daube was familiar with the accompaniment style of "Bach" (presumably C. P. E.), which he praises in his *General-Baß*,[3] and the *goût-moderne* designation of his six published lute sonatas suggests the influence of the French-speaking Berlin court.

---

[1] A comparison of articles on Daube in eighteenth-, nineteenth-, and twentieth-century lexica produces a bewildering array of biographical discrepancies and bibliographical contradictions. The most accurate biographical information available is found in Michael Karbaum, "Das theoretische Werk Johann Friedrich Daubes."

[2] Reichert (*MGG*, vol. III, col. 27) and Buelow (*The New Grove*, vol. V, p. 253) state that Daube was a theorbist at the Berlin court of Frederick the Great at the age of eleven. Karbaum, who searched the Berlin archives with no result, feels that this assertion goes back to the above mentioned document, which, however, does not establish Daube's appointment or function at the court, nor his age ("Das theoretische Werk," p. 13). Reichert says that Daube was born in 1733 and died in 1797 "im 64. Lebensjahr," but Karbaum, based on an obituary notice written by Daube on the death of his wife, deduces that he was born "before 1730" in the former area of Hessendarmstadt (ibid., pp 10–11).

[3] See p. 204, Eng. trans., pp. 259–60.

I

The cosmopolitan *Aufklärung* atmosphere of eighteenth-century Berlin was enthusi-
astically fostered by King Frederick, who invited to his court the most prominent writers
and artists of Europe. The city became known for the publication of literary dialectics
and musical criticism, and as a flourishing center of musical performance. Regular
musical activities included meetings of the Friday Academy (one of the first amateur
chamber music organizations in Berlin), frequent opera productions reflecting Frederick's
preference for German composers, Italian singers, and French dancers,[4] and court *Abend-
musiken* featuring the monarch performing on the flute.

Among the principal musicians with whom Daube must have come into contact
in Berlin were Quantz, the king's flute teacher; C. P. E. Bach, the king's accompanist;
Karl Heinrich Graun (1704–57), Kapellmeister, whose works dominated the Berlin
operatic scene; Johann Gottlieb Graun (1698–1771), concertmaster; Johann Friedrich
Agricola (1720–74), composer and later director of the opera; Christoph Nichelmann
(1717–62), assistant to C. P. E. Bach; Franz Benda (1709–86), violinist; and lutenist
Baron. The compositions of this group included *galant* chamber music, Italian-style
opera, keyboard pieces in the *empfindsamer Stil*, contrapuntal sacred music, and the solo
songs of the "first Berlin school." Whatever Daube's position may have been in this
milieu, there emerges in his later works an acquaintance with the rich variety of musical
styles and wide range of aesthetic ideas which recalls the associations of his Berlin years.

In 1744 the sixteen-year-old Prince Karl Eugen left Berlin to assume the title of
Duke of Württemburg at Stuttgart-Ludwigsburg, taking with him "einen Lautenisten
Nahmens Taube."[5] In July, soon after Karl Eugen's coronation, Daube received his official
appointment as chamber lutenist, and after 1750 he also became chamber flutist, a well-
paid position which he held until May 1755. During this period Daube also found time
to compose and write. In 1746 J. U. Haffner of Nürnberg published Daube's Op. 1,
"Six sonates pour le Luth dans le goût moderne,"[6] and by the summer of 1754 Daube
had completed his first theoretical work, *General-Baß in drey Accorden*; this was published
in 1756 with a dedication to Karl Eugen. It was also during this period, in 1746, that
Daube married Susanna Margaretha Schubhart.[7]

In May 1755 Daube was suddenly dismissed from his position, possibly because of
the gradual demise of the lute, or possibly because of the increasing importation of
Italian musicians after Nicolò Jommelli (1714–74) became Karl Eugen's Kapellmeister.[8]
The improbability of reinstatement in either case might explain why Daube's letters of
petition to the duke stated not only his preference for musical employment, but also his
secretarial qualifications and knowledge of Latin, French, and Italian. In 1756, the year

[4] Helm, *Frederick the Great*, p. 73.

[5] From the *Spezialdekret* authorizing Daube's appointment. Cited in Karbaum, "Das theoretische Werk," p. 20.

[6] These sonatas are now missing, according to Hans Neemann in the forward to his edition of Daube's "Trio in
D-Moll für Laute, Flöte (Violine) und Klavier" in *Alte Haus- und Kammer-musik mit Laute* (1927). See also Heinrich
Lemacher, *Handbuch der Hausmusik*, p. 355.

[7] Karbaum, "Das theoretische Werk," p. 21.

[8] Karbaum, "Das theoretische Werk," p. 22. See Abert, *Jommelli*, p. 69.

his *General-Baß* appeared in print, Daube obtained the poorly paid position of second orchestral flutist, in which he remained until 1765.[9]

In many respects Karl Eugen's musical establishment at the Württemburg court was modeled upon that of Frederick the Great at Berlin. Like Frederick, the young duke was an enthusiastic dilettante musician, "a good player on the harpsichord,"[10] who frequently participated in the musical activities of his court; like Frederick, Karl Eugen constructed a magnificent building in which to stage theatrical works.

The theatre is immense, and is open at the back of the stage, where there is an amphitheatre, in the open air, which is sometimes filled with people, to produce effects in perspective; it is built, as are all the theatres which I had yet seen in Germany, upon the Italian model.[11]

The operatic productions given here likewise resembled those of the corresponding Berlin repertory – music in the Italian style, usually performed by Italian singers and French dancers. Also, as in Berlin, there was an ample complement of instrumentalists. In 1745 Daube was listed among thirty-one instrumentalists in the Kapelle which, during his tenure, almost doubled in size.[12] The orchestra at Karl Eugen's court became known as one of the finest in Germany. Christian Friedrich Daniel Schubart (1739–91) described it as consisting of "the foremost virtuosos in the world."[13] Among these were violinists Antonio Lolli (renowned for his technical ability), and Pietro Nardini (famous for his cantabile style). Although many of Daube's orchestral colleagues were also known for their compositions, the major works heard at court were those of Karl Eugen's current Kapellmeister, Giuseppe Antonio Brescianello (1744–51), and Ignaz Holzbauer of Vienna (1751–3), who subsequently assumed a similar position in Mannheim. In 1753 Jommelli was appointed Kapellmeister at Stuttgart, and "from this time on the musical taste of this region became entirely italianized."[14] Also heard were the ballet pantomimes of Florian Deller (*c*. 1730–1774), composed for Karl Eugen's famous French dancing master, Jean-Georges Noverre (1727–1810).

The italianate atmosphere of the Stuttgart Hofkapelle is perhaps responsible for the pseudonym, "Colomba," with which "der lautenist Taube" signed some of his compositions.[15] ("Colomba" and "Taube" mean "dove" in Italian and German respectively.) More subtle influences of Daube's twenty-one years in Stuttgart appear in his later works, especially in *Der Musikalische Dilettant* of 1773. Daube's absolute command of the chamber music idiom, his knowledge of effective scoring, and familiarity with current stylistic traits (including the Italian cantabile and symphonic violin figuration), bespeak a rich and intensive musical experience gained through the interaction of performance and composition. Certainly the musical environment of the Württemberg court must have

[9] Karbaum ("Das theoretische Werk," p. 23) says that no notice of Daube's reinstatement appeared in the *Württemburgischen Staatshandbüchern* until 1758.

[10] Burney, *Present State* (2/1775), vol. I, p. 105; *Musical Tours*, ed. Scholes (1959), vol. II, p. 38.

[11] Burney, *Present State* (2/1775), vol. I, p. 104; *Musical Tours*, ed. Scholes (1959), vol. II, p. 37.

[12] Sittard, *Geschichte* (1890), vol. II, pp. 30, 58.

[13] Schubart, *Ideen* (1806), p. 156.

[14] Schubart, *Ideen* (1806), p. 150.

[15] Pohlmann, *Laute*, p. 79.

been stimulating. In 1772 Dr. Charles Burney wrote that "the operas and musical establishments of [Karl Eugen], used, during the . . . direction of Jommelli, to be the best and most splendid in Germany. . . ."[16] Once again, as in Berlin, Daube was involved in the musical life of a major European court at the very height of its brilliance.

The year 1765 marked two important events in Daube's life – the publication, once again by Haffner, of his "Sonata in F für Cembalo" in Vol. XI of the *Oeuvres mélées*,[17] and his move from Stuttgart to Augsburg. The latter involved more than a mere change of location. Until this time Daube had worked amid the court chamber music and operatic productions fostered by his royal patrons. The musical life of Augsburg, however, was rooted in a long tradition of Catholic church music and, more recently, of Lutheran church music.

Ever since [Augsburg] became the residence of a bishop, church music has blossomed remarkably there. . . . For several centuries the vespers and choirs have been excellently appointed. Even now pieces from that venerable, ancient time, which completely satisfy the ear and heart of the connoisseur, are performed there. . . . As is well known, the reformation divided this city into two parts. . . . The Lutherans . . . ushered in the German church chorale with such fervour that it can be compared with the best German cities. Even today in the Barfüßerkirche one hears this singing in its original purity.[18]

Catholic church music in Augsburg also impressed Burney during his visit of 1772: "The music of the mass was in a good style; there was an agreeable mixture of ancient and modern. . . ."[19] – a striking comment, since the same criterion of good style was advocated by Daube in *Der Musikalische Dilettant* of 1773. Perhaps the Augsburg musical scene provided the opportunity for Daube, already well versed in the chamber and operatic styles, to assimilate also the ecclesiastical style, and thereby to achieve the balance betweens "ancient and modern" which characterizes that work.

Daube's move to Augsburg also represents the growing tendency of German musicians to leave the relative security of royal patronage in favor of the independence and financial uncertainty of the free-lance musician and writer. Fortunately, the latter third of the century saw the development of a commercial trend in music; a sharp rise in music publishing and journalistic activities, as well as an increasing number of public concerts and an expansion of the bourgeoisie dilettante market for instruments and instruction,[20] provided new opportunities for native musicians.

Augsburg, in addition to being a center of church music, was the seat of an academy established by J. D. Herz and chartered by Emperor Franz I in 1753.[21] From this group –

[16] Burney, *Present State* (2/1775), vol. I, p. 100; *Musical Tours*, ed. Scholes (1959), vol. II, p. 36.

[17] In *Oeuvres mélées contenant VI. sonates pour le clavecin de tant de plus célèbres compositeurs . . .* , Partie XI (Nürnberg: Haffner, 1765). This series, published between 1755 and 1765, contains seventy-two sonatas in twelve volumes. Other composers represented include C. P. E. Bach, G. G. Krebs, L. Mozart, G. A. Scheibe, and G. C. Wagenseil (RISM, vol. II, pp. 271–2). For excerpts and discussion, see Lange, *Beiträge*, pp. 9–11, 12, 27, Anlage pp. 3, 5–7, 8, 27. For a brief description, see Newman, *Sonata in the Classic Era*, p. 322.

[18] Schubart, *Ideen* (1806), p. 211.

[19] Burney, *Present State* (2/1775), vol. I, p. 117; *Musical Tours*, ed. Scholes (1959), vol. II, p. 42.

[20] Gericke, *Musikalienhandel*, pp. 11–15.

[21] Karbaum, "Das theoretische Werk," p. 28.

which included such prominent members as Johann Christoph Gottsched (Leipzig), Johann Heinrich I (Kassel), Georg Sulzer (Berlin), and Johann Joachim Winckelmann (Rome) – Daube received a journalistic opportunity and the title of "Rath and erster Secretär der Kaiserlichen Francischen Akademie der freyen Künste und Wissenschaften."[22] In all probability, Daube had previous contacts in Augsburg through his published lute sonatas, which had been sold there by the publishing firm of J. J. Lotter.[23] But his main contact with the Academy seems to have been Baron von Milkan, a gentleman associated with the Württemburg court, who was appointed Director generalis of the Academy in 1757.[24]

About 1769 Daube's work as a correspondent for the Augsburg Academy took him to Vienna, where he would spend the remaining twenty-eight years of his life in another of the great musical centers of Europe.

Indeed, Vienna is so rich in composers, and incloses within its walls such a number of musicians of superior merit, that, it is but just to allow it to be, among German cities, the imperial seat of music, as well as of power.[25]

Thus Burney summed up his impressions of the musical life of Vienna in 1772. His vivid descriptions paint a colorful picture of the setting in which Daube produced the majority of his theoretical works – *Der Musikalische Dilettant: eine Wochenschrift / eine Abhandlung des Generalbaßes (1770/71)*, *Der Musikalische Dilettant: eine Abhandlung der Komposition (1773)*, *Beweis . . . gottesdienstliche Musik (1782)*, and *Anleitung zur Erfindung der Melodie (1797/98)*.

After arriving in Vienna, Daube resided modestly in the Leopoldstadt. His address was "Haus Nr. 145 zum Goldenes Rössel" until the death of his wife in 1790, and thereafter "Hofriemerhaus Nr. 345" until his death, mentioned in a brief obituary in the *Wiener Zeitung* of 30 September 1797.[26]

Although evidence of Daube's connection with the Augsburg Academy during this period is sparse, it is known that *Der Musikalische Dilettant* (1770) was advertised in the *Augsburger Kunstzeitung*,[27] and that, about the same time, the Augsburg Academy became an outlet for the distribution of the publications of Johann Thomas Edler von Trattner (1717–98), the Viennese publisher of *Der Musikalische Dilettant* (1773). Moreover, in 1773 the *Augsburg Akademiezeitung* officially sought to merge with the *Wiener Realzeitung* and the related *K. K. Anzeigen*,[28] for which Daube may have worked as a journalist.[29]

[22] Karbaum, "Das theoretische Werk," p. 33. Reichert seems unconvinced that Daube actually lived in Augsburg, despite his association with the academy ("Daube," *MGG*, vol. III, cols. 27–8).

[23] Layer, *Catalogus Musicus II*, p. 22.

[24] Karbaum, "Das theoretische Werk," p. 32. See F. Freude, "Die kaiserlich francischen Akademie der freien Künste und Wissenschaften in Augsburg," in *Zs. d. historischen Verein für Schwaben und Neuburg*, vol. XXXIV (1908), pp. 1ff.

[25] Burney, *Present State* (2/1775), vol. I, p. 368; *Musical Tours*, ed. Scholes (1959), vol. II, p. 124.

[26] Karbaum, "Das theoretische Werk," pp. 36, 45.

[27] Freystätter, *Zeitschriften*, p. 19.

[28] Karbaum, "Das theoretische Werk," pp. 34, 128. See *Realzeitung*, vol. III (1773), Preliminary Announcement.

[29] Karbaum ("Das theoretische Werk," pp. 34, 180) recognizes Daube's hand in an article in the *Anzeigen*, vol. III/48 (Vienna: von Ghelen, 1 Dec. 1773), pp. 382ff, entitled "Gellertische Urtheile von der Musik," which presents views and opinions found in Daube's treatises. The continuation, "Von einiger Componisten," deals with composers with whose works he was familiar.

The only tangible documentation of Daube's activities in Vienna is provided by his publications and related notices, but circumstances surrounding several of his works[30] suggest that he continued to compose – not only in connection with his publications, but also, as was the custom, for specific occasions. Nor would Daube have neglected performance; a lute was among the few possessions he retained until his death.[31] But we can only make an informed guess as to Daube's position in the musical-social structure of the city.

The imperial court, center of the Austro-Hungarian Holy Roman Empire, played an influential role in the cultivation of music, encouraging operatic, sacred, and chamber music.

One of the main musical positions at court was that of Kapellmeister, even though, due to war-related economic measures, the court band *K. K. Hof- und Kammermusik* had reached a low of twenty members by 1772. In 1771 Kapellmeister Florian Gassman (1723–74) founded the *Tonkünstler Societät*, the oldest organized music association and first public concert institute in Vienna. Each year it presented two double concerts for the benefit of widows and orphans of Austrian musicians.[32] Since the Hofkapelle formed the core of the *Tonkünstler Societät*, the artistry of the imperial musicians became available, on occasion, to the public. Also available a few years later were the popular *Liebhaber Konzerte* "in der Mehlgrube" and "im Augarten."[33] However, important as these performances may have been in initiating public concerts in Vienna, they were, at the time, exceptional events.

Far more prevalent than public concerts were the *Akademien* for invited guests, given in the elegant residences of the Viennese aristocracy. Hanslick compares the *Tonkünstler Societät* to the sun, around which revolved innumerable planets – the private Kapellen and dilettante gatherings of the nobility – but notes that the planets were the predominant force.[34] Yet the musical activities of the imperial court were emulated throughout Vienna. Many distinguished noblemen supported a Kapelle of performers and composers, and required a constant supply of *galant* entertainment music for *Akademien*, table music, birthday celebrations, serenades, etc. Other noblemen, acting as patrons on a more casual basis, occasionally ordered a composition or invited professional musicians to perform in their homes. Burney describes an after-dinner concert at which Haydn quartets were played by "M. Startzler, . . . M. Ordonetz; count Brühl, . . . and M. Weigel."[35]

The inclusion of a titled performer in the above ensemble was not unusual, but rather indicative of the fashion for dilettantism among the nobility, many of whom studied an

[30] Namely, the six quartets to be noted below and a song (later included in *Der Musikalische Dillettant* of 1771) entitled "Der Trost des durchlauchtigst-kaiserlichen Hauses bey der höchsten Versammlung in Wien im Heumonate 1770. Besungen von Hr. F. A. v. Raab: in die Musik gebracht von Hr. Daube." Karbaum ("Das theoretische Werk," p. 43) thinks the reference is to a reunion of the imperial family in July 1770.

[31] Karbaum, "Das theoretische Werk," p. 245.

[32] Hanslick, *Geschichte* (1869), pp. 6, 8.

[33] Hanslick, *Geschichte* (1869), p. 69.

[34] Hanslick, *Geschichte* (1869), p. 36.

[35] Burney, *Present State* (2/1775), vol. I, p. 294; *Musical Tours*, ed. Scholes (1959), vol. II, p. 100.

instrument, voice, or even composition, and performed at the chamber music gatherings of élite society. In this, too, they followed a royal example, for Empress Maria Theresia (1717–80) and her children all studied music with their own Hofklaviermeister, Georg Christoph Wagenseil (1715–77) and later Joseph Anton Steffan (1726–1800).

The whole imperial family is musical: the Emperor [Joseph, reigned 1765–90] perhaps just enough for a sovereign prince, that is, with sufficient hand, both on the violoncello and harpsichord, to amuse himself; and sufficient taste and judgement to hear, understand, and receive delight from others.[36]

Dilettante activities, spreading from the court throughout the nobility and bourgeoisie, flourished in late eighteenth-century Vienna with an enthusiasm unmatched in any other city. In 1782 Mozart wrote to his father that "there are a crowd of dilettantes here, and very good ones at that, both men and women. . . ."[37] But whereas amateur musicians in most German-speaking areas organized into public *Dilettantenvereine* during the 1760s and 70s, the Viennese preferred to retain the more intimate *Dilettantenkreise* of family and friends – a practice which made it difficult for a musician new to the city to become known.[38] It was to this large but exclusive audience that Daube addressed his *Dilettant* treatises of 1770/71 and 1773.

Despite Daube's publications and his ability to serve as a performer, composer, or teacher in the *Dilettantenkreise*, the only trace of evidence to link him with this sphere of activity is the dedication of his last work, *Anleitung zur Erfindung der Melodie* (1797/98), to Herr Ignaz Grafen von Fuchs.

The warm tone of Daube's dedication, his reference to previous explanations of composition and musical style, his statement that the *Anleitung* owed its existence mainly to the count, and his inclusion of the count's family in the closing salutation, all suggest that Daube was well acquainted with the family and may even have served as their music teacher. Moreover, the 20,000-item music library of von Fuchs contained all of Daube's theoretical works, plus a symphony and six quartets in manuscript,[39] (perhaps written for one of the count's invitational *Hausabendmusiken*).

Despite the scarcity of formal public concerts, the enjoyment of music pervaded eighteenth-century Vienna. The imperial city resounded with music for all occasions, encompassing a wide variety of styles and pervading all strata of society. According to Johann Friedrich Reichardt (1752–1814) in 1783, "The court cultivated music with a passion, the nobles were the most musical that perhaps there ever had been. The entire fun-loving populace took part in the joyous art . . ."[40]

From the streets one could hear military bands, dance music, garden divertimentos, and "Wirthshaus" or "Tafelmusik." Burney reported that "there was music every day,

[36] Burney, *Present State* (2/1775), vol. I, p. 257; *Musical Tours*, ed. Scholes (1959), vol. II, p. 88.
[37] Bauer and Deutsch, *Mozart: Briefe*, vol. III, p. 208, Eng. trans., p. 804.
[38] Hanslick, *Geschichte* (1869), pp. 68, 69.
[39] Karbaum, "Das theoretische Werk," p. 42. See E. Schenk, "Eine Wiener Musiksammlung der Beethoven-Zeit," in *Festschrift Heinrich Besseler* (Leipzig, 1962), pp. 377–88.
[40] Hanslick, *Geschichte* (1869), p. 64. From "Autobiographien," *Allgemeine Musikalische Zeitung* (1813), p. 141.

during dinner . . . at the inn" where he stayed.[41] Nocturnal serenades and impromptu music-making also were prevalent.

At night two of the poor scholars of this city sung, in the court of the inn where I lodged, duets . . . very well in tune, and with feeling and taste. . . . After this there was a band of these singers, who performed through the streets a kind of glees, in three and four parts: this whole country is certainly very musical. I frequently heard the soldiers upon guard, and centinels, as well as common people, sing in parts.[42]

Music of a more formal nature was also available to everyone in church. Burney marveled at the abundance of musical services.

. . . there is scarce a church or convent in Vienna, which has not every morning its *mass in music* . . . set in parts, and performed with voices, accompanied by at least three or four violins, a tenor and base, besides the organ; and as the churches here are daily crowded, this music . . . must, in some degree, form the ear of the inhabitants. . . . And it seems as if *the national music of a country was good or bad, in proportion to that of its church service.*[43]

There are no records to link Daube directly with church music, but several aspects of his pamphlet *Beweis, daß die gottesdienstliche Musik* (1782) would seem to indicate that his activities during his Vienna years, and perhaps earlier, may have included the composition and/or performance of sacred music.

Nevertheless, the scanty documentation does suggest a shift of emphasis in Daube's activities during his Augsburg and Vienna years. While he continued to compose and – we can safely assume – to perform, his writing increased. The resulting lifetime of attainments encompassed many areas of musical endeavor. As a performer, Daube's experience included chamber, opera, and probably church styles. As a composer, he produced symphonies, solo songs, lute pieces, chamber music for many combinations, and possibly sacred music. And as an author, his surviving works (apart from his journalistic ventures) include treatises on several major topics in music theory – thorough-bass, composition, and melodic invention.

In the forward to his last work, *Anleitung zur Erfindung der Melodie*, dated 2 January 1797, during the apparent poverty of his later years, Daube spoke of his adopted city with fondness and pride. He recognized the musical wealth around him and sketched the musical scene as he saw it near the end of his twenty-eight years in Vienna.

Is Vienna not a genuine nursery, in which great men are raised? – To whom is Hayden unknown? To whom the exalted Mozart? The musicians Albrechtsberger, Bethoven, Bemucky, Eibler, Förster, Freystädtler, Gallus, Hoffmeister, Kletzinsky, Kozeluch, Kreith, Kromer, Mancini, Müller, W. Pohl, Schmid, Salieri, Süßmayer, Täuber, Wanhal, Weigl, and many others.[44] And one encounters so many virtuosos on diverse instruments! – Even among the fair sex there are some already skilled in composition, such as Mad. Auerhammer, the blind Fräule v. Paradies, Fräule v.

---

[41] Burney, *Present State* (2/1775), vol. I, p. 335; *Musical Tours*, ed. Scholes (1959), vol. II, p. 114.

[42] Burney, *Present State* (2/1775), vol. I, pp. 225–6; *Musical Tours*, ed. Scholes (1959), vol. II, p. 78.

[43] Burney, *Present State* (2/1775), vol. I, pp. 226–7; *Musical Tours*, ed. Scholes (1959), vol. II, p. 78

[44] [Daube:] Please pardon me, if I have not included everyone according to his character. Among friends of harmony, no disharmony should have the upper hand! –

Kurzbek, Mad. le Bret, Madem v. Meyer, Mad. le Comte, Mad. Beyer, etc. There are many very dexterous instrumentalists, on the fortepiano as well as on the violin and wind instruments, who moreover are mere dilettantes. And there is, so to say, almost an overabundance of professional virtuosos. – In all of Europe, it would be difficult to find such accuracy of performance, in the church, as well as at the opera and in chambers. – What then is the reason? No other, than that connoisseurs from the high nobility esteem the dedicated sons of music, especially when they perform with virtuosity (*Virtu*).

It seems fitting that Daube should have spent his last years in late eighteenth-century Vienna for, in the sequence of residences throughout his life, he followed the shifting center of musical gravity. Just as he had known Berlin at the height of its musical splendor and experienced the musical flowering of the Württemburg court, so also he witnessed an era of unprecedented greatness in Vienna, "the imperial seat of music."

DAUBE'S THEORETICAL WORKS

General-Baß (1756)

Daube's first treatise, *Thorough-Bass in Three Chords*, dedicated to Duke Karl Eugen von Württemburg, forms the harmonic basis of his later theoretical works.

General-Baß / in drey Accorden, / gegründet / in den Regeln der alt- und neuen Autoren, / nebst einem hierauf gebauten Unterricht: / wie man / aus einer jeden aufgegebenen Tonart, nur mit zwey Mittels- / Accorden, in eine von den drey und zwanzig Tonarten / die man begehret, gelangen kann, / und der / hierauf gegründeten Kunst zu präludiren, / wie auch zu jeder Melodie einen Baß zu setzen, / daß also / durch diese neue und leichte Anleitung, zugleich auch zur Composition / unmittelbar der Weg gebahnet wird / von / Johann Friedrich Daube, / Hochfürstlich-Württembergischen Kammer-Musicus. / Leipzig 1756 / Verlegts Johann Benjamin Andrä. / Buchhändler in Frankfurt am Mayn.

Shortly after Daube's *General-Baß* appeared, it was severely criticized in the *Historisch-Kritische Beyträge* by Friedrich Wilhelm Marpurg (pseudonym Dr. Gemmel), who unjustly interpreted it as an inaccurate plagiarism of Rameau's system. His criticism, in a tone of sarcasm and ridicule, was continued sporadically in the same periodical.[45] Despite, or perhaps because of, the sharp-quilled Marpurg, the *General-Baß* became Daube's best-known work. Copies are extant in widely scattered European libraries, and one was found among the books of Haydn.[46]

Later writers, such as François-Joseph Fétis, have appreciated Daube's simplification of methods. "In spite of Marpurg's severe criticism, Daube's works include some very fine things . . . [for] it was something to recall, in his time, that harmony has its simple elements."[47] Hugo Riemann, who devoted several pages to a discussion of Daube's *General-Baß*, likewise reverses Marpurg's verdict: "Daube is . . . more logical than Rameau

---

[45] Marpurg, *Historisch-Kritische Beyträge* (1754–78), vol. II, pp. 325–66, 464–74, 542–7; vol. III, pp. 465–86; vol. IV, pp. 196–246.

[46] Deutsch, "Haydns Musikbücherei," pp. 220–21.

[47] Fétis, *Biographie universelle* (1883), p. 433.

himself in carrying out the completely new theory of the meaning of the harmonies and in the attempt to actually succeed with a few basic concepts."[48]

The notion of Daube's dependence upon Rameau, begun by Marpurg, reappears in almost all later evaluations of the *General-Baß* until that of Karbaum, who pointed out Marpurg's interpretive blunders in an extensive commentary.[49] That Daube's "drey Accorden" are invariably discussed in relation to Rameau's three fundamental chords is not, in itself, surprising, considering Rameau's dominant position in eighteenth-century harmonic theory and the similarity of the chords themselves. What does seem strange is that Daube's reply to Marpurg has consistently been overlooked, a very surprising oversight since it, too, was printed in the *Historisch-Kritische Beyträge*. Daube's short, calmly worded letter includes the following passage:

He accuses me as though I had borrowed from the writings of Rameau, none of which was even available for me to read, except *Démonstration du principe de l'harmonie*, which I obtained to look at for a few hours five years ago. Neither could I have had it sooner than the summer of 1754, when my work had already been submitted to the publisher.[50]

The interesting point now becomes – not whether Daube's "drey Accorden" resembled Rameau's three fundamental chords (they did), nor whether Daube borrowed from Rameau (he apparently did not), but rather the fact that it was possible for Daube to arrive independently and pragmatically at the same conclusions that Rameau had reached by theoretical speculation.[51] The realization of this possibility in Daube's work signals a triumph for the *galant* ideal of simplification (one facet of the eighteenth-century concept of natural law as an understandable and useful order), and thereby lends an extramusical validity to the codification of the tonal system as a felicitous eighteenth-century achievement.

Der Musikalische Dilettant (1770/71)

The remainder of Daube's theoretical works were written and published in Vienna and, with the exception of one short pamphlet, can be considered a comprehensive *Musical Dilettante* series.

The first to appear was a weekly periodical published by Kurtzböck during 1770 and 1771. In the copy from the Musiksammlung der Österreichischen Nationalbibliothek (Vienna), the two yearly volumes are bound together, with two title-pages at the beginning and another before the 1771 portion. The fact that not all extant copies of this work contain all three title-pages undoubtedly accounts for many of the variants in bibliographical listings. The earliest title-page gives the following information:

---

[48] Riemann, *Musiktheorie* (1898), p. 489.

[49] Karbaum, "Das theoretische Werk," pp. 47–112.

[50] Marpurg, *Historisch-Kritische Beyträge*, vol. III (1757), pp. 69–70.

[51] The difference between Rameau's speculative approach in 1722 and Daube's practical approach in 1756 illustrates the subtle shift in point of view from rationalization to observation of facts discussed by Becker in *The Heavenly City*, pp. 21–2.

Der / Musikalische Dillettante / eine / Wochenschrift / Wien / gedruckt bey Joseph Kürzbocken
N. Oe. Landschafts- / und Universitätsbuchdruckern. / 1770.

The 1771 title-page (when present) appears in front of the original title-page and includes
a subtitle.

*Der / Musikalische Dillettant / eine / Abhandlung des Generalbasses / durch alle 24 Tonarten, mit
untermengten Opernarien, u. Solis, Duet- / ten und Trio für die meisten Instrumenten, /* von / Johann
Friedrich Daube / Rath und erster Secretair / der kaiserl. Franciscischen Akademie der freyen /
Künste und Wissenschaften in Wien / und Augsburg / Erster Band / Mit röm. Kaiserl. aller-
gnädigstem Privilegio / Wien / gedruckt bey Joseph Kurtzböck K. K. illyrisch- und orientalischen
Hof- wie auch N. Oe. / Landschafts- und Universitätsbuchdruckern. / 1771.

Another 1771 title-page, identical except for "Zweyter Band," marks the yearly division
in some copies.

Neither title-page mentions that the periodical was meant to continue. But a notice
in the *K. K. Realzeitung* in March 1771 makes it clear that future issues dealing with
other subjects were planned.[52] Nevertheless, the Kurtzböck publication was terminated
that year, at the conclusion of the discussion of thorough-bass.

This useful musical work for beginners and connoisseurs of music contains not only a short,
basic, and clear treatment of the origin, continuation, and growth of music, but chiefly a
fundamental method in thorough-bass and composition . . . moreover it soon will deal with musical style and the invention of melody. Further, the amateur will find well-written musical pieces
for the keyboard and other instruments . . .[53]

The "musikalische Stücke" which comprise half of each weekly issue have no relationship to the concurrent instruction in thorough-bass, which progresses systematically
by keys, but are independent works for diverse combinations of instruments and voices.
Many are anonymous. Most can probably be attributed to Daube.[54] Other composers
represented include Daube's Stuttgart colleagues Jommelli and Deller, the Neapolitans
Baldassare Galuppi (1706–95) and Giuseppe Sarti (1729–1802), and the Viennese Wagenseil, Joseph Starzer (1726–87), and Haydn.

The thorough-bass material presented in *Der Musikalische Dilettant* (1770/71) is essentially an abridged and simplified version of *General-Baß in drey Accorden*. At the end of
the *General-Baß*, Daube had mentioned that instruction in composition would follow
"in the second part." No sequel ensued. But fourteen years later, beginning what was
intended to be a continuing *Dilettant* series, Daube needed to acquaint his new, Viennese
audience with his theory of thorough-bass. Then, with his harmonic basis established,
he hoped again to proceed with the long-planned work on composition. Thus viewed,
Der Musikalische Dilettant (1770/71) represents a second attempt to lay the preparatory
groundwork for a comprehensive series.

---

[52] It is listed among seven German musical periodicals begun between 1761 and 1780 in Kirchner's *Die Grundlage des
deutschen Zeitschriftenwesens* (vol. II, pp. 109, 335).

[53] *Kaiserlich Königliche allergnädigst privilegirte Realzeitung der Wissenschaften, Künste und der Kommerzien*, vol. 2/11
(Vienna: Kurtzböck, 11 March 1771), pp. 177–8.

[54] Karbaum, "Das theoretische Werk," p. 169, n. 1.

Der Musikalische Dilettant (1773)

Daube's treatise on composition finally materialized as

Der / Musikalische Dilettant: / eine / Abhandlung der Komposition, / welche / nicht allein die neuesten Setzarten der zwo- drey- und mehrstimmigen Sachen; / sondern auch die meisten künstlichen Gattungen der alten Kanons: der / einfachen und Doppelfugen, deutlich vorträgt, und durch ausgesuchte / Beyspiele erkläret. / Von / Johann Friederich Daube, / Rath und erster Seckretär der Kaiserl. Franciscischen Akademie der freyen / Künste und Wissenschaften in Wien und Augspurg. / Mit Röm. Kaiserl. allergnädigsten Privilegio. / WIEN, / gedruckt bey Johann Thomas Edlen von Trattnern, / kaiserl. königl. Hofbuchdruckern und Buchhändlern. / 1773.

This book has often been confused with the earlier *Dilettant*, and in the article "Daube" in *Die Musik in Geschichte und Gegenwart*, this subtitle is erroneously connected with the 1770 publication. There are three main points of distinction between the two works: the 1773 *Dilettant* deals with composition rather than thorough-bass; it originated as a book rather than a periodical; it was published by von Trattner rather than Kurtzböck.[55]

The publisher of *The Musical Dilettante* (1773), von Trattner, was one of the richest and most eminent commoners of Vienna. An orphan who gradually rose to the position of court book dealer and book printer to Empress Maria Theresia, von Trattner printed and published more than any of his predecessors and was the most important Viennese music dealer of his time. Instead of following the custom of depending on newspaper advertisements, von Trattner even put out his own catalog. For this reason the scarcity of his announcements in the *Wienerisches Diarium* gives a misleading picture of the wide scope of his musical endeavors.[56]

Nevertheless, two notices about Daube's *Musical Dilettante* (1773) did appear in the *Wienerisches Diarium*. In April 1773, von Trattner ran an elaborate announcement of his plan to extend the earlier work into a complete series.

Now since the first treatise on thorough-bass through all twenty-four keys has been recognized as good and useful in printed and written reviews, the author hopes that the following three treatises will gain similar approval. The first of these deals with composition. This art, which formerly . . . was very difficult, and could only be learned with much effort, is presented here in the easiest and clearest manner. The beginner is lead by the hand, as it were, from combining two intervals . . . to the greatest difficulties of composition. With each [step], he will find the reason for . . . everything he sets down: Why is it placed here? Why is it made up of these intervals rather than others? Essential for many! The following treatise will comprise musical style, considering melody, as well as harmony, in the high, middle, and low styles, through all kinds of pieces for church, opera, and chamber. Here examples by renowned composers will be presented and analyzed. The invention of all types of melody will be described in the last treatise. It will begin with the very shortest pieces and proceed to the longest. Later it also will show, easily and clearly, the expression of all human emotions (*Affekten*) through melody and harmony. And so, ultimately, one will discover a method by which even an older person can write with verve in the current taste.

---

[55] Advertisements in the *Wienerisches Diarium* show that the Kurtzböck publication of 1770/71 was still available in January 1773, and that the von Trattner publication of 1773 was still available in May 1775.

[56] Gericke, *Musikalienhandel*, pp. 68–71.

The . . . [musical] examples . . . have made the work very costly. So, in order to make these three treatises available to the amateurs sooner, the author has joined with a society of able men who have agreed to have them printed by subscription. Thus, friends of music are informed that the society has decided to let them have these three volumes for a very reasonable price. . . .[57]

From this announcement it can be seen that the projected series would have resulted in a total of four *Dilettant* publications: the Kurtzböck periodical on thorough-bass (1770/71), the von Trattner treatise on composition (1773), a work on musical style, and a work on the invention of melody. When the fourth treatise finally did appear in 1797/98, it was not published by von Trattner, nor identified as part of the *Dilettant* series. But the correspondence between the contents of this work as announced in 1773, and as published twenty-four years later, is so close that one can only conclude that it was completely planned, or even written, when the original announcement was made. This idea, in turn, suggests that the third *Dilettant*, the proposed work on musical style, might also have existed in nearly final form at this time, although no trace of the work has yet come to light.

Regardless of the fate of the remainder of the series, Daube's 1773 treatise on composition was to have been the continuation of an ambitious enterprise. To have given it an advance announcement in the *Wienerisches Diarium*, von Trattner must have regarded it as a major work of considerable importance and current interest. A second notice, issued upon publication, listed its contents and advertised its step-by-step explanations of musical examples, stating, "The method of teaching is new, and amateurs will encounter much that they seek in vain in other musical writings."[58] Six entire pages also were devoted to a review, which was full of praise for Daube and his treatise.

The work announced in a special paper last spring, The Musical Dilettante by Johann Friedrich Daube, left the von Trattner press a few days ago. . . .

Since we [were] already familiar with the author through his previous publications, we eagerly perused his newly released work. We must say that basic principles and clarity prevail; even the very short Preface contains expressions and precepts which cannot be other than useful to amateurs and prospective composers. . . .

In our opinion, this treatise on composition can be very beneficial to beginners and amateurs of musical knowledge and also give experienced composers occasion for further reflection. We do not know of any author who has written so soundly, clearly, and concisely about music as the author of this work, as every musical scholar and lover of truth must attest.[59]

Despite the considerable publicity and initial acclaim which would seem to have assured *The Musical Dilettante* (1773) a secure position in musical literature, it soon fell into oblivion and was scarcely noticed for 200 years. The title appeared routinely in encyclopedia listings of Daube's works, but never received the critical attention given to his *General-Baß*.

---

[57] *Wienerisches Diarium von Staats, vermischten und gelehrten Neuigkeiten*, No. 33 (Vienna: von Ghelen, 1773), Ankündigung.

[58] *Wienerisches Diarium von Staats, vermischten und gelehrten Neuigkeiten*, No. 12 (Vienna: von Ghelen, 9 Feb. 1774), appendix.

[59] *Kaiserlich Königlich allergnädigst privilegirte Anzeigen aus sämmtlichen kaiserl. königl. Erbländern*, vol. III / 50 (Vienna: von Ghelen, 15 Dec. 1773).

The only modern commentaries on *The Musical Dilettante* (1773) are by Peter Benary and, more recently, by Michael Karbaum, who shares Benary's views and expands upon his presentation. Benary expresses surprise that this work was overlooked for so long. Although he does not mention the well-known Marpurg criticism or bibliographical confusion as possible factors, he suggests another explanation for the dominance of the *General-Baß* among Daube's works.

The picture of Daube acquired from "Generalbaß in drey Accorden" undergoes such a fundamental modification, in the sense of enrichment, expansion, and progress, through this much less noticed work, that one involuntarily asks why it did not set the tone for the classification and estimation of Daube in the history of music. The handiest explanation for this may well lie in the fact that always, but above all since [Hugo] Riemann, the theory of composition has been pushed into the background by music theory in the narrower sense, thus essentially the theory of harmony, because that is easier to describe and represent.[60]

Benary considers *The Musical Dilettante* (1773) important, not only among Daube's writings, but also as a work commensurate with those of Daube's well-known contemporaries. In his view, it is more "advanced" than the composition treatises of Johann Philipp Kirnberger (1721–83) and Johann Georg Albrechtsberger (1736–1809) – and even in the immediate vicinity of the composition method of Heinrich Koch (1749–1816).[61] After an extensive and enthusiastic review of the section on the free style, Benary briefly discounts the contrapuntal section as being on a lower level, but concludes that

the "Musical Dilettant" by Joh. Fr. Daube represents a highly significant theory of composition. In it the author of the work, "Generalbaß in drey Accorden" advances the limited boundaries of music theory to an actual compositional method. Theory is included only so far as it appears necessary for explaining certain specifics. The . . . fundamentally new position which Daube takes up may perhaps have become clear. Once again it appears that the great names which have gone down in music history frequently cause essentially more meaningful achievements of the so-called minor masters (*Kleinmeister*) to be obscured and forgotten. We venture to say that the significance of this work of Daube, which has remained almost unnoticed, cannot be emphasized enough.[62]

Wie die Leydenschaften

The year after the publication of the *Dilettant* treatise on composition, in August 1774, the *Frankfurter Anzeigen* announced that Hessen-born "Herr Taube, Secretär bey der Florentinischen musikalischen Societät,"[63] was preparing a work on the expression of the affects through music, and claimed that connoisseurs who had read the manuscript

[60] Benary, *Kompositionslehre*, p. 133.
[61] Benary, *Kompositionslehre*, p. 133.
[62] Benary, *Kompositionslehre*, p. 140.
[63] Meusel (*Lexicon*, vol. II, p. 288) states that he had held this position "seit 176. . . ." Nothing more is known of this association. However Karbaum ("Das theoretische Werk," p. 34) discovered that "Herr Johann Baptista Rondinelli Scarlatti, Secretair der berühmten Florentinischen Akademie der freyen Künste" was welcomed as an honorary member of the Augsburg Academy in 1770, adding that whether this reception may perhaps represent a gesture of reciprocation remains a hypothesis.

had high praise for its author.[64] Ten years later Johann Nikolaus Forkel (1749–1818) cited this notice without comment as to whether the work had achieved publication.[65] No copies, either published or in manuscript, have been found.

Karbaum speculates that this work would have been the missing part of the *Dilettant* series, even though the announced subject of the third volume was musical style rather than the affects.[66] It does seem probable that Daube had written the entire series by this time. Moreover, the notice in the *Frankfurter Anzeigen* appeared about the time when the publication of the third *Dilettant* might have been expected. But whether Daube changed the topic of the third *Dilettant* in the series (indicating only one lost work), or whether he wrote an additional unrelated work, perhaps for a publication of the Florentine Musical Academy (possibly indicating two lost works), remains unknown.

Beweis, daß die gottesdienstliche Musik (1782)

Daube's next published work was a short pamphlet on church music, which until 1964 was mentioned in only one source – *Der Portheimische Zettelkatalog*, a private catalogue compiled by a Viennese gentleman who collected information on less well-known figures about whom he had read.[67] He listed seven sources on Daube and two of his works, the 1770 *Dilettant* and the *Beweis*. A copy of the latter finally came to light in 1964 in the Musikabteilung der Bayerischen Staatsbibliothek in Munich:

Beweis, / daß die gottesdienstliche Musik / von den allerältesten Zeiten an, unter / allen Völkern des Erdbodens fortge- / währet, und auch in Ewigkeit / dauern werde. / Von Daube. / Wien, / bey Joh. Ferd. Edlen von Schönfeld. / 1782.

Daube begins this work by extolling the virtues of music, citing biblical examples of music for worship. After comparing the effectiveness of music with that of the sermon, and condemning the "enemies" of his art by means of a quotation from "Schakespear," he criticizes the current use of operatic melodies and secular dance styles in church music, musical settings unsuitable for texts of meditation and worship, and poor performance of such pieces, implicitly giving preference to the conservative church style as appropriate for sacred music.[68]

Daube expresses fear that such practices may lead to a disdain of church music and a desire to abolish it. He argues against this possibility on biblical grounds, and on the basis of Greek and Roman esteem of music, concluding that, on the strength of such a heritage, there is no doubt that "the purest harmony of music will continue with us into the next world, so that we may sing eternal offerings of praise and thanksgiving."[69]

Having thus established his *Beweis* ("proof") of the continuance of sacred music, Daube devotes the few remaining pages to his ideas for reform. He maintains that composers tire

[64] *Frankfurter Anzeigen*, vol. V (August, 1774), p. 518. From Karbaum, "Das theoretische Werk," p. 155.
[65] Forkel, *Musikalischer Almanach* (1784), p. 41.
[66] Karbaum, "Das theoretische Werk," p. 207.
[67] *Der Portheimische Zettelkatalog*, Entry 464, Stadtbibliothek Vienna.
[68] Daube, *Beweis*, pp. 12–13.
[69] Daube, *Beweis*, p. 18.

of repeatedly setting the Latin Mass, and suggests that, except on the highest holidays, it might be better to say a [low] Mass, followed immediately by a performance of some church music on the text of the Gospel of the day. Since each Sunday or holiday requires a different text, composers would have ample opportunity to adorn the solemn service through the expression of different affects.[70] Church music of this sort would be performed better, and create an enthusiasm leading to higher pay and greater opportunities for beginning and native musicians.[71]

The format Daube proposes – an opening Gospel verse set tutti or with four voices and instruments, followed by two recitative and aria pairs, a short recitative, and the conclusion, with an appropriate verse from a song presented tutti, "whereupon the remaining verses might be sung by the entire congregation"[72] – resembles that of the Protestant church cantata of northern Germany, where he spent his youth. Daube also volunteers to prepare a model of both text and music. This offer – the only indication that he may have composed sacred music – holds forth the possibility that a church archive in Vienna may some day yield a cantata-like work by J. F. Daube.

Daube concludes that the musician's required realm of knowledge and ability is vast and that his endeavors should be appreciated rather than made more difficult. Just consider, he exclaims, how much talent, prolonged effort, opportunity, and money are required to become a true virtuoso! At the English universities of "Oxfort und Kambridge," where regular professors are appointed to teach music publicly, a doctor's degree in music requires twelve years – longer than in any other field. The famed Handel was a doctor of music. "May any . . . hindrance to the progress of such a protracted and difficult science be a remote [possibility]!"[73]

Anleitung zur Erfindung der Melodie (1797/98)

Daube's last work appeared under two different titles and was printed by several publishers. However, the content of the various editions is identical. The Täubel edition in the Musiksammlung der Österreichischen Nationalbibliothek contains a dedication to Herr Ignaz Grafen von Fuchs, which states that the *Erfindung* "owes its existence mainly to you."

Anleitung / zur / Erfindung der Melodie / und ihrer Fortsetzung. / von / Johann Friedrich Daube, / Rath und erster Secretair der von weyl. Kaiser Franz I. gestif- / teten Akademie der Wissenschaften in Augsburg. / Erster Theil. / Mit Römisch- Kaiserlichem Privilegio. / Wien, 1797. / Gedruckt bey Christian Gottlob Täubel. *Anleitung / zur / Erfindung der Melodie / und ihrer Fortsetzung.* / von / Johann Friedrich Daube, / Rath und erster Secretair der von weyland Kaiser Franz I. / gestifteten Akademie der Wissenschaften in Augsburg. / Zweyter Theil, / welcher die Composition enthält. / Mit Römisch- Kaiserlichem Privilegio. / Wien, 1798 / In Commission der Hochenleitterschen Buchhandlung. (Also, both volumes, Wien: J. Funk, 1798.)

[70] Daube, *Beweis*, pp. 18–19.
[71] Daube, *Beweis*, pp. 20–21.
[72] Daube, *Beweis*, pp. 18–19.
[73] Daube, *Beweis*, pp. 21–2.

This work also appeared as

Anleitung zum Selbstunterricht in der musikalischen Komposition, sowohl für die Instrumental- als Vocalmusik, 1. Tl. *Von Erfindung der Melodie und ihrer Fortsetzung,* 2. Tl. *welcher die Composition enthält.* – Wien: Schaumburg in Kommission, 1798 (both volumes). (Also, both volumes, Wien: Binz, 1798.) (Also, second volume only, Linz: Commission der Akademischen Buchhandlung, 1798.)

Michael Karbaum describes the *Erfindung* as one of the few attempts "to integrate melodic instruction as a permanent component of a compositional system."[74] A detailed listing of the contents is found in works by Ernst Ludwig Gerber (1746–1819)[75] and Carl Ferdinand Becker (1804–77).[76] Gerber also gives his appraisal of Daube's *Erfindung*: "Remarkably full of good quality and practical value! . . . indeed the discovery and organization of all these compositional ideas and aids bring honor to the insight and discernment of the author. . . ."[77]

As discussed above, this book was to have been the fourth work in the *Dilettant* series. Although the first volume did not appear until the year of Daube's death, and the second volume posthumously, it was probably written much earlier – perhaps between 1770 and 1773 – when the series was announced. Karbaum notes that while it has the distinction of being the last theoretical work published in eighteenth-century Vienna, its style and approach are more representative of the 1770s.[78]

The Musical Dilettante (1773) contains several references to future instruction in the invention of melody, and at one point[79] Daube gives "the amateurs a little foretaste of what we promised about the invention of melody at the beginning of this work" (i.e., this series). Although no separate section on melody is included in the 1773 treatise, Daube does touch on several aspects of melodic invention and variation within the broader compositional context, just as he had done in the context of thorough-bass. In the *Erfindung der Melodie*, with attention directed specifically toward the melodic element, Daube expands and develops these ideas in a manner totally consistent with his earlier works, and thus brings his comprehensive *Dilettant* series to a conclusion.

DAUBE'S *THE MUSICAL DILETTANTE* (1773): A SYNOPSIS

When Daube's *Musical Dilettante* appeared in Vienna in 1773, the dilettante was a familiar figure on the musical scene, and a profusion of musical activities flourished among royalty and bourgeoisie. Thus the title calls to mind a cultural phenomenon of Enlightenment Europe and raises expectations of a dedication honoring a noble dilettante patron. But Daube, publishing by subscription, simply addresses "the reader," and sets forth his

---

[74] Karbaum, "Das theoretische Werk," p. 224.
[75] Gerber, *Neues Lexikon* (1812–14), vol. II, pp. 851–2.
[76] Becker, *Darstellung* (1836), p. 449.
[77] Gerber, *Lexikon*, p. 853.
[78] Karbaum, "Das theoretische Werk," p. 224.
[79] See pp. 28–9, Eng. trans., pp. 58–9.

intention "to present this knowledge in the clearest and easiest way, so that the dilettante might be able to use it for his enjoyment."

"Dilettante" derives from the Italian "dilettare," meaning to enjoy oneself or to take delight in something[80] and refers to "a person who practices singing or an instrument for pleasure, without making music their main occupation, or supporting themselves through this activity."[81] Therefore dilettantes, even those who attained a "professional" proficiency, stood in contrast to professional "musicians," many of whom earned their livelihood working as composers, performers, and teachers for noble dilettantes, whose status, affluence, and leisure enabled them to cultivate music purely for their delight and edification.

The Enlightenment dilettante, with a "cultivated enjoyment of leisure," might be interpreted as the "Renaissance man" in eighteenth-century guise.[82] Enlightenment humanists shared the Renaissance view that man, in his perfection, could rise above the necessities of life to distinctively human pursuits. Optimistically, they believed that the means to human perfection lay in efforts to rationalize and understand every branch of knowledge, simplified and related through common principles of nature.[83] Their "objective was to bring enlightenment to the *Liebhaber*, the *dilettante*, the *man of taste* . . . [who,] in the eighteenth century, was prone to be a man of culture with wide intellectual interests. . . ."[84]

Seen in this context, Daube's *Musical Dilettante* (1773) exemplifies the humanistic attempt "to bring enlightenment to . . . the dilettante." Its suitability for this purpose is seen in Daube's emphasis on *galant* chamber music and concertante part-writing. Of the three functional styles recognized by eighteenth-century theorists – church, chamber, and theater – Meinrad Spiess equates the chamber style with the *galant*.

Chamber music, also called *galanterie-music*, takes its name from the rooms and salons of the nobility, where it is usually performed. Whoever looks for delight, artifice, invention, art, taste, affection (*tendresse*) will find them all in the so-called Concerti Grossi, Sonatas da Camera, etc. in which

[80] Daube's choice of *Der Musikalische Dilettant* for his title, rather than the German "Liebhaber" (sometimes used in the text), suggests both the pleasure of studying music and the strong Italian influence in the southern part of the German-speaking countries – a verbal hint confirmed by certain Italian musical style traits within the work itself. Neither Adelung's *Wörterbuch* (Leipzig, 1796), nor Sulzer's *Allgemeine Theorie* (Leipzig, 1771–4) contain an entry for "Dilettant." But according to Adelung, "the Liebhaber, *Ital. Dilettante*, is one who has an excellent taste for fine arts and artworks without being an artist himself. Not all amateurs (*Liebhaber*) are also connoisseurs (*Kenner*)" (*Wörterbuch*, vol. II, col. 261).

[81] Koch, "Dilettant," *Lexicon*, (1802), col. 431.

[82] In some ways the eighteenth-century dilettante recalls the universally educated *uomo universale* or *donna universale* of the Renaissance. Seeking to prove the propriety of musical study, sixteenth-century humanists had appealed to the authority of Aristotle, who distinguished between "liberal and illiberal occupations", (i.e., those fit and those unfit for a freeman). The *artes liberales*, according to Aristotle, are not animal necessities, but are peculiar to the imagination and emotions of man. "Valuable in themselves," they are pursued for the sake of knowing how "to guide our leisure," which "offers . . . the very joy of living." Because music has an intrinsic value in "the cultivated enjoyment of leisure," it attains to this higher category of study proper for a freeman (in *Aristotle: Selections*, Eng. trans., Philip Wheelwright, pp. 285–7).

[83] These idealistic pursuits were encouraged by humanist philosophers such as Lessing, who held that a person's nobility or worth lay in their striving for truth ("Eine Duplik," *Sämtliche Schriften*, vol. XIII (1897), pp. 23–4).

[84] Duckles, "Johann Adam Hiller's 'Critical Prospectus for a Music Library'," pp. 177–8.

one cannot fail entirely to be pleased to hear all the high, middle, and low voices concert with each other, imitate each other, and compete for attention, all with neatness and zest.[85]

Kirnberger likewise says that "since chamber music is for connoisseurs and amateurs, pieces can be written in a more learned and artificial manner than those intended for public use, where everything must be more simple and cantabile, so that everyone will grasp it."[86] Both Spiess and Kirnberger corroborate Daube's inclusion of strict-style techniques within a *galant* context, where "concerting" voices reflect the polite dialogues of elegant society. Other features making Daube's works especially suitable for dilettantes are his simplification of harmony, limitation of variation figures, workable formulae for constructing canons, clear explanations of numerous musical examples, and occasional references to other disciplines. Moreover, Daube's lucid, methodical approach contributes greatly to the ease and pleasure of composition, as he leads the dilettante "an der Hand"[87] through modern *galant* or free-style part-writing from two voices to chamber symphonies, and older ecclesiastical or strict-style techniques from canon to fugue.

The opening chapter, "Harmony in general," immediately reveals the unique textural signature of *The Musical Dilettante*. Contrary to expectations, Daube does not review his harmonic system, but considers the multifarious effects of various textures, inversions, scorings, timbres, instrumentations, voicings, and dynamics, which will be interwoven into the compositional process. It soon becomes apparent that Daube's "Harmonie" indicates not only a specific chord or chords, but also the vertical structure in both the chordal and textural sense – thus harmonization, texture, or sound in general. Although Daube advocates clarity and variety, he is not concerned with an adjectival catalog of textural possibilities. Rather, his purpose seems to be to awaken a wide spectrum of sound concepts in his readers' memories, and to encourage them to approach composition by imagining the aural dimension of music beyond the *Dilettante*'s printed pages. Thus Daube at once asserts the validity of the ear in composition and corroborates his belief that the final aim of music is to please the ear and move the soul through the expression of the affects. The best harmonization of a melody, he concludes, "complements the expression of [its] affects. . . ." He then moves on, expecting the dilettante to be familiar with chordal harmony from his earlier works.

In *General-Baß in drey Accorden* (1756) and *Der Musikalische Dilettant* (1770/71), Daube recognizes three chords as the basis of harmony. He believes that the many other combinations of tones arise "from the retention and anticipation of one or several intervals of the three main chords."[88]

Daube's "first" or "ruling chord"[89] refers to the major or minor triad built on the first degree of the scale.

[85] *Tractatus Musicus* (1746), pp. 161ff, Eng. trans. in Ratner, *Classic Music*, p. 7.

[86] Sulzer, "Cammermusik," *Allgemeine Theorie*, vol. I (1771), p. 189.

[87] *Wienerisches Diarium von Staats, vermischten und gelehrten Neuigkeiten*, No. 33 (Vienna: von Ghelen, 1773), Ankündigung.

[88] For critical commentaries on Daube's harmonic system see Karbaum, "Das theoretische Werk"; Benary, *Kompositionslehre*; Riemann, *Geschichte*; and Shirlaw, *Theory*.

[89] This appellation is reminiscent of Riepel's picturesque designations of scale tones as positions in the social hierarchy. The tonic, for instance, is the master-farmer ("der Meyer") and the dominant is the chief farm-hand ("der Oberknecht") (*Anfangsgründe*, vol. II (1755), p. 65).

His "second chord," the ii$^6_5$, is built upon the fourth scale degree. Although it corresponds to Rameau's controversial "chord of the fourth degree" or "chord of the added sixth," Daube is more consistent about the structure of this chord than Rameau, who retains the triad plus "added sixth" above the fourth scale degree, and the chord built in thirds upon the second degree, as equal alternatives. This flexibility is reflected in Rameau's theory of "double emploi," whereby the root of the ii$^6_5$ may be either the second or fourth scale degree – whichever provides the stronger fundamental bass (root movement by fourths or fifths) to the following chord.[90] The resulting choice of a strong fundamental bass from ii$^6_5$ to either V or I is foreign to Daube's system, since, in the "natural order" of his three-chord progression, the second chord normally moves to the third chord (V), rather than to the first.[91]

Daube's "third chord" is the V^7. Although built upon the fifth scale degree, Daube considers the essential element to be the seventh scale degree, the "main indicator of the key." The dissonant seventh of the chord is optional, as is the dissonance of the second chord, "written only when it repeats the preceding tone," as, in C major for example, the C in the second chord and F in the third chord.[92] The third chord leads back to the first, which "should naturally follow the third chord . . . [although] the rules of art may permit a partially similar chord to follow instead."

Daube also recognizes two derivative chords involving chromatic alterations. The "chromatic chord" (augmented sixth) is derived from "combining the intervals of two keys." As the enharmonic equivalent of a third chord outside the key, it can be used for distant modulations. Seldom used by earlier composers, this chord now occurs occasionally "in the middle of a piece" and, like the diminished seventh, quite often in recitative.

Currently, says Daube, the diminished seventh chord also is granted "civic rights" in all minor keys. Combined from the second and third chords, it may take the place of the third chord, except in cadences. Since it, too, can wear the enharmonic "mask," it is convenient for effecting modulations.

In *The Musical Dilettante* (1773) Daube usually modulates by chromatically altering a harmony which is "partially similar" to a new third chord, since "the new third chord must precede the first chord in that key . . . at least the main indication of the key must be there, namely the new sharp." The "double meaning" of this altered chord (secondary dominant), "which can be seen from two points of view," refers to its shift of function within the three-chord progression as it is chromatically altered and repositioned in a new key.

Daube's chords retain their identity in any arrangement of their tones, i.e., inversion. Like Rameau, Daube emphasizes the position or function of the chord in the key, rather than the interval figures above a given bass note, as the means of identifying chords. Kirnberger represents a more conservative approach. Although he often speaks of chords

---

[90] Rameau discusses this concept in chap. 9, "Origine de la Dissonance Harmonique, & de son double emploi," *et infra*, of his *Génération harmonique*.

[91] See p. 62 and n. 36 to text.

[92] In *The Musical Dilettante* (1773), Daube's only references to the preparation of dissonance are made in regard to the bass part. His soprano lines, in keeping with the precepts of the free style, contain numerous examples of dissonances approached by leap. Compare Kirnberger, *Kunst*, vol. I (1771), pp. 80–90, Eng. trans., pp. 99–108.

in terms of their key position, and explains their derivation by inversion, he classifies them by figured-bass numerals, thus giving the inversion intervals priority over the position of the root in the scale of the key.[93]

In an era when the harmonic foundation of thorough-bass was being replaced by treble-dominated textures and clearer key definition, Daube's system reduces the "frightening" profusion of interval-combination "chords" above an actual figured bass (as well as Rameau's root-defined chords above an abstract fundamental bass) to a minimal progression of three chords, which owe their existence less to a dominating bass line than to the newer concept of harmonic function. Despite ornamental tones and incomplete harmonies, each of Daube's chords retains its integrity as long as it carries out its appropriate harmonic function. This built-in flexibility of a standardized formula provides for harmonic diversity without obscuring the basic progression, since it underlines the invariable, function-bearing representative of each chord.

In distilling Daube's three chords to their functional essence, the first chord is represented by the first degree of the scale; the second chord by the fourth degree, upon which it is built; and the third chord by the seventh degree, the "main indicator of the key."[94] Therefore the tones 1, 4, and 7 of the scale constitute the invariable and essential components of Daube's three chords, which, in turn, embody the three functions of cadential harmony.[95]

The beauty and timeliness of Daube's harmonic system lie in its practical manifestation of the "classic" ideals of clarity and simplicity; at a time when most theorists still were entangled in a web of thorough-bass figures, Daube recognizes the functional component as the essence of each chord, and identifies ornamental tones and chromatic alterations as "artificial" variants of a simple, "natural," three-chord progression.

Daube enriches his definitions of "The three motions" (Chapter 2) with practical advice and the aesthetic concepts of art and nature. Parallel motion, due to its simplicity and spontaneity, is most natural. It enhances "delicately singing passages" in church, opera, and chamber styles. Contrary motion, with its greater complexity and intervallic variety, "was engendered by art and established by practical usage." It prevents mistakes and gives rise to beautiful melodic motives. In oblique motion "nature and art play an equal part." An embellishment of harmony, "the most magnificent symphonies are impressively adorned with it when the wind instruments have sustained tones."

Introducing free-style part-writing with "Combining two voices" (Chapter 3), Daube addresses the preliminaries of setting a good second voice to a given melody. He distinguishes between composition for two equal voices, similar in range, contour, and rhythmic motion, and composition for melody with bass, in which bass melodies and non-chord tones create an aesthetically complementary, but distinct part.

---

[93] Kirnberger, *Kunst*, vol. I (1771), pp. 34–80, Eng. trans. pp. 54–98.

[94] Daube does not use cognates or translated equivalents of Rameau's terms – "notte sensible," "tonique," "dominante-tonique," "quatriéme notte" (*Traité*, 1722), and "sousdominante" (*Nouveau Système*, 1726) – nor (as discussed above) were his "three chords" derived from those of Rameau.

[95] The functional nature of Daube's harmonic system corroborates the research of Leonard Ratner, who applies the "1–4–7–1" approach to cadential harmony in *Harmony: Structure and Style*.

Daube explains that melody tones comprise "essential tones to which the other voice must be set" (i.e., chord tones) and tones which "are given no bass or separate harmony" (i.e., non-chord tones). Of the latter, those on the beat are appoggiaturas, those after the beat are passing tones.

Using the three chords as a frame of reference, Daube discusses the harmonization of "essential tones," recognition of non-chord tones, voice-leading, bass melodies, cadence formation, interpretation of ambiguous accidentals, key relationships, and simple modulations. He recommends the natural "succession of the three chords, except when the melody occasionally requires that the second chord be omitted. . . ," or when a 7–6 descent in the melody requires parallel sixths or thirds, a progression which provides variety of motion.

Interesting with regard to the transitional era which it represents, is the *rapprochement* Daube effects between the contrapuntal and harmonic methods of teaching composition. The harmonic approach is clearly evident in his three-chord system and classification of non-chord tones according to their arsic or thetic rhythmic positions.[96] The contrapuntal method is apparent in his progression from two to many voices in the tradition of Fux's *Gradus ad Parnassum* (1725), and by traces of the progressive rhythms of species counterpoint in his two-part examples.[97]

Eighteenth-century theorists disagree about beginning composition instruction with two voices.[98] Kirnberger objects that without a background of four-voice writing, one would not know which tones could be omitted. Taking Daube's perspective, however, the question turns from the omission of chord tones from a four-part context, to the selection of chord tones from a simple harmonic pattern – his three-chord progression – the functions of which can be represented by few voices or many. "The main harmonic framework," says Daube, "depends upon three-part composition." Therefore, whoever masters "Combining three voices" (Chapter 4), will "find it easy to construct a harmony of many voices."

Daube divides three-part composition into the natural style, based on simplicity of all musical elements, and the artificial style, which incorporates variety through the complexities of art. Harmonically, the natural style is characterized by a restriction to the three chords; texturally, by the differing roles of the three voices.

For the natural style, and for "singing" passages in the artificial style, Daube favors a flowing, "spontaneous," cantabile melody. The bass follows the tonal implications of the melody and complements its rhythmic motion, using passing tones "to always promote the singing style." Last to be written, the middle voice "neither ascends above [the first], nor introduces anything concerting or imitative, but simply proceeds with the bass according to the rules of harmony." Sometimes it parallels the upper voice in thirds or sixths, despite the incomplete harmonies which occasionally result.[99]

[96] See n. 26 to text.
[97] See n. 30 to text.
[98] Those who favor beginning with two parts include Fux (*Gradus*, 1725), Marpurg (*Abhandlung*, 1753–4), Padre Martini (*Esemplare*, 1774–5), and the Rev. John Trydell, whose *Two Essays* form the basis of "Musick," *Encyclopaedia Britannica* (1771). Those opposed include Rameau (*Traité*, 1722), J. A. P. Schulz ("Zweistimmig. (Musik.)" in Sulzer, *Allgemeine Theorie*, vol. II (1774)), and Kirnberger (*Kunst*, 1771–9).
[99] See n. 47 to text.

In Daube's artificial category, nature and art are combined "to please the greatest number of listeners." Harmonically, the artificial style uses more chromaticism, artificial ties, and foreign resolutions (i.e., resolutions containing accidentals "foreign" to the key). Texturally, the voices are more equal. A hierarchy in which the main melody "constantly asserts its authority" is replaced by mutual accommodation, often involving "the exchange of motives between voices, so that sometimes one and sometimes the other has the most prominent role." Such concerting may comprise a non-imitative dialogue, or may include voice-crossing and imitation. The latter creates a more polyphonic texture, which Daube associates with the "so-called sonatas *a tre*, in which . . . the bass often plays a melodic motif from the upper voices." But, cautions Daube, such repeated phrases should contain something bright, lively, playful, skipping, distinctive, pleasant, singable, or brilliant.

Daube's frequent juxtaposition of singing and brilliant styles within the "beautiful continuity" of the melody represents the *galant* taste for "something new and unexpected." Daube heightens these surprises by giving the singing style a "delicate *piano*" with "thin accompaniment," and the brilliant style an "intense *forte*" with "vigorous movement" in the accompaniment.

Such contrasts also emphasize "beautiful symmetry,"[100] or "good division of the main melody" (i.e., overall form) which requires that phrases contain an even number of measures, and that a passage heard in the first half of a piece recur in the second.[101] The symmetry of phrases and sections should be clearly articulated by changes in texture, as well as style and dynamics, since "continuously full harmony is not pleasing to the ear." Thus texture is a primary agent to vary sound, clarify style, and delineate structure. Having established these basic structural principles, Daube subsequently applies them to quartets and chamber symphonies.

The eighteenth century witnessed a transition from the solo and trio sonata to the string quartet as the prevalent chamber-music ensemble. But despite the growing popularity of the quartet, most treatises still dealt with four-part textures in the context of either counterpoint and fugue or thorough-bass realization. In "Combining four voices" (Chapter 5), however, Daube steps over the threshold into the realm of free-style string quartet composition. This was a new frontier in music theory.

Discussing the natural style, Daube concentrates on the new member of the ensemble – the viola – in relation to the other voices. Its role as a replacement for the harpsichord in the trio sonata is apparent in its assignment to those "tones which are still left after three voices have been composed. . . ." The viola may never ascend above the upper voice, but should have a good melodic line even at the expense of an occasional incomplete harmony. It often doubles the bass, especially at the beginnings and ends of phrases.

The artificial style incorporates "ties, imitations, modulations . . . and all the special alternations [of style and texture] encountered in three-part composition." Here a more sophisticated viola part is included as an integral member of the ensemble, and "can contribute greatly to the enhancement . . . of a piece . . ." through imitative phrases, concerting parts, or as a high bass.

[100] See pp. 97–8.
[101] See n. 61 to text.

Daube describes several types of quartets: those with the first voice in the brilliant style against a simple harmonic background, those with the melody divided between two voices while the others accompany, and those with all four voices concerting among themselves.[102]

Many characteristics of Daube's "four-part scores" suggest the *quatuor concertant* repertoire. These include "a harmonic vocabulary of mainly primary chords, which accommodates . . . textural and melodic action – often brilliance. . . ," a melodic style frequently drawn from concerto and Italian opera (corresponding to Daube's brilliant and singing styles), predominantly symmetrical phrase structure, and part-writing in which "dialogue is the main textural stance."[103]

Daube also distinguishes several genres – symphony, concerto, sonata, and trio – which may guide the stylistic derivation of a four-part Allegro. The symphonic type alternates "the rushing and brilliant with the singing style." In the concerto style, "the first voice has various solos . . . lightly accompanied." Simple three-part sonatas are "distinguished by . . . the alternation of four-part and two-part harmony. . . . [while] the first violin continues . . . with singing passages in the style of Italian arias. . . ." The fourth type resembles the artificial three-part sonatas described in the preceding chapter. In slow, cantabile movements, Daube suggests creating variety by interrupting a *piano* passage with "a single *forzando* tone," using "pizzicato" accompaniment, and repeating the melody with "muted violins." Daube's plural, "violins," suggests that some of these four-part scores might be performed by several players per part, in the manner of string chamber symphonies.

During Daube's lifetime a new style of orchestration was developing to enhance concurrent changes in musical style. In "Composition in five and more parts" (Chapter 6), Daube opens another frontier in music theory by offering the earliest instruction on the idiomatic orchestration of chamber symphonies with winds.

Daube's use of sustained wind tones with active string figuration illustrates "the most salient feature of the changing orchestration."[104] Sustained tones, says Daube, "have been introduced into symphonies in the current taste, where they enliven and strengthen the brilliant passages."

Then, in a manner reflecting the growth of the symphony, Daube gradually adds pairs of wind instruments to four-part strings – first horns, which "to a large extent . . . comprises the current taste in symphonies," then oboes or flutes, and finally oboes and flutes – an ensemble which accurately reflects the current chamber orchestra.[105] Daube's instruction concentrates on effective, idiomatic writing for winds, which "in brilliant passages . . . have mostly sustained tones." Elsewhere, the upper woodwinds play "short singing passages . . . in thirds or sixths," and concert together, or "even with the horns," which also may play "short solos" in the middle range, possibly accompanied by a bassoon. Short phrases and frequent rests allow wind players to breathe, and contrib-

---

[102] See p. 112.
[103] Compare Levy, *Quatuor Concertant*, pp. 46, 104–06, 134–5, 247, 326.
[104] Carse, *Orchestration*, p. 139.
[105] Compare J. A. P. Schulz, "Symphonie. (Musik.)," in Sulzer, *Allgemeine Theorie*, vol. II (1774), pp. 1121–2.

ute to the "diversity of the harmony," as groups of instruments alternate in soloistic or supportive roles.

Scoring and textural variety are not autonomous considerations, however, but aid in clarifying the musical design: basic blocks of texture, instrumentation, and dynamics set off stylistic contrasts in accordance with principles of symmetry and recurrence. The bold-stroke symphonic medium requires harmonic simplicity, "because the brilliant and fleeting melody is not consistent with great artifice."[106] Yet, as Daube mentions elsewhere, brief double counterpoints provide variety, and motivic imitations prove very effective.

Daube's concept of the symphony rings true to his cosmopolitan heritage in Berlin, Stuttgart, and Vienna, which had "the most famous and largest orchestras of the eighteenth century each in their own period of bloom."[107] In Daube's discussion, the contrapuntal and motivic practices of Berlin, italianate melodies of Stuttgart, progressive orchestration and stylistic contrasts of neighboring Mannheim,[108] and idiomatic wind writing of Vienna,[109] all appear in ascending order of importance. By emphasizing orchestration Daube remains consistent to his interest in texture, becomes an innovator among theorists, and aptly represents the chamber symphony, which characteristically displays "the splendor of instrumental music."[110]

"Variation" (Chapter 7), a chapter "more concerned with melody" than with the composition of several voices, links the preceding, free-style harmonization of melodic figures to the subsequent, strict-style imitation of melodic figures. Daube's use of variation as a stylistic common denominator comes out repeatedly in later chapters, as he adapts strict-style techniques to free-style aesthetic and musical values. But although Daube considers variation a valuable resource in all styles, his main example is in the popular theme and variations form.[111]

Teaching that "variations flow from the chords themselves," Daube elaborates each tone of his three chords, progressing rhythmically in a manner suggestive of species counterpoint.[112] Several of Daube's motives are reminiscent of the *Figurenlehre*, a theory of musical composition based on the analogy of music and rhetoric.[113] Daube's schematic approach and counting of figures in his examples also recalls *ars combinatoria* invention, in which a given number of items are recombined and permuted.[114] Daube also points out that different registers, articulations, rests, and dotted rhythms, will yield even more

---

[106] See n. 75 to text. Daube also encourages facile key relationships in "the natural construction of a long melody" (i.e., a complete movement) in *Der Musikalische Dillettant: eine Abhandlung des Generalbasses* (Vienna: Kurtzböck, 1770/71), pp. 91–2.

[107] Carse, *XVIIIth Century*, p. 29.

[108] Daube's use of winds in the singing style, surprise dynamics, general pauses, a "rocket," and absence of figured bass also recall the Mannheim style, which Carse calls "virtually a school of orchestration" (*Orchestration*, p. 186).

[109] Schubart, *Ideen* (1806), p. 77.

[110] Sulzer, "Symphonie. (Musik.)," *Allgemeine Theorie*, vol. II (1774), p. 1122.

[111] See n. 83 to text.

[112] See n. 30 to text.

[113] See Mattheson, *Capellmeister* (1739), vol. II, chap. 14 and Lenneberg, "Mattheson" *JMT* (1958), vol. II/1, pp. 47–84 and vol. II/2, pp. 193–236. For a later eighteenth-century view of figures, see n. 93 to text.

[114] See nn. 9 and 87 to text.

figures, and that keyboard and harp call for bass variations, since "one is guided by the instruments" – a comment redolent of the idiomatic, improvised variation-finales popular at public virtuoso concerts.

As a basis for variations, Daube recommends choosing the customary menuet or short aria with a good, simple bass. Daube's theme, a cantabile style Andante, contains a figure identified as an Italian vocal ornament.[115] His individual variations demonstrate both consistent figuration and contrasting motives, since "the rushing style should always be interrupted by something delicate and melodious. . . ."

"Variation" gathers together many musical strands, both past and present – the traditions of species counterpoint, *Figurenlehre, ars combinatoria*, and the changing practices of improvised ornamentation. In his theme and variations, Daube weaves this heritage into a musical form which embodies the structural clarity and melodic style of his era, and fosters the budding idiomatic virtuosity which would come to full flower in the next century. Yet Daube's main purpose is to teach variation as a means of elaborating a simple line from his three-chord progression into an attractive, figural melody; this premise of melodic construction governs not only his free-style chamber music, but also the strict-style techniques of imitation, canon, double counterpoint, and fugue.

"Imitation" (Chapter 8) provides practical instruction on free imitation, rarely found in the theoretical literature of the time. Daube considers imitation "indispensable" in church, theater, and chamber music. "Nothing good . . . can be accomplished without [imitation]. . . . It unites art with nature" (i.e., it employs an artistic technique to distribute a natural melodic motif throughout the "Harmonie").

Daube's remarks on "similar imitation" focus on range, spacing, and spontaneous-sounding alternations between a steady, thorough-bass foundation and a melodic, concerting bass, often placed in an appropriately higher register.

When preserving "the continuity of the key," Daube eschews strict contrapuntal imitation. Instead, drawing a figure from one harmony, he imitates it freely within the following harmony of his three-chord progression. Two- and three-part examples illustrate this technique with running passages and sustained tones, motivic fragmentation, rhythmic displacement, and motives in thirds before a cadence.

An example for horns and bassoons then demonstrates that, with four parts, "the first imitation occurs a fifth lower or a fourth higher" (i.e., fugally), and shows a modification for natural horn, while an excerpt for flutes and oboes illustrates various pairings of motivic fragments and a homophonic approach to the cadence. Discussing the importance of these developmental procedures, Daube concludes perceptively that "the fame [of those symphonies which have won general approval] rests not on the diversity of many thoughts, but rather much more on a good arrangement of a few melodic motives, on the way they are fragmented, and . . . used in the appropriate place."

Because Daube approaches composition as a performer, rather than as a historically minded theorist, he features free imitation as an element of concertante part-writing

---

[115] See Ex. 91 and p. 143. For a study of differences in national style among sets of variations, see Fischer, "Arietta Variata," p. 404.

rather than as a modern stepchild of strict canon and fugue. Hence Daube's selection of imitative figures "in accordance with the nature of the instruments," his awareness of "the continuity of a good melodic line in the upper voice," his preference for brief imitations and impromptu responsiveness among the parts, his decorative use of imitation to enliven textures on a simple harmonic palette (similar to techniques of Rococo art), and hence his belief that free motivic imitation is more useful and natural than canon, because here "the composer still has the freedom to continue his melody spontaneously."

"Canon" (Chapter 9) proceeds from the simplest types to the most artificial "monuments of antiquity . . . in vogue 200 years ago." Surprisingly comprehensive, Daube's practical, canonic recipe book indicates his valuation of strict-style canon in an era of free-style homophony, stylistic contrast, and emerging conflict of rules and genius.

Daube appreciates simple, vocal canon as a traditional plaything for dilettantes and offers the inverted retrograde canon, "dedicated only to the friendship of two persons . . . sitting opposite one another," with each singing the notes "as they appear from his point of view."[116]

As a composer and teacher, Daube also values canon as a preparatory discipline for writing fugue and double counterpoint, and for understanding that "for the most part, . . . canon is based on the variation of the previous measure. . . ."

Daube does not restrict canon to the church style of "the ancients," but intersperses simple canonic passages "in the theater and chamber . . . as short solos within . . . a large piece."[117] To Daube, the sound of lightly scored canonic polyphony, "between the rushing or brilliant passages in a large Allegro, with . . . each of the three parts played by a different instrument . . . ," provides yet another resource for textural variety and stylistic contrast. Daube's incorporation of canon, fugato, and invertible counterpoint into *galant* symphonic and chamber music – rarely explained in treatises – is his most unique and historically significant treatment of the strict-style techniques. Still in an incipient stage in 1773, this practice increased toward the end of the century, when references to the "learned style" were familiar topics in the works of Haydn and Mozart.[118]

In presenting canon as an ingredient congenial to the music of his era, Daube reconciles a number of differences between the older and newer styles. He adapts canon to the *galant* ideals of (1) simplicity, by retaining his three-chord harmonic system for canonic writing, and by favoring simple canons over hidden devices (riddle and crab canons); (2) clarity, by making imitations more perceptible through long tones, rests, a running bass, and diverse instrumentation; (3) homophony, by constructing canonic voices in the same range to form a good, interdependent melody from the upper tones; (4) melodiousness, by insisting that canonic contrivances not interfere with the natural "singing style" or characteristic figural rhythms of individual canonic lines; (5) stylistic contrast, by amalgamating brief canonic passages into larger forms; (6) freedom, by encouraging spon-

[116] See n. 107 to text.

[117] However Daube considers the more artificial types appropriate only for the church style, and then only when justified by the text and accompanied by free, non-imitative parts. See p. 168.

[118] See, for instance, Mozart's Serenade in C minor for Winds, K. 388 (1782 or 1783), III, and Symphony No. 41, K. 551 (1788), IV and Haydn's Symphony 99 (1793), IV, and String Quartet, Opus 76/6 (1797), I.

taneity and the breaking off of canonic passages – vaguely symbolic of the genius' breaking of rules (canons), and the new questioning of authority which surfaces more noticeably in "Simple fugue" (Chapter 10), since there "more freedom is allowed."

"Simple Fugue – fugal imitation without a consistent countersubject – deals with both "regular fugues," carried out "according to certain rules," and "unbound or approximate fugues," which freely incorporate "the imitation of one or two main motives," as in "our good current pieces – symphonies, opera arias, and concertos. . . ."[119]

Daube's preference is for fugue themes, moderate in length and range, which incorporate several figures.[120] Although he gives no range restrictions (possibly because of the mainly instrumental context) his subjects encompass a fourth to a ninth. Subjects may be "either lively and bright or serious," as in the decorated alla breve, dance rhythms, and concerto style of Daube's various examples.[121] Most begin with the soprano, recalling Viennese church fugue entries of the time.[122]

Daube describes three "regular fugue beginnings" and their correct "repetitions" (i.e., real or tonal answers).[123] His tonal adjustments are conventional, but his explanation of them in terms of key-defining half steps within a chordal context (rather than in terms of modes or scales) shows his strong tonal orientation. Daube's ideas on irregular subjects, which "do not begin [or end] on the octave or fifth of the key,"[124] differ from those of contemporary theorists, since his chordal orientation leads to certain unconventional answers, and to an unusually large number of answers at the subdominant level.[125]

Later entries, treated more freely, "may occur at other intervals."[126] Episodes may present contrasting material or utilize figures drawn from the subject.[127] Daube's guidelines on length of episodes, keys of secondary expositions, and stretto also admit of "variants," for he never intends "to set limitations where none is possible."

Daube's concept of a fugue imbued with "the freedom of the moderns,"[128] stands delicately and temporarily balanced between the "rules of the ancients" and the increasingly thorough fugal codifications of many eighteenth-century theorists.[129] In Daube's hands, fugue is still the vital, pliant technique of his formative years (as in the works of Handel, which Daube admired),[130] interpreted according to *galant* principles of creative

[119] See n. 118 to text.

[120] See nn. 119 and 143 to text.

[121] See n. 141 to text.

[122] These customarily began with the soprano and moved downward, or with the bass and moved upward through the other voices (Horsley, *Fugue*, p. 160).

[123] Much fugal terminology originated after Daube's time. For instance, although eighteenth-century French and German theorists described the tonal answer, the terms "tonal" and "real" were not used outside Italy until the twentieth century (Horsley, *Fugue*, pp. 101, 155).

[124] See n. 124 to text.

[125] This occurs because the chord membership of the last tone partly determines whether the imitation begins in the third chord (dominant level), or second chord (subdominant level), or whether both are possible. See nn. 120, 123, and 125 to text.

[126] This recalls Martini's *attacco* subject. See n. 130 to text.

[127] This type is often called "strict" fugue. See n. 144 to text.

[128] See Ex. 168.

[129] The resulting nineteenth-century conservatory concept of fugue as a regulated form rather than a flexible "procedure" of composition, effectively "set limitations" to fugue and led to its decline as a valid means of musical expression.

[130] See *Beweis* (1782), p. 22 and *Erfindung* (1797), preface.

freedom. By recording this attitude toward fugal composition, Daube again diverges from the mainstream of theoretical thought, but represents the use of fugue in late eighteenth-century chamber music more clearly than any other writer.

Daube's presentation of "Double counterpoint" (Chapter 11) combines traditional methods with his practical, modern approach. He treats only double counterpoint,[131] and only the three intervallic inversions in common use – the octave, tenth, and twelfth.[132] Standard features include tables of interval inversion, and the preliminary procedure of writing the inversion underneath the original two voices. Following the tradition of differentiating subject and countersubject for easy recognition, Daube suggests a slow subject with a rapid countersubject entering slightly later.[133] He also illustrates the common practices of converting one type of counterpoint to another, amplifying a line at the third (or sixth), and using auxiliary voices for greater freedom of melodic action, especially at cadences.[134]

Daube's *galant* orientation is apparent in his brilliant-style symphonic excerpt (Example 192), with free, auxiliary voices between widely separated contrapuntal lines. Moreover, while he touches on the essential topics of double counterpoint, he gives only those rules practical for free-style writing. And although Daube does not insist that his three-chord progression govern intervallic counterpoint, his tonal, harmonic approach appears in several guises: his unconventional procedure of writing the figurated countersubject before the more sustained subject, resulting less in "note-against-note" counterpoint than in "melodic figure against harmonic underpinning" composition; his addition of accidentals to reduce the modal implications that may result from side-slipping to another tonal center when inverting at the tenth or twelfth; and his extremely free adaptation of melodic inversions to a key and fixed harmonic plan. Not surprisingly, Daube's only example of strict (real) melodic inversion produces a mirror image of the melody without violating the half steps of the key.[135]

While Daube appreciates the use by "the ancients" of double counterpoint for melodic extension, and its continuing position in the church style, he also advocates interspersing short contrapuntal passages into arias or symphonies, and applying contrapuntal inversion to melody and accompaniment textures.[136] Used in these ways, which reflect current trends, double counterpoint can "show forth art and beauty" in *galant* music. Thus Daube reconciles old and new, strict and free, while presenting an indispensable ingredient for the study of double fugue.

"Double fugue" (Chapter 12) combines fugal imitation with invertible counterpoint. After discussing "artificial" simple fugue, in which the invertible countersubject first appears with the answer,[137] Daube moves on to double, triple, and quadruple fugue

---

[131] See nn. 150 and 174 to text.

[132] Although Marpurg treats invertible counterpoint at seven different intervals (*Abhandlung*, vol. I (1753), chap. VIII), Daube, together with Kirnberger (*Kunst*, vol. II/2 and 3 (1777 and 1779)) and the majority of late eighteenth-century theorists, limits his instruction to the three most commonly used inversions.

[133] See n. 154 to text.

[134] See nn. 155 and 163 to text.

[135] See Exx. 187 and 224 and nn. 167, 212 and 213 to text.

[136] See n. 168 to text.

[137] See nn. 177 and 178 to text.

proper,[138] usually presenting multiple subjects at once or in quick succession at the beginning.[139] Techniques covered include the invention of subjects suitable for inversion at
the octave, tenth, and twelfth, derivation of voices, stretto, augmentation, diminution,
melodic inversion, and combinations of these.

Despite Daube's thorough treatment of artificial techniques, however, he reaffirms
his *galant* ideals throughout his final chapter. Emphasizing clarity, he recommends the
judicious placement of rests, differentiation of multiple themes through rhythm, time of
entry, and length, and use of different instruments for each line. "Noble simplicity"
of melody and harmony becomes increasingly important as textures become more
complex, and Daube reiterates the homophonic concept that "the ear always hears only
one melody with regard to the upper voice." Daube also values the artificial techniques
of "the ancients" for their inherent variety, since multiple invertible counterpoint
produces an array of harmonic permutations, while melodic inversion offers numerous
linear possibilities.

Moreover, brief contrapuntal passages interspersed into a basically homophonic *galant*
idiom provide variety of sound and texture – perhaps the most salient concern in Daube's
free-style part-writing instruction. Thus, by adapting strict-style techniques to *galant*
aesthetic values and a cadential harmonic system, Daube encourages the stylistic integra-
tion which, before his death in 1797, had become a hallmark of the greatest classic
masterworks.

Johann Friedrich Daube's work reveals the insights of a broadminded, cosmopolitan
musician, whose unique and practical approach reflects the music, more than the theory,
of his time. In *The Musical Dilettante* (1773), Daube offers his comprehensive view of
musical composition in "the clearest and easiest way" for the "enjoyment" of amateurs.
In doing so, he focuses on the dilettante as a late eighteenth-century cultural phenomenon, captures the essence of the *galant* chamber style, and reconciles diverse elements
into a musical style in which "art and nature are united to produce true beauty."

[138] See n. 174 to text.
[139] See n. 195 to text.

The
Musical Dilettante

A

Treatise on Composition,
which
clearly explains and illustrates by means of selected examples,
not only the newest styles of composition for pieces
in two, three and more parts, but also
most artificial species of ancient canons
and of simple and double fugues.

by

Johann Friederich Daube,

Counsel and First Secretary of the Imperial Franciscan Academy
of Liberal Arts and Sciences in Vienna and Augsburg.

with most gracious Imperial Roman privilege.

Vienna

printed by Johann Thomas Edlen von Trattner,
royal and imperial court printers and booksellers.

1773

CONTENTS
OF THE ENTIRE WORK

PREFACE

A well-laid foundation in thorough-bass can rightfully be called the guide to composition. The reason is that thorough-bass consists of the knowledge of chords and their succession. Composition, on the other hand, is the skillful combining of these chords with melody in such a way that the expression or depiction of the affects may result. Furthermore, every melody is constructed of tones which are intervals derived from chords, although, strictly speaking, this does not take into account the passing tones which are frequently required for the formation of the melody.

It is, to be sure, actually quite possible to have the practical science of thorough-bass at one's fingertips without understanding composition, but it is impossible to be able to compose without knowing the rudiments of thorough-bass. For to invent a certain melody and set a bass to it by ear is only the very slightest part of the art of composition. To do this, of course, one does not need to understand the theory of thorough-bass, although without this knowledge one is certainly not even in a position to provide the shortest melody with a well-founded accompaniment. And even should one happen upon a good accompaniment by frequently hearing similar passages, one is still at a loss to suggest the slightest basis for it. Thus it is always safer to learn thorough-bass solidly, and in its entire range, before venturing to compose. In composition there are great difficulties to be mastered, particularly for a professional musician who wants to learn it thoroughly.

We will make every effort to present this knowledge in the clearest and easiest way for amateurs, especially those who have read our treatise on thorough-bass[1] and understand the succession of chords, together with the relationship of keys. We assure the reader that all unnecessary prolixity is avoided and that anything which is not essential and useful at the present time is excluded. The basic principles, the arduous difficulties, and those things which were formerly obscure should be explained and revealed here in such a way that the amateur might easily be able to learn and use this pleasant science for his enjoyment. We now turn to the explanation of harmony.

---

[1] Throughout this work "our treatise on thorough-bass" refers to Daube's *Der Musikalische Dillettant* (Vienna, 1770/71), the first work in the *Dilettant* series, rather than his *General-Baß in drey Accorden* (Leipzig, 1756).

HARMONY IN GENERAL

Harmony is an arrangement of several tones or voices which are combined artificially so as to best obtain the final aim, which is to please the ear. It is presented in various ways: through the realization of the thorough-bass, whenever nothing but chords, all of which must be harmonic, are heard on the harpsichord etc.; or by various other instruments each playing a separate melodic line as, for example, in a fugue, where much artistic [elaboration] is displayed, or in a slow piece consisting mostly of chords. Here this same harmony is already more widely dispersed, while the diverse note values which occur, and similarly the passing tones, ornaments, etc., direct the harmony toward an effect altogether different from that which might result from a realization of the thorough-bass. Now if the harmony is expressed by voices [4] and instruments together, the result can be even better, provided the execution is good. Every amateur knows how much singing contributes to the expression of the affects.[2] The human voice always remains the most noble means of expressing them,[3] particularly when it has been well supported by nature and art. What even nature alone is able to do in this regard, and how it directs even the purest part of the harmony toward expressing certain affects, is found by listening to the sacred hymns which are sung by many persons together. The melody of these songs is the simplest and altogether the most artless, and the harmony, which is sung by people, most of whom understand nothing at all about music, consists of the unison and the octave. These two intervals, sung here by natural, untrained voices, are usually quite well in tune, and, despite the great poverty of this harmony, the final aim, which is to move the soul, is nevertheless very often achieved.

Indeed, the effect of harmony is multifarious.[4] A chord in which the intervals are spread out far from one another creates an altogether different impression than a chord in which they are quite close together. Furthermore, the ruling chord[5] in C major, for

---

[2] The doctrine of the affections or emotions (*Affektenlehre*), a codification of emotions and the means by which they could be represented in music, was to have been the subject of Daube's third, and missing, *Dilettant*.

[3] Beyond the general eighteenth-century admiration for the human voice as the most natural instrument, Daube's proclivity toward a vocal, "singing" style probably was influenced by his contact with the Italian bel-canto style which flourished in the southern German-speaking areas.

[4] As Daube proceeds, it becomes clear that *Harmonie* denotes both texture and chordal harmony (as opposed to the linear element of *Melodie*), and that his opening chapter invites the reader to explore the realm of texture and sound.

[5] Daube's "ruling chord" or "first chord" is the tonic chord. See the Introduction (p. 19–21) for the "three chords" in Daube's harmonic system.

example, sounds excellent when it is heard in the middle of the scale. Its effect is good on the organ, harpsichord, or piano, but still better when played by two violins and a violoncello. If it is heard on wind instruments of one family or of several, with or without string instruments, the effect is different in each case. This in turn is changed (let us not say further improved), if the first inversion is heard with the violoncello projecting the bass E quite emphatically with a *forzando*, and then slurring to F [Example 1].

Ex. 1

The second inversion, with G in the bass, does not have such a good effect, particularly if C is on top, [5] but it, too, can sound good if E is on top, or the bass is sustained in the low register [Example 2].

Ex. 2

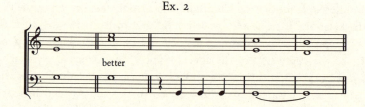

The reason is that the G, apart from this, is the root of its own natural harmony. However, if it is to appear as a bass with the harmony of the ruling chord, its effect cannot be as good, because in this chord it is properly regarded as an upper voice, especially when the proper root is on top, as shown here in the first measure of the first example. On the other hand, if the upper voice has E, which naturally lies closer to the G, the effect is better, because the sixth [between the outer voices] is pleasing to the ear. See the second measure. However, if the G is situated in the lower bass register, and is heard before the harmony of the ruling chord appears, the effect is excellent, especially if it is followed by the G harmony, or even a different one, over the stationary bass G.

Although the effect of the ruling chord in the middle tones of the scale is very good, it nevertheless is made even better by spacing its intervals far apart, as when two flutes play E and G, or E and C in the upper register [Example 3].

Ex. 3

The effect is very different when two oboes play these tones in the middle octave, particularly in thirds, [6] which sound more pleasant than sixths on these instruments, in contrast to the flutes [Example 4].

Ex. 4

The effect is changed once more when these two diverse wind instruments are heard together, and again if violins are added. If horns, too, join these instruments, the completely full harmony produces a magnificent musical expression. However, if the violins are muted, and the other instruments blow *piano*, this doubled chord can be expressed delicately. Placing the oboes an octave below the violins is an unusual arrangement which also creates an exceptional effect. It remains true that the characteristic tone quality of each instrument also contributes greatly to the expression of the affects. The unison is said to exactly coincide among all instruments, and yet everyone, even one uninformed about music, hears the difference between each of the instruments. All instruments used during antiquity as well as at the present time differ from one another in tone quality, [a characteristic] which results from the nature of the instrument and remains peculiar to it alone. Chords in which the tones are kept close together in the very low bass register are ineffectual on any instrument and of no use whatever. Yet they are more readily acceptable if the third [above the bass] is omitted, since then only the interval of a fifth or sixth is heard. Thirds and seconds are used to advantage in the upper register, but very rarely in the lower register unless the melody were found in the tenor. Even the very low double basses make a good impression only with a full complement of many diverse instruments, while violoncellos are much more useful in lightly scored things, or solos, in concertos, with the voice, in arias, etc.

In order for the harmony to have a good effect, it is also necessary to avoid always maintaining the complete full-voiced harmony, even if the piece is supposed to be comprised of four, five, or more voices. The third, however essential it may be, [7] can nevertheless be excluded at times, as when the fifth is paired with the bass, and its octave is better than the third in the middle part [Example 5].

Ex. 5

However, a bass tone which can be just a third below the top voice is always preferable to any other bass, in which case the fifth can be put in the middle part. Sixths have a good effect when their bass is played by either the second violin or the violoncello, but in this case the rest of the harmony should not be so heavy as to disturb the effect of the sixths. The diminished fifth, the augmented fourth, or so-called tritone, make a particular impression, especially in slow, delicate pieces in close two- or three-part harmony. However, should the piece be generally full-voiced, as may be the case in a church piece, chorus, or symphony, the other intervals can also be added. Here, however, a fine judgement is required, since even in the largest things the full-voicing must sometimes be interrupted for the occurrence of a delicate passage. In this full texture, however, the voices should very seldom lie close together. On the contrary, it is always better for the voices to be separated from one another. Every scholar of music knows that, through the separation of their voices, even the strongest dissonant chords lose a large part of their harshness or discord, whereby they, in alternation with other chords, help to contribute greatly toward the beauty of a piece. The effect is very clearly perceived by the ear.

[8] In three-part composition, where the third can more readily be omitted, the second chord also makes a good impression when the adjacent intervals of a fifth and sixth are heard together, with the fifth then slurring down a step [Example 6].[6]

Ex. 6

In a four-part piece, however, the third can also be included. In the third chord, the third and seventh are preferable to the fifth, if the piece should be in three parts [Example 7].[7]

Ex. 7

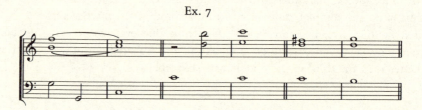

On the other hand, when the seventh is major, it can be combined with the second. Likewise, the second and augmented fourth are readily used together in three-part composition. Look at the two foregoing examples. The diminished seventh chord[8] calls

---

[6] Daube's "second chord" is ii$^6_5$, sometimes ii^6 or IV. In Ex. 6, m. 2, both *d″* and *b′* have a stem in the original.

[7] Daube's "third chord" is V[7], sometimes V or vii. In Ex. 7, the *b′–c″* slur is editorial.

[8] One of Daube's "artificial" chords, the diminished (*klein*) seventh may substitute for the "third chord" except in cadences. See n. 12 for a discussion of "art" and "artificial."

for close intervals and always makes a good impression. However, if the piece has only three voices, the diminished seventh, and likewise the ninth in similar cases, is accompanied by the third [Example 8].

Ex. 8

[9] The other artificial chords welcome the separation of their tones. Now if a piece should include many such harmonies, particular care must be taken, at least when changing to a different chord, that one tone might always be able to remain stationary, and that chiefly in alternation between the two voices. For example:

Ex. 9

In general, variety in harmony, just as in melody, is very necessary, both in view of the succession of chords and the distribution of the chord tones, provided that it is to contribute to the pleasure of the ear and the expression of the affects. Everyone knows that even if a well-constructed melody were given to a hundred or more skillful composers to be harmonized, and these harmonizations were all worked out strictly according to the rules of composition, yet, throughout all hundred compositions, the melody in combination with the harmony would inevitably produce a different impression each time.[9] Then, one might ask, which is the best? That one is best which is adapted to the nature of the melody and complements the expression of those affects which are characteristic of it.[10] These are things which are taken into consideration by even the most experienced composers, for whom it is otherwise quite an easy thing indeed to write the harmony for any naturally flowing melody. In the course of this book we will endeavor to elucidate all of this even more clearly by means of the accompanying examples.

---

[9] Daube's awareness of the potential for variety in the large numerical possibilities for selection and combination of musical elements suggests the *ars combinatoria*, used earlier by Mersenne, Kircher, Printz, and Ziegler, and by Daube's contemporary Riepel. This concept, important in mathematical theory of the period, was set forth by Leibniz in his *Dissertatio de arte combinatoria* (1666). Applied to music, "*Musica Combinatoria* . . . shows how to combine sounds by changing their position and shape in as many ways as possible" (Brossard, *Dictionaire* (1703), p. 58, Eng. trans., p. 63). See Ratner, "*Ars combinatoria*," p. 345. See n. 87.

[10] Daube shows a typically eighteenth-century interest in rational judgement. Other writers who judge a harmonization by its reflection of the expressive character of the melody include Rameau, *Traité* (1722), p. 324, Eng. trans., p. 341; Kollmann, *Essay* (1799), p. 82; Kirnberger, *Kunst*, vol. II/1 (1776), p. 19, Eng. trans., p. 297.

2

THE THREE DIFFERENT MOTIONS
OF THE VOICES

If we consider harmony from the point of view that it may serve as the accompaniment for melody, it has its limitations as far as [10] the succession of chords is concerned. However, if the voices which have been formed from the chords can move in different directions in relation to one another, and thereby carry their own separate lines,[11] then harmony can be accorded the same almost limitless variety as that which is inherent in melody. In music there are three different motions by which the voices move back and forth. The first is called parallel motion. This consists of two voices ascending or descending together in the same tempo, that is, in notes of equal value. This motion can be called the natural one. Art plays a very small part in it.[12] Nature has given it the unison and the octave, as we hear in the echo, and eventually the third above and below (sixth) were added by the process of imitation. The alternation of the third and octave, and of the sixth and unison may be attributed to art. Thus parallel motion can also provide the easiest introductory method for the construction of two voices. In doing this a beginner has only to observe that the second voice can proceed in either thirds or sixths with the first, and then, in accordance with the thorough-bass method, that the ending must be an octave or unison rather than a third or sixth, provided that it has been preceded by a closing formula or cadence [Example 10].

Ex. 10

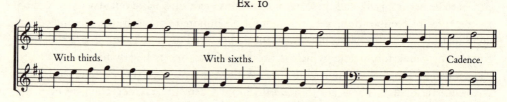

With thirds.   With sixths.   Cadence.

[11] The idea of having the voices "carry their own separate lines" is mentioned by many theorists, including Riepel, *Anfangsgründe*, vol. V (1768), p. 3 and Kirnberger, *Kunst*, vol. I (1771), pp. 143–5, Eng. trans., pp. 160–62. While some writers, such as Riepel, Kirnberger, and Fux (*Gradus* (1725), Ger. trans., L. Mizler (1742), p. 60, Eng. trans. in Mann, *Counterpoint*, pp. 21–2) describe the three motions as contrapuntal progressions of perfect and imperfect consonances, others, especially those discussing thorough-bass performance rather than composition, define the three motions as Daube does – in terms of relative direction without intervallic specifications. These include Löhlein, *Klavier-Schule* (1765), pp. 88–9; C. P. E. Bach, *Versuch* (2/1759), pp. 24–5, Eng. trans., p. 191; and Petri, *Anleitung* (2/1782), p. 225.

[12] Here Daube introduces the dichotomy of art (*Kunst*) and nature (*Natur*), a theme which recurs on many levels throughout the *Dilettante*. In general Daube equates art or artifice with musical complexity, intellectual ingenuity, harmony or texture (as opposed to melody), and complexities such as chromaticism and the bound style of "the ancients," while nature – more prevalent in music of "the moderns" – is represented by simplicity, spontaneity, melody, diatonic harmony, and an appeal to the ear as opposed to the intellect. ("Artificial" likewise meant "made by art," and did not carry the connotation of "synthetic" which it acquired later.) For eighteenth-century discussions of these terms see J. A. P. Schulz's "Kunst; künstlich." in Sulzer, *Allgemeine Theorie*, vol. II (1774), pp. 625–6 and Adelung's *Wörterbuch*, vol. II (1796), pp. 1830–35.

This method of composing two parts is regarded with particular favor when two voices – namely two sopranos, or two flutes, two oboes, etc. – are set in the middle of a scale. The upper register is still more advantageous to the flutes. Slow rather than quick passages are preferable for the voice. Parallel motion may be included in any piece. It is sometimes desirable in the church style as well as the opera and chamber styles.[13] Everything of a delicately singing nature can be enhanced by it. The appropriate place to use parallel motion will be pointed out even more clearly during the course of this work.

Another motion in harmony is called contrary motion and characteristically occurs when the melody of the main voice ascends [11] into the upper register while the other voice descends, or the reverse. This type of motion already has been very highly recommended in our thorough-bass treatise, because it is among the most important points in the study of thorough-bass. It likewise deserves to be designated as the surest way to prevent mistakes in composition. It was engendered by art and established by practical usage. From contrary motion, there arise the most beautiful combinations and melodic motives (*Glieder*) which must serve as the substance (*Körper*) of the main melody (*Hauptmelodie*). But moderation also must be observed here, because otherwise an all too strong or continuous use of contrary motion can actually be detrimental to the main melody.

Variety in music is always most pleasant. The advantages and usefulness of contrary motion may be judged from the fact that it has all the intervals in its domain, so that even the unison and the octave may appear in a two-voice piece.

Ex. 11

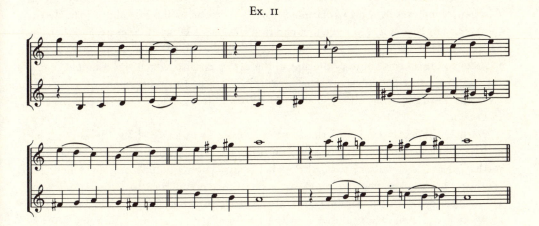

Here [in Example 11] we see that it is possible to begin with a unison or an octave, as well as with the other intervals. The beginning may be a consonance or dissonance, but the end must usually be a consonance. The first example shows a very simple usage including only the intervals within the key. Here contrary motion begins with the diminished fifth, and the harmony is an alternation of the third and first chords. The second example begins with a third and already contains an interval foreign to the key.

---

[13] The three functional styles recognized by eighteenth-century theorists. Parallel motion was less to be expected in the church style, due to the latter's traditionally contrapuntal nature. See pp. 132, 217 and n. 157.

This is done [12] so that the E in the bass or lower voice could coincide with the last tone, B, [of the upper voice] and yet a different note could be set in the lower voice against each tone of the upper voice. For more on this subject, examine the key of E minor in the treatise on thorough-bass. The third example begins with the diminished seventh and resolves into the first chord, as is customary. The third chord follows, and then the first chord again. After this, although the third chord does reappear, it does not resolve into the first chord, but rather into one partially similar to it, namely the third chord in D minor, and this harmony in turn goes to a chord partially equivalent to its first chord, namely the compound seventh chord in G major.[14] The following harmonies have the same resolution as those in the first two measures, except that they are set one tone lower. In our thorough-bass method, the treatment of the artificial resolution of chords[15] is demonstrated by several examples. The fourth example shows that with this type of motion the various voices may also be allowed to commence with a unison. The first tone, by virtue of the following F-sharp, belongs to the harmony of the second chord in G major. The subsequent interval of a second results from the retention of the tone in the upper voice, and here is to be considered more as a passing interval which occurs only in order to proceed from the unison and likewise to allow contrary motion to be introduced. The F-sharp and C which follow belong to the third chord in the key of G major, and then comes a harmony partially similar to its first chord, namely the third chord in A minor, which is succeeded by the octave A. The fifth example is especially worthy of a beginner's attention. It begins with an octave followed by the third chord in A minor, which resolves into a harmony partially similar to the first chord, namely the third chord in D minor. Now the first chord in the key of D minor appears, and then the partially similar third chord in G major followed also by the first chord in G major. In order to propel this contrary motion to the octave A with which this example began, the chromatic chord[16] which is partially equivalent to the foregoing chord now appears, with the G-sharp being the half step closest to it from below, just as the B-flat is from above.

We have diligently explained these examples here in order to show the novice how each harmony should always be reasoned out from the previous one. In our thorough-bass method, page 305, we said that, although the first chord should naturally follow the third chord in any key, nevertheless the rules of art may permit a partially similar chord to follow instead. [13] All of composition, indeed even the melody itself, is based upon this, as we will endeavor to demonstrate in the proper place. There are also many cases in which a bass note indicates what is to follow, even when the melody may not yet show it [Example 12].

---

[14] A diminished triad plus a major third. Daube often calls it the compound (*zusammengesetzt*) major seventh chord.
[15] "Artificial resolutions" are those resolving to a chord other than the expected "first chord." They include resolutions to "partially similar" or "partially equivalent" chords, in which one or more notes belong to the first chord, while one or more are different – often chromatically altered to change the expected triad into a new dominant chord.
[16] The second of Daube's "artificial" chords is the augmented sixth chord.

Ex. 12

Here the melody indicates that the third chord could be used twice before the final tone [i.e., tonic note], but the bass sounds the A which corresponds to the upper G and E only once before going to D from the first chord. The reason for this is the following. In the thorough-bass method we mentioned that the harmony of the first chord must follow that of the third chord. The exceptions to this rule are the aforesaid partially similar chords, and the deceptive cadence. Now if the harmony of the first chord does not appear immediately in the melody, nevertheless, according to the preceding rule, the root of the first chord is set to it, as shown in the example. Moreover, bound tones such as the G which occurs twice here,[17] very seldom are given their own bass, and besides, this second G can also be regarded as an appoggiatura, which never has a bass of its own. If this rule is observed, one may (provided only that one or several tones from the third chord are previously sounded in the melody) choose to take the melody to different tones or degrees, to which the bass can be added. In that way the succession [of chords] always remains proper to the root of the first chord. More about this below.

We now turn to the explanation of the third motion of the voices. This is called oblique motion and consists of one voice moving through various tones while the other voice sounds only a single tone. This tone may be sustained as a long note or expressed by rapidly reiterated notes, provided that the pitch remains the same. Oblique motion is the most artificial and beautiful in composition. It also quite often incorporates one of the two motions described above, whereby both are heard at the same time. Often a combination of all three motions occurs, but always for the pleasure of [14] connoisseurs of music. Without this principal motion, very little of beauty can be accomplished in composition. And oblique motion is quite unique, in that nature and art play an equal part in it. No type of musical piece can do without it entirely, with the exception perhaps of a few little pieces for trumpets or horns. Most of the affects can be expressed by it. In general, it may be said that true beauty in music is dependent upon oblique motion. In most opera arias in the current taste, one can hardly find a measure without this type of motion, and indeed, the most magnificent symphonies are impressively adorned with it when the wind instruments have sustained tones.[18] Thus it also can rightfully be called an embellishment of the harmony. Indeed, in the proper place we will even attempt to demonstrate that the invention of melody itself is partially indebted to oblique motion.

---

[17] Ex. 12: the *e″* and *g″* are not tied in the original.

[18] See Chapter 6, *passim*. Compare Riepel on sustained wind tones in symphonic writing, *Anfangsgründe*, vol. IV (1765), p. 72.

We have purposely described these three motions in harmony rather extensively since, as a rule, they are treated much too briefly in other writings. It is known that the advantages resulting from a clear and detailed explanation can be extremely important to a prospective composer. Of what use is the knowledge of harmony, if one does not know how to activate it by means of the proper motions? For want of this it would very closely resemble an inanimate body. Even if one wanted to set a harmony in motion by means of the repeated statement of one chord, it would please no one. Why? What is lacking here is melody – the change or progression of tones, and the change of motion itself. But a phrase in which a single change occurs already has been subjected to one of the three types of motion.

In the treatise on thorough-bass we brought up various aspects of this subject and demonstrated that even accompanying or thorough-bass playing is dependent upon the three motions. Anyone who fully understood that truth will certainly not doubt their aforementioned usefulness in composition. Therefore we recommend the thorough-bass treatise. A beginner would do well to read it over and appropriate it even before proceeding to the combining of two voices. The resulting benefits will be evident soon afterwards.

3

COMBINING TWO VOICES

[15] It is reasonable to begin the study of harmony with two voices. Whoever knows how to write these well, will subsequently not find it difficult to add a third one also. Here, however, we are speaking only of altogether simple harmony which as yet requires very little judgement. Two-part harmony[19] can conveniently be divided into two classes:[20] one, which simply pertains to an upper voice and a bass; and the other, which is com-

[19] In this preliminary chapter on part-writing, Daube does not use the term "duet," which implies concerting between the two parts (a technique developed in Chapters 4–6). According to J. A. P. Schulz, "two-voice pieces . . . are of two types: the most distinguished and difficult are those for two concerting voices, and are called duets" (Sulzer, "Zweistimmig. (Musik.)," *Allgemeine Theorie*, vol. II (1774), pp. 1286–7, corroborated by Kirnberger in "Duet. (Musik.)," ibid., vol. I (1771), pp. 282–3). Compare Türk, *Klavierschule* (1789), p. 394, Eng. trans., p. 387; and Koch, "Duett," *Lexicon* (1802), cols. 497, 501.

[20] Some other theorists also recognize two types of two-part writing, distinguished less by range than by a basically homophonic texture (similar to Daube's "two equal voices") and a more polyphonic texture (similar to Daube's melody/bass type). This stylistic distinction, noted about 1760 by Quantz (*Sechs Duette für zwei Flöten*, vol. I, Preface), is explicitly described thirty years later by Koch, *Versuch*, vol. III (1793), pp. 320–21, Eng. trans., pp. 204–05.

posed of two equal voices.[21] To make a correct setting of the former type, choose any key (as was analyzed and explained in our thorough-bass method) and put a tone from this key in the upper voice, noticing at once, however, to which chord this tone belongs. Then write the lowest tone, namely the root of this chord, in the bass.

In the key of C major, for example, if we set the E in the upper voice, we immediately discover that this tone is to be found in neither the second nor third chord, but that it belongs in the first chord, the root of which is C. Therefore this C is set in the bass, because it best harmonizes with E as well as G [Example 13].

Ex. 13

In two-part composition it is also permissible for the root to provide the bass for its octave, but this should not be done with the other intervals of this chord. The second bass note is [16] E. This tone is used in the bass when C or G is in the soprano. It serves as an alternate for C and always has a good effect [Example 14].

Ex. 14

G also can appear in the bass whenever the bass moves in sixths with the upper voice, a progression which provides variety in two-part composition and is permitted throughout all degrees of the key. It is in just this way that the G is brought into the bass for the formation of a cadence [Example 15].

---

[21] Daube's melody/bass type, a standard eighteenth-century texture, relates to the thorough-bass tradition (in which the bass provides the harmonic foundation for a treble *Melodie-Instrument*) and also forms the skeletal framework for many ensemble pieces, including symphonies. Riepel, for instance, speaks of letting the second violins play in unison with the firsts, while the violas move in octaves with the bass line (*Anfangsgründe*, vol. III (1757), p. 35). Pieces for two equal (usually treble) parts reflect the generally accepted later eighteenth-century view that the harmony is so clear and orderly that the two treble voices can lead the ear adequately through the rhetoric of key and cadential formula – an assumption especially well founded in Daube's simplified three-chord harmonic system. See Quantz, *Sechs Duette für zwei Flöten* (c. 1760), vol. I, Preface; Kirnberger, *Kunst*, vol. I (1771), p. 171, Eng. trans., pp. 184–5; and Koch, *Versuch*, vol. III (1793), pp. 320–21, Eng. trans., pp. 204–05. See also Ratner, *Classic Music*, pp. 108–09, 120–23.

Ex. 15

Since we already have pointed out all of this in the thorough-bass method, it can be reviewed there. We now have demonstrated the position of each interval of the first chord in the bass. However, we still must speak about those tones which may occur here even though they really belong to melody rather than harmony. They are called passing tones. Their origin and use are described in our thorough-bass method on pages 51 and 84. They are used to great advantage in composition and are, in fact, necessary, since whenever the upper voice sustains a long note, the bass should continue with a moving part, because constant motion is the soul of music. Thus, if one part stands still, as it were, or sustains a long note, the other part must maintain the motion. To be sure, there are also cases in which all the voices proceed very slowly, but these are too far out of fashion, and are more suitable for songs of lament and mourning, than for encouragement and cheer, which [17] after all, should be the principal purpose.[22] Here are the locations of passing tones in the first chord [Example 16].[23]

Ex. 16

In the first example we see two passing tones, namely D and F. These result from the movement of the root, C, to its third, which includes the D in between, and then from the movement of E to its third, G, which likewise passes through the tone F between them. In the second example two additional passing tones are shown, namely B, the half step below the root, and A, a [whole] step above the fifth, G. With both of these tones,

---

[22] Daube's phrase, "the soul (Seele) of music," which hints at the current fascination with bringing the mechanical to life, also is used by Leopold Mozart and others (Violinschule (3/1789), p. 27, Eng. trans., p. 30). Riepel likewise comments that "a slow movement such as an Adagio is sad," and that "today most music lovers are no longer pleased to listen to sad things, except in church" (Anfangsgründe, vol. IV (1765), p. 32). See n. 41.

[23] Ex. 16: m. 2, upper voice, the last note is a whole note in the original; lower voice, the last note is a half note in the original; m. 3, no crosses over f and a in the original.

however, the bass line must return directly to the intervals of the first chord.[24] In the first case this is because the next tone below B does not belong in the first chord, and since B is a passing tone already, it certainly should be followed by a tone in the C chord. In the second case the same is to be noticed with A, where the bass likewise may not ascend to B. However, if the bass ascends or descends in running sixteenth notes, even this can take place [Example 17].

Ex. 17

Just as the main consideration in writing a simple bass voice is not the passing tones, but rather only that the first and third notes harmonize well with the upper voice, so the same should likewise apply in writing the upper voice. Here there is an almost constant admixture of passing tones, especially when the melody is in the singing style or includes stepwise [18] ascending and descending passages. Let us give a few illustrations of this [Example 18].[25]

Ex. 18 Passing Tones in the Upper Voice

---

[24] Daube categorizes unaccented neighbor tones (upper and lower auxiliaries) with passing tones because of their weak rhythmic position. There was general agreement among contemporaneous theorists about this terminology.

[25] Ex. 18: m. 3, upper voice, notes 2–3 are sixteenths in the original.

Here we see that the first note of each quarter measure always belongs to the harmony of the first chord. Later we will also show that if the first note has been heard once already, and subsequently occurs in this [rhythmic] position, it might also pass as an appoggiatura[26] set against a bass which actually belongs with the second note. This, then, is the way to write a bass to the intervals of the first chord. Now in a harmony of two equal voices mostly thirds and sixths will occur. Therefore, if the first voice has E, the second voice can have either C or G [Example 19]. If the first voice has C, the other voice takes E, the sixth [below]. On the other hand, if the first voice should have G, the second takes either E, or else C, the fifth [below].

Ex. 19

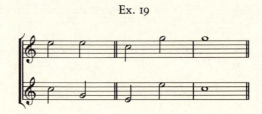

[19] If the first voice contains subdivided passing tones, the second voice can have just as many [Example 20].

Ex. 20

Imitations can also occur. If the first voice introduces a few passages, the second voice can then repeat them while the first voice sustains a tone in the harmony of the first chord [Example 21].[27]

---

[26] Daube categorizes reiterated suspensions (and accented passing tones) with appoggiaturas because of their strong rhythmic position. Like Daube, many eighteenth-century German writers used the term "Vorschlag" to denote prepared, reiterated dissonance, as well as the unprepared or free appoggiatura approached by leap. C. P. E. Bach says that "at times appoggiaturas (*die Vorschläge*) repeat the preceding note, at times they do not . . ." (*Versuch* (2/1759), p. 64, Eng. trans., p. 87). See n. 43. In harmonizing a melody of diverse note values, the recognition of non-chord tones in any rhythmic position is of critical importance in determining the correct chords, whereas in elaborating a 1:1 counterpoint to another species, the required consistency of melodic motion may be achieved by adding either arsic or thetic non-chord tones between the original pitches. Hence what Kirnberger – thinking contrapuntally – calls an irregular passing tone (a transitional "Durchgang," which "goes through" on the beat) (*Kunst*, vol. I (1771), pp. 194–5, Eng. trans., p. 210), Daube – thinking harmonically – calls a "stumbling block" appoggiatura (a "*Vorschlag*" which "strikes before" the chord tone and may not easily be recognized).

[27] Ex. 21: m. 1, lower voice, notes 4–7 are sixteenths in the original.

Ex. 21

All of these passages may be accounted for within the harmony of the first chord, for, as has been said already, the passing tones do not belong to any chord.

We hope that our demonstration of two-part harmony in the first chord has been clear. A beginner should carefully reread this opening discussion of two-part composition and draw up a few examples according to this prescription, so that in the future he will not find it difficult to comprehend artificial constructions either. We now turn to the second chord which shows even more variety since it is made up of four intervals, as is known from the thorough-bass method where its root was indicated in every key. We want to continue with the key of C major, in which the root of the [20] second chord is F. This tone must harmonize with all three upper voices [Example 22].

Ex. 22

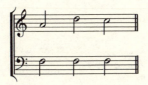

However, when the F itself is in the upper voice, the bass takes A [Example 23]. If two bass tones are needed for this F, the D can also be used. The fifth of this chord, C, is seldom found in the bass except when it is held over from the root of a preceding first chord, in which case the F can then also appear in the upper voice against the retained bass C.

Ex. 23

Two bass tones can be set to the sixth, D, or the fifth, C, when either of these appears in the upper voice [Example 24].

Ex. 24

The bass parts derived from the harmony of the second chord are rich in passing tones. These can occur particularly when the upper voice has sustained notes [Example 25].

Ex. 25 Passing Tones in the Bass

The four-part harmony of this chord gives rise to these passing tones. To these is added E, the tone below F. On the other hand, when the upper voice sounds passing tones in this chord, the bass usually remains on the root or its third [Example 26].

Ex. 26 Passing Tones in the Upper Voice

Here the procedure followed in the first chord is to be recommended, [namely,] that in those cases involving running passages, one should concern oneself mainly with the first note which, however, must be founded on the harmony of the bass. Now if two equal voices are to be composed, here again passages of thirds and sixths should be considered. The location of these intervals is evident from the chord itself. When the third is omitted from the chord, still there is always the sixth, and the reverse.

Ex. 27

Ex. 28 With Passing Tones in Both Voices

One sees [in Examples 27–8] that the tones F and A can be accompanied in thirds as well as sixths. When the C is part of this harmony, it calls for only the sixth, A, whereas D, on the other hand, prefers only the third, F. And all this proceeds from the harmony of this chord, as is further proven in the thorough-bass method. Imitation can also occur in this chord [Example 29].

Ex. 29

Whoever has insight into the richness of melody will find it easy to arrange a great many various imitations.

The harmony of the third chord, as is known, also has four parts, the root in this key being G. Now if the tones of the G harmony are sounded successively in the upper voice, the root can be set to each of them [Example 30], all of which is known already from our treatise on thorough-bass.

Ex. 30

[m. 2, bass note *c* in original]

[23] Sometimes, for a change, the third of the chord also must appear in the bass [Example 31]. However, should the two voices move in sixths or thirds, a procedure which is used for variety and in certain other situations, the remaining intervals also can appear in the bass. Even the F, for instance, can be set with a soprano B, if it has been preceded by the second chord.

Ex. 31

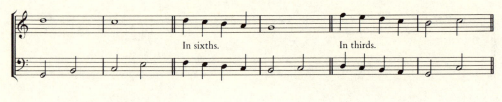

Otherwise the actual bass tones are the root, G, and the third, B. The rest of the chord tones more properly contribute to the bass melody. They are also employed when two bass notes are set to a long note in the upper voice. If the root descends a tone, the seventh of this harmony, namely F, appears in the bass. When the bass forms a sixth or third with a long note in the upper voice, the following bass note can be either the root or its third [Example 32].

Ex. 32

Passing tones in the bass, when mingled with the tones of this harmony, contribute to the formation of the bass melody [Example 33].[28]

Ex. 33 With Passing Tones

---

[28] Daube repeatedly emphasizes the importance of the bass melody, not only as a good harmonic foundation, but also as a flowing, cantabile line in itself. See, for instance, p. 82. Other theorists also concern themselves with the formation of a cantabile bass line. C. P. E. Bach expresses the opinion that "good bass themes, evolving naturally, are among the master touches of composition" ("Ein gutes Baßthema mit einer ungezwungenen Ausarbeitung gehöret mit zu den Meisterstücken der Composition.") (*Versuch* (2/1759), pp. 322–3, Eng. trans., p. 426). Riepel writes that the bass "must have a flexible, spacious (*weitläufigers*) cantabile" (*Anfangsgründe*, vol. I (1752), p. 18). Scheibe speaks of using first inversions to make the bass more "singing" (*Musikalische Composition* (1773), p. 355), and Portmann encourages inversions to create a light, natural, flowing bass line (*Leichtes Lehrbuch*, (1789), p. 51).

When two equal voices are to be constructed, passages in thirds and sixths make a good impression in this chord also [Example 34].[29]

Ex. 34

When a tone in the upper voice is sustained, the second voice sounds two or more tones against it. This also has a good effect [Example 35].

Ex. 35

When passing tones and chord tones are intermingled, the second voice may move either in sixths or thirds, with just as many passing tones as the upper voice, or else sound only the plain intervals of the chord [Example 36].

Ex. 36 With Passing Tones

The alternation of passages in thirds and sixths produces a good effect, especially with two vocalists or wind instrumentalists. The imitation of a running passage can be arranged in this chord also [Example 37].

Ex. 37

[29] Ex. 34: m. 1, upper voice, note 1 is *d″* in the original; Ex. 36: m. 2, upper voice, note 9 is *c″* in original.

The discussion of these three chords can be very useful to an amateur composer. One sees here a complete correspondence to the thorough-bass method: how to write a correct bass to a melody and how the bass, through the inclusion of passing tones, may be made melodic; likewise, how to construct two equal voices, knowing which intervals may be most prevalent there; and finally, how to arrange imitation.

We now turn to the [process of] combining these three chords in two-part composition, in which regard we must refer again to the explanation of the key of C major in the thorough-bass method, where we have shown the various ways in which these three chords can succeed one another.[30]

Ex. 38

In this example [Example 38] the three chords proceed in order until the seventh measure where the third chord follows directly upon the first chord, and then these two chords alternate until the end. In constructing a bass to the upper voice, one merely examines each melody tone to determine to which chord it belongs and, since some tones are found in two chords, one simply heeds the order of succession of the three chords. In the first measure here we find C and E in the upper voice. Both tones belong to the first chord and consequently, especially at the beginning, the root C, is used. The second measure contains D and C. Both of these tones belong to the harmony of the second chord, therefore the root, F, must be set in the bass. The third measure contains four tones, all of which belong to the third chord in C major. The root, G, or for a change its third, B, accompanies these tones. The fourth measure has two tones which, however, do not both belong in the same chord, and so two different bass tones should be set to them. The first

---

[30] The next four examples constitute a set, in which Daube's various elaborations of the original melody show traces of species counterpoint, widely known through Fux's *Gradus* (1725), Ger. trans., L. Mizler (1742). In this example Daube uses first species (1:1) and second species (2:1) rhythmic relationships; in the next, third species (4:1); the following hints of fourth species (syncopated); the last is fifth species (free). Although this reference may seem surprising in a *galant* context, "species counterpoint was taken over bodily into the music of the classic style. . . . Much classic music that is thoroughly *galant* in spirit will reveal a two-part counterpoint in the first or second species when the elaboration is lifted away . . ." (Ratner, "*Ars combinatoria*," p. 358; see also his *Classic Music*, pp. 109–13).

tone, E, belongs in the first chord, and the following A in the second chord. Therefore, the two roots, C and F, must be put in the bass. The third chord usually must follow the harmony of the second chord, just as happens here when the subsequent soprano D is accompanied by G in the bass. Then E follows in the bass, because the upper voice has C. In the sixth measure F and D reappear, both of which are found in the second, as well as the third chord. Here one would have the choice of employing only one chord, namely the third chord, or using the bass tones from both chords. We [27] have done the latter, because in that way the succession of the three chords takes place and the bass is made more melodic, while at the same time forming a cadence. The following C belongs in the first chord again, and the bass likewise sounds the octave C, an interval which occurs readily after a regular cadence. Now the second chord is omitted, because the B is not a member of it, but rather of the third chord, and so the bass sounds D, the sixth [below]. This bass is good because of the contrary motion [from the previous interval], and because it brings about [parallel] sixths with the following bass E and soprano C. The subsequent G in the upper voice could be part of the first chord as well as the third chord. We have chosen the latter and put B, the sixth [below], in the bass. Since G appears once again in the soprano, the bass may very well accompany it with the root, C, the second time. The B in the upper voice once again belongs in the third chord, and the root, G, accordingly appears in the bass. The final interval must be an octave.

Now, in order to substantially increase the motion of the bass line, one may simply introduce passing tones here and there, whereby a bass melody is also obtained. However, in doing this, one must make certain that the root or its third in each chord usually appears as the first, or at least as the third note. The melody also will be further improved if it is interrupted occasionally by short rests, of which more is to be said in the future.[31]

Ex. 39

[31] See n. 49.

Here [in Example 39] the bass always has four notes for each chord, with the first note being the root or its third, except in the seventh measure, where the bass D is a sixth below the soprano, which demonstrates that the bass may also ascend and descend [28] in thirds or sixths with the upper voice, chiefly because the third above the root is also present in these passages, as the following E and B here, which are the thirds above the roots of the first and third chords respectively.

Now if one wanted to vary the melody of the upper voice by means of appoggiaturas, which were to be written as large notes, the bass nevertheless could remain as it is, despite the many dissonances that then would be heard against it. For the amateur's pleasure we would like to include this example also [Example 40].

Ex. 40

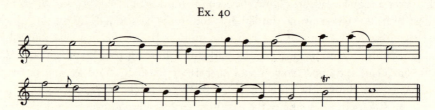

These appoggiaturas or retarded tones already have been described on page 97 of our thorough-bass method. The practice of using them is good, yet must not be carried to excess. They can contribute to the enhancement of the melody, but also to the weakening [of its quality]. On the other hand, whoever knows how to vary a simple melody well, can make even the poorest melodic line attractive. Since the entire art of variation also originates in the three chords, we want to give a little sample of it [Example 41].

Ex. 41

[m. 1, upper voice, the dots are missing in the original; m. 9, upper voice, the final appoggiatura is *b′* in the original]

[29] The preceding groundwork is as simple as possible, because it is meant to serve only for the study of two-part composition of the type in which a bass accompanies the upper voice. We have endeavored to improve this upper voice to some extent through the addition of appoggiaturas. Now this improved melody has been varied according to

the harmony of the three chords, resulting in a tolerable melody. Since the melody includes skipping passages, a running bass may not be used here. For this reason we have kept the original plain bass. Oblique motion is best in such cases. We have pursued this example diligently for the purpose of giving the amateurs a little foretaste of what we promised about the invention of melody at the beginning of this work.[32] Therefore, a beginner in composition should not become impatient if his essays do not immediately turn out well for him, particularly where the melody is concerned. This can soon be improved with ambition, time, and a good introductory method, especially when diligence is coupled with a desire to compose.

In constructing a bass to the usual melody, one must pay special attention to the place where the melody modulates into another key, in order to locate the melody tones in the three chords of the new key as soon as possible. Notice, in doing this, that the harmony of the new third chord must precede the first chord in that key.

Ex. 42

[30] Here [in Example 42] one does not clearly perceive where the key changes, unless it might be at the cadence in G major. Now and then in the thorough-bass method it was said that, in keeping with the natural course of the melody and harmony, one could not proceed to another key until the first chord of the old key had been heard. Now since

---

[32] Daube is referring to the projected fourth volume of the *Dilettant* series, which finally appeared without that title in 1797/98 as *Anleitung zur Erfindung der Melodie und ihrer Fortsetzung*.

this chord appears in the fourth measure, the melody and harmony of the fifth measure can already be considered to be in the key of G major. Therefore, the C and A in this measure belong to the harmony of the third chord, especially since the preceding C-major chord bears a great resemblance to the second chord in G major. The intervals of the first chord in the new key are introduced already in the sixth measure. In the eighth measure another change takes place. The F appears and is retained. Here one could regard such a continuation of the melody as a movement back into the key of C, if the ninth and tenth[33] measures were not repeated once more a tone lower. Because the G-major chord is indicated in this repetition in the twelfth measure, the tenth measure can just as properly be part of the first chord in A minor. Now it still depends upon where the harmony of the third chord is located since, according to our rule, it usually should precede the first chord. At least the main indication of the key must be there, namely the new sharp. Now since the ninth measure contains three tones, of which the latter two are in the third chord of A minor, the first tone, F, which is not in that chord, must be considered an appoggiatura to the main note, E, or else a chord which also contains the F must be sought. Should the former alternative be preferred, C could be placed in the bass, and the F in the eighth measure would then be from the harmony of the third chord in C major. This phrase would be correct, but the transposition to B minor which would subsequently have to take place cannot ensue because these two keys are much too distant from one another.[34] We have chosen the other alternative, all the more since it promotes the natural melodic line of both parts. It is known that minor keys have another chord, namely the diminished seventh chord, and it is this which here takes the place of the third chord in A minor, since they are differentiated by only one tone. Its root is G-sharp, which indeed is always the main indication of the key of A. Therefore D, the first tone in the [tenth] measure, may pass for an appoggiatura which, strictly speaking, is given no separate bass. The eleventh measure, due to the retention of the E, can be regarded as the compound major seventh chord of G major, or else as the harmony of the third chord in G major, if we want to consider the retained E in this measure as an appoggiatura, just the same as the one in the next measure. [31] The D in the thirteenth measure and the A in the fourteenth measure are to be regarded as appoggiaturas also, which is why the bass disregards them, taking its cue from the following note instead. If an amateur considers the bound or retained tones from this point of view, he will very soon arrive at an understanding of the derivation and position of the ninth, and of those sevenths and other harmonies which are not naturally situated in our three chords.

There are also appoggiaturas which consist of half steps that are not tones indicative of a new key [Example 43].

---

[33] "eighth and ninth" in the original.

[34] Vogler likewise recommends avoiding modulations more than one sharp or flat distant (*Tonwissenschaft* (1776), pp. 70–73). It should be noted, however, that Vogler is concerned mainly with unity in the conservative church style, Daube with directing the beginner as simply as possible. Contemporaneous music certainly contained bolder key relationships than these, and Daube's earlier *General-Baß* (1756) deals with all of them.

Ex. 43

The key of C major, as is known, has no sharp nor flat, and yet both can occur in that key without the melody modulating into another key. These accidental sharps and flats appear as appoggiaturas. In view of this, the bass never harmonizes with them, but rather with the following note, even though its value makes it much shorter than the appoggiatura. Here F appears at once in the first measure where, despite the fact that it naturally belongs in this key, it is regarded as an appoggiatura, in that the subsequent E is the main note to which the bass is set. This appoggiatura occurs here only to fill the space between the opening G and the E, and this is done by the F in between. The F-sharp which occurs in this same measure is an appoggiatura to the following G, and therefore the bass conforms to the latter, and the [presence of] the F-sharp is likewise disregarded. The last note in the second [32] measure is a passing [C-] sharp which subsequently is used as an appoggiatura to D. Therefore one again considers the following note, D, which calls for F in the bass. At the very beginning of the measure, however, this F is set against the C-sharp, but viewed as if the D were there instead of the C-sharp. Now this tone is the root of the second chord, and so, according to the aforementioned rule, it must be followed by the root of the third chord or by another bass drawn from this harmony, if it is to be done strictly according to the nature of the key. Meanwhile, the tone A is retained in the upper voice and makes another appoggiatura to G, but this does not affect the bass voice here either, since it always completely disregards the presence of the appoggiatura. In the fifth measure two sharp appoggiaturas appear and are dealt with in a similar manner.

Appoggiaturas marked with a sharp are always slurred upward a half step to the following tone. On the contrary, those appoggiaturas marked with a flat are slurred downward a half step to the following tone.

Ex. 44

Ex. 44 (cont.)

In this example [Example 44] there are three flat appoggiaturas which come about in a merely incidental way, and therefore are not treated according to their derivation, but rather, as was said, are accompanied by that bass which really belongs with the next note. The treatment of appoggiaturas is one of the main points confronting the amateur composer. They are the [33] stumbling block of many who are not yet thoroughly proficient. Then there are also short passages, or so-called ornaments (*Manieren*), which include both the sharp and flat appoggiaturas described here [Example 45].

Ex. 45

These appoggiaturas which occur in rapid succession are more pleasing if they are performed quickly rather than slowly. Yet the appoggiaturas found in the first measure can more readily be expressed rather slowly, because the first appoggiatura consists of a whole tone, to which the ear is naturally accustomed. The bass C harmonizes with only the second and fourth note, G, while the first and third notes here again are regarded as absent. The [first] half of the third measure combines the two types of appoggiatura described previously, and the bass F is set to the second and fourth notes. The same thing is found in the fourth and fifth measures. The main rule for the knowledge of these different types of appoggiatura, and for a well-founded bass setting of them is the following: set the bass according to the order of succession of the three main chords, except when the melody occasionally requires that the second chord be omitted from the accompaniment, which is easily determined either by the tones of the melody, by the preceding or succeeding chord, or, with a little training, ultimately by the ear.

[34] A FEW GENERAL REMARKS PERTAINING TO
THE CONSTRUCTION OF A BASS

For the beginner's sake, we want to review very briefly the fundamental principles of two-part composition as follows. A beginner should choose any key he pleases, even if it might be the most difficult to realize or play on an instrument. Then, in accordance with the explanation given in our thorough-bass method, he should examine the key to locate certain tones from all three chords in both the upper and lower registers. After this, he should set in the bass either the root, or its third, which corresponds to each tone now found in the upper voice. If he wants the upper voice to move with the bass in thirds, sixths, or a combination of both intervals, he has only to observe which tones call for the sixth or the third, as is always indicated by the harmony of the chord. It is to be noticed further that the bass for the first note in the opening measure should be the root of the first chord, even if this happened to be the octave of the upper voice. If a formal cadence takes place at the end, the last bass note must likewise be the octave of the upper voice, namely the root of the first chord. The reason for this is that the unison and the octave are the most perfect consonances, indeed, in a certain sense, they are but one. Now since these intervals have the best ratios, and thus take priority over the other consonances, and great priority over the dissonances, it is appropriate to use them for closing and likewise for beginning a piece when the melody of the upper voice requires it. For example [see Example 46], if the first note in the upper voice were A, one would, following this advice, set A in the bass also. If C-sharp were to occur above, one would immediately see that this tone, since it is to be found in neither the second nor third chords, belongs in the harmony of the first chord. Further, should one see B, which is in both the second and third chords, one would merely have to determine whether it is followed immediately by A or C-sharp. If one of these two tones occurs, B belongs to the harmony of the third chord. But if the B is either sustained or repeated [m. 3], or if it is followed by G-sharp, the first half (or the first note if it is repeated) is included in the second chord, and the second half (or the repetition) is included in the third chord. If G-sharp follows, B is accompanied by D in the bass, and G-sharp is accompanied by E [m. 5]. The same situation exists with the D also, since this tone belongs in both the second and third chords. Therefore, one merely determines whether the following tone belongs to the harmony of the first or the third chord. [35] If it is the latter, the D must be accompanied in the bass by the octave or its third from the second chord. If on the contrary, the D is followed by a tone from the first chord [m. 8], it must be accompanied by the root, E, or its third, namely G-sharp, from the third chord, unless a formal cadence succeeds this D, in which case the harmony of the second chord will accompany the D (but in a two-part piece a bass D or F-sharp), whereupon a bass E is set to the subsequent C-sharp in the upper voice. This E is repeated because B or G-sharp must follow the C-sharp or A in the upper voice, if it is to be a [formal] cadence.[35] Furthermore, the tones A and E also appear in two chords. Here the very next tone always gives a clear indication

---

[35] A perfect authentic cadence involving I_4^6 as in mm. 10–11 of Ex. 46. Note the reference to the soprano-bass octave earlier in this paragraph. See also p. 79.

of the harmony to which the previous tone belongs. An example will reinforce what has
been said [Example 46].

Ex. 46

Experience shows that the third chord or its intervals must always be followed by the
first chord, except in a deceptive cadence. All good, natural melodies should also be based
upon this [principle]. The only exception permitted would be a harmony consisting of
simple progressions in thirds or sixths [Example 47].[36]

Ex. 47

Here is the exception at the beginning of the second measure. The melody, instead of
going to C at the end of the first measure, goes to A, which is the lowest third of the
second chord. The following progression in thirds proceeds along the same lines until
the end of the fourth measure, whereas the subsequent sixths in the seventh measure

---

[36] Daube's other exception to the normal "order of succession" of the three chords occurs "when the melody occasionally
requires that the second chord be omitted." See p. 62. Other variants include deceptive cadences and "artificial
resolutions" (i.e., resolutions involving accidentals). Ex. 47: m. 7, beat 3, figure was 6 in original. Exx. 47–8: mm. 8,
the bass has whole notes in the originals.

proceed in the order of succession of the three chords. Now when such a succession of tones appears in a melody, there is nothing better to do than to set the bass to it in sixths and thirds. Even in doing this we find that the natural melodic line itself would suffer, and that in setting a melody which goes against the order of succession of the three chords, one would very seldom produce anything of merit. Indeed, one would inevitably come across a hundred good melodies all composed according to the natural order, before finding a single one which runs against or contrary to it. We will demonstrate this even more clearly in the future, when we discuss the invention of melody.

The melody of the foregoing example can be improved by simply replacing the A in the second and fourth measures with C, but then the bass must be altered accordingly [Example 48].

Ex. 48

[37] We see that the initial melody is capable of imitation, because, [on the one hand] the C and G in the second measure are also found in the harmony of the first chord, and because, on the other hand, the first and third notes of the first measure form a very suitable bass for the second measure, since they are also taken from the harmony of the first chord. In the same way, imitation finds a most favorable opportunity in the third and fourth measures, and could even be continued to some extent in the fifth and sixth measures. In short, the entire process of combining these two voices is based on the natural succession of the three chords. Yet a beginner has to notice that the three different motions which were discussed previously are observed even in two-part composition, whereby melody and harmony are combined properly from the beginning, and the listener is provided with a beautiful variety upon which the life of a piece depends.

We now want to consider briefly the style which is composed of two equal voices.[37] If a countermelody is to be set to an [existing] melody, one proceeds again as above, except that the second voice is written in the same violin or piano clef etc. as the first

[37] Of special interest in this medium are the *Sechs Sonaten für zwei Oboen* by Juan Bautista Plà, one of two famous Spanish oboist brothers, colleagues of Daube at the Württemburg court. (Schott Edition 5898.) Ex. 48, m. 8, bass has whole note, and ex. 49, m. 4, upper voice appoggiatura is *d′* in originals.

voice, whereby the intervals or harmonizing tones are brought close together. One determines to which chord the different tones of the melody belong, and then sets in the second voice a harmonizing tone from the same chord, which can be either the third, sixth, or else sometimes the fifth, fourth, indeed even the seventh, as we have pointed out already in the explanation of each chord.

Ex. 49

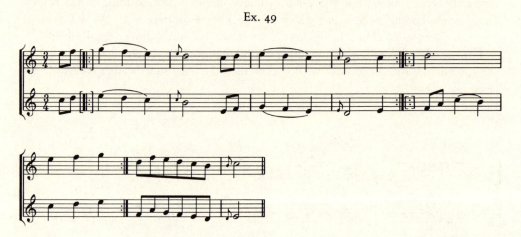

The beginning [of Example 49] demonstrates that the second voice might very well move in thirds with the upper voice. The end of the second, and the continuation of the third and fourth measures present a succession of sixths. Because the sustained D in the fifth measure belongs in the second and third chords, the other voice also may be allowed to have tones from both chords, as happens here. [38] The following melody [Example 50] is also suitable for a succession of thirds and sixths. The previously described three motions of music are to be observed most strictly here also. The occasional whole- or half-step appoggiaturas which arise during a progression of thirds or sixths occur in both voices. However, if the second voice has the root, namely a fifth or fourth [below] etc., only the upper voice sounds the appoggiatura.

Ex. 50

The D with the appoggiatura in the second example belongs to the harmony of the third chord, so for a change the second voice can sound the root, G, which does not take an appoggiatura unless it were to be made from below by holding over a half-step F-sharp. In the next measure A is in the upper voice, while the second voice has the root, F, because both voices belong in the harmony of the second chord.

Before we conclude this discussion, we must still consider briefly the extraneous harmonies caused by the retardation and the anticipation. These already have been explained on page 97 of our thorough-bass method, and their origin has been shown on page 100. They can also occur in two-part composition, in fact, to even greater effect than in composition in four or more parts. The reason for this is that here only one tone can be discordant instead of possibly several.

Ex. 51

[m. 2, upper voice, the *d'* is dotted in the original]

[In Example 51] E, G, and B are retarded in the first example, C and E in the next. Now since the second voice proceeds by half measures, while the first [39] remains behind, the resulting delay gives rise to various intervals not naturally included in the three main chords.

But if the first note is shortened by half, and is advanced to its neighbor tone while the other voice proceeds according to its true note values, a harmony sometimes results which likewise does not naturally belong in this key. This displacement of notes can occur in ascent or descent in either voice [Example 52a–b], but not in both at once unless a third voice were present.

Ex. 52

(a)

Ex. 52 (*cont.*)

(b)

With displaced sixths.

[*b*: m. 6, the lower voice has *b′* in the original]

It quite often happens that one comes across a melody containing such side-slipping of tones, which certainly creates a pleasant effect. Here one considers only the first note in the first voice, and then sets a harmonizing tone in the other voice according to our instructions. Now these two voices may constitute the interval of a third, seventh, fifth, etc. This is all the same. Even a succession of fifths is allowed here, if one voice is advanced to create sixths [Example 53].

Ex. 53

Retardation   Anticipation

[40] These passages are more unusual. They must be handled carefully. The progression of the second voice is not always determined in this case from the first note of the upper voice, since the second note, which otherwise is but a passing tone, must sometimes be considered also. The first example illustrates this. The second C, together with the following D, and the F in the second voice, is in the second chord in the key of C major. The tones under the next two slurs, namely D–E and E–F are not found together in the same chord [anywhere] in this key. Therefore, the first tone under each of these two slurs is considered to be a retardation. But the following two tones, namely F and G, again belong together in the third chord, and are accompanied by B in the second voice. If the retarded notes were crossed out, this example would consist of a simple succession of sixths.

In this discussion we have stated and demonstrated that the tones or notes of an upper voice comprise three different classes. Either they are tones to which another voice must actually be set under the guidance of the three chords. This always concerns the first of two notes of equal value. The second class consists of appoggiaturas which are slurred to the proper tone and are given no bass or separate harmony, except in the aforementioned case, that is, in progressions of thirds and sixths with two equal voices. This, once again, concerns the first note, which either is retained from before, or else appears as an appoggiatura to embellish a long note.[38] The third class consists of passing tones, which likewise are given no bass or complete harmony. If they are accompanied, again, it is done in thirds and sixths. These are always the second of two notes of equal value.[39] The proper position of each tone in these three classes has been clearly explained. Retardations also belong here, that is, in the second class. Anticipations are included in the third class.

4

COMBINING THREE VOICES

This discussion is one of the most important in the entire [study of] composition. Whoever knows how to combine three voices well, will likewise find it easy to construct a harmony of many voices. The main harmonic framework depends upon three-part composition. Indeed, [41] the entire effect of the harmony proceeds chiefly from that basis. It can conveniently be divided into two classes, natural and artificial construction.[40] In the former class all three voices are merely drawn from the three chords, and the upper voice constantly asserts its authority as the primary voice, while the second voice neither ascends above it nor introduces anything concerting or imitative, but simply proceeds with the bass according to the rules of harmony. In this way, the melody of the upper voice is never interrupted. One sees many pieces of this type, even by renowned masters, in which neither the second voice nor the bass have any imitation. The second class, on the contrary, is a product of the aforementioned artificial construction. Here nature and art must be united to produce true beauty. The second type is characterized by the three motions of the voices, the imitation of a melodic motif in all three voices, concerting in some passages, the alternation of the brilliant and singing styles, beautiful symmetry or division of the main melody, along with the varying of the harmony by means of *forte* and *piano*.

Let us take up the former type first. Here it is necessary that we re-examine each chord separately. The amateurs of the preceding discussion will consent to this more readily since one is dependent on the other.

The first or ruling chord has the most perfect triad. The effect of this harmony is the best and, although it differs in accordance with the instruments that are used (for two violins and a violoncello make a different impression than two flutes etc., two oboes,

---

[38] Thus Daube also refers to reiterated suspensions and accented passing tones as appoggiaturas. See n. 26.
[39] Thus Daube also refers to neighbor tones (upper or lower auxiliaries) as passing tones. See n. 24.
[40] See n. 12, and pp. 87–8.

two horns, etc.) yet, as was said, it always produces an effect better than that of the other two chords. Now if E from this chord occurs in the melody, the bass for it will be C, and the G which is still available in this chord is left for the second voice [Example 54]. If the upper voice has G, the second voice is given E and the bass, C. If C is found in the melody, E is put in the bass, and G again in the second voice. Sometimes the lower octave C also goes with an upper C in the melody, in which case the second voice takes E.

Ex. 54

[m. 4, the two upper parts have quarter rests at the end in the original]

We see here once more that the alternation of passages in thirds and sixths might be put to good use between the two upper voices as well as with the bass itself. The remaining considerations pertinent to this first chord have already been explained in the preceding chapters. Still, we might say here that the root, C, may be sustained in the bass as well as in an upper voice, while the harmonies of all three chords are heard one after another, provided that [the succession] commences and closes with the first chord [Example 55]. The same freedom may be taken with G also. The reason is that both tones are found in two chords: C in the first and second; and G in the first and third.

Ex. 55

Oblique motion is the basis of these phrases. Another example can be found in the foregoing explanation of the three motions of harmony.

The second chord, as is known, consists of four tones. If D occurs in the melody, the bass has the root, F, and the second voice takes C if this tone precedes it, or A [Example 56]. But if C occurs in the upper voice, A can be set quite suitably in the second voice while the bass retains F. If F is found in the melody, the bass sounds either A, or else another F, leaving D or C for the second voice. If one finds A in the upper voice, the second voice is given C and the bass retains F. The tone D comes in the bass when preceded by F, since it then provides variety or contributes to the formation of a melodic bass line. C appears in the bass if it was already on that tone during the previous chord.

Ex. 56

These seven previously described examples all have their basis in the succession of the three chords. They consist of the alternation of passages in sixths or thirds, which always requires two voices. In constructing three-part examples it is well to make certain that all three voices do not always proceed at the same rate of motion. The possible alternatives consist of one voice proceeding, while the other two voices move at a slow pace; two voices progressing at the same speed while the third moves twice as fast; and also, one voice proceeding slowly while the other two move rapidly.[41] Only toward the end or the conclusion [may all the voices] have the same rate of motion.

Since the third chord is likewise four-part, one once again has a choice of using either the third or fourth tone in three-part composition. The most reliable way is to take the second voice to the tone nearest the preceding one, or even to keep it where it is already. Now if G is situated in the upper voice, either B or G can serve as its bass [Example 57]. In the first case, the second voice takes D, or F if it was on this tone previously. In the other case, it can have B as well. If D is in the melody the second voice is given B and the bass, G. However, if B is in the upper voice, then the bass may take G or D, the sixth [below], while the second voice is given D in the first case, and F or G in the second case. If one sees F in the upper voice, the bass must go to either G or B while the second voice takes D. If a bass F should precede this chord, it may likewise remain stationary in this harmony, where it then is looked upon as having the same status as the G itself. In this case, the two upper voices can be on D and B, or G and B. This inversion of the bass is quite frequent nowadays.

Ex. 57

[41] This gear-like rhythmic differentiation of voices (recommended in several contexts) recalls the mechanical orientation of the century, which nourished a fascination with clocks and machinery. Musically it suggests a vestige of species counterpoint and Baroque rhythmic relationships, although most of Daube's longer, free-style examples do not carry them through at length. (See, however, Ex. 78.) This suggestion could not be considered common in late eighteenth-century composition manuals, but it is offered by Riepel in *Anfangsgründe*, vol. II (1755), p. 87. See also p. 170.

These seven examples were described above. If one peruses the key of C major in the thorough-bass method, one will find all these inversions of the harmony of the three chords. The principle is the same.

Therefore, let this suffice for the manner of writing three parts within each chord. We now want to show how these three chords succeed one another and take place alternately from the beginning to the end [Example 58].

Ex. 58

[m. 12 upper part, a half note in the original]

Since this example contains nothing other than the simple succession of the three chords, it will be easily comprehended by an amateur, provided he understood the explanation of each chord. One sees that the harmonious triad has been retained throughout the example, and even its occasional absence is due to the melodic requirement of one or another voice. The harmony should not be incomplete whenever the full harmony can benefit the melody of any voice. On the other hand, if the complete harmony is detrimental to the melody and hinders the nature of a voice line, it is better that the harmony forfeit an interval. This is demonstrated in the first measure. The upper voice begins with C and ascends two tones. The bass also begins with the root, an octave from the upper C. Therefore the second voice should sound E or G here, but since neither of these tones forms a good melody for the second voice, it is better, especially at the beginning, for the piece to open with only the octave than for the melodic line to suffer on account of the complete harmony, all the more so since the third above the root is supplied at once by the quicker progression of the bass, which improves the empty harmony to some extent. The bass F in the second measure is held over into the beginning of the third measure, whereby this tone is looked upon as having the same status as the root of the third chord. In the fourth measure a rest occurs in both upper voices, but the bass continues alone with rapid notes so that the movement will not be interrupted. The tone that is subsequently tied over in the upper voice provides an opportunity for the other two voices to progress at an equal pace through an alternation of thirds and sixths. On the second quarter of the seventh measure, the second voice preferably goes to the octave C, for the sake of the melody, rather than completing the triad by [47] going to G. This tone is still missing in the next measure. The first quarter contains only the octave, but then the bass rests while both upper voices proceed together with intervals of the ruling chord. Now [m. 9] the preceding four measures are repeated, except that the upper voices have exchanged their melodies. The sustained G of the upper voice is now an octave lower in the second voice, while the first voice sounds the melody previously heard in the second voice.[42] This explanation is certain to be of use to an amateur composer if he reads it attentively and compares it with the example itself. He will see how natural three-part composition is to be handled, and how the chords conform to the upper voice, alternating among themselves, yet always according to their order of succession.

Now let us take up this example once again, and accompany it with other voices, so that the beginner may see that a given melody might be treated in different ways. A melody with a wide variety of note values can likewise have various harmonies set to it, all of which are correct according to the rules of composition but different in effect, as has been mentioned above. The main rule in large pieces is never to interrupt the melody of the first voice, or to hinder it at all with the harmony. Accordingly, it is a great mistake for the second voice to cross above the first voice occasionally, except in concerting passages, where the two voices are supposed to alternate.

Ex. 59

---

[42] Here Daube informally introduces the technique of invertible counterpoint, discussed in Chapter II.

The harmony here [in Example 59] shows more variety than in the previous accompaniment. The rapid movement of the two lower voices has given them a life of their own, whereby they aid the main melody itself by making the few quarter notes seem all the more brilliant. The alternation of fast and slow tones contributes significantly toward heightening the effect of a melodic line. The bass remains stationary in the second measure, despite the presence of the second chord to which the root F really belongs. However, we have said several times before that if the preceding bass note were also present in the harmony of the very next chord, it then could be retained because, by virtue of the preceding root, it would have acquired the same status as the proper root. All three motions of the harmony are also to be found in this example. The first measure displays oblique motion, with the first voice proceeding slowly and the other two voices rapidly. Parallel motion also occurs, where the second voice and the bass move together in thirds. The second measure contains oblique motion, but then the third measure already exhibits contrary motion, since the second voice descends and the other two voices ascend. Contrary motion of the voices is very evident from the ninth measure until the end. The two upper voices ascend in parallel motion in thirds, while the bass descends, not reascending until the penultimate measure where the upper voices descend again. Something more is to be said regarding the harmony of the ninth and tenth measures. In the former, A appears in the bass. This tone is the third beneath C, and since the upper C is also to be found in the second chord, an A may very well be set in the bass, especially because it contributes to the bass melody.

[49] The following measure [m. 10] has D and C in the bass, although a beginner might not be able to guess why they are there. The D in the bass is a passing tone here, since E is the main note; the following C is from the harmony of the second chord, as is the first half of both long notes, D and F, in the first and second voices. The harmony of the third chord immediately succeeds this inversion of the second chord. An exchange (*Verwechslung*) of intervals also takes place in this example.[43] In the third measure, the second voice has D, which is used here for the formation of the melody of this voice. Actually it should follow the C, because it is only a passing tone which does not belong in this harmony, but it nevertheless is placed in front of the C, which can be called an exchange.

However, if the melody includes tones which belong in different keys, these foreign sharps or flats must be treated according to their own key. Ties can appear, and similarly the opportunity to bring about the deceptive cadence can present itself, since all of these occur quite often in three-part composition, as here [Example 60]:

---

[43] This idea of "exchange" (instead of Daube's usual term, "Vorschlag" or "appoggiatura," for an accented passing tone) hints of *ars combinatoria*, in which objects are rearranged in as many ways as possible. (See nn. 9 and 87.) Riepel, who discusses non-chord tones in connection with counterpoint, uses the term "verwechselte Noten" for accented or thetic passing tones, apparently because the consonance or chord tone which would normally occur on the strong (part of the) beat has been exchanged (*verwechselt*) for a generally dissonant ornamental tone (*Anfangsgründe*, vol. V (1768), p. 10). Similar usages occur in Portmann (*Leichtes Lehrbuch* (1789), p. 36), Petri (*Anleitung* (2/1782), p. 164), and Scheibe (*Musikalisches Composition* (1773), pp. 266, 282). See n. 26 and the Introduction, p. 22.

Ex. 60

[50] In constructing compositions of three and more parts, it is essential to set a well-founded bass with the melody at once, even before working out the second soprano voice. However, since no rule is without exception, one can be made here also, especially with artificial composition in three parts, which will be treated later.

In the first measure the melody has a G, the first half of which accordingly belongs in the harmony of the first chord, whereas the second half is regarded here as a retardation, or as an appoggiatura to A. From this point of view it is given the root, F, which really belongs with A, and the second voice has D and C, which are from the harmony of the second chord. The third measure has an F-sharp. This tone has been borrowed from the harmony of the third chord in G major, which is why the corresponding harmony is also employed. The second voice takes D, and the bass retains the previous C, because this tone naturally occurs in the borrowed chord. Now since it belongs in G major, it must be followed by its first chord, or at least one similar to it. Both occur. The ruling chord in G major now appears, immediately followed by F again in the melody, which indicates that the original key of C major may have returned, because the F is from the third chord in that key. This F, together with the D a third lower, is retained into the beginning of the fourth [measure].[44] The bass disregards the retained tones and sounds C against them. These two tones can be called retardations as well as appoggiaturas, and are treated as if E and C were there instead. Therefore the half step before G, namely F-sharp, is set with the following E and C. The origin of a seventh such as the F-sharp to E here is found in the division of a long note, since the lower third is put with the first half, and the lower

[44] "fourth chord" in the original.

seventh with the other half, so that in this way the alternation of consonance and dissonance might always be possible. Whoever takes a liking to such three- and four-part settings, will find more of them on page 424 in our thorough-bass method. Something new is introduced again in the sixth measure. The B-flat in the melody belongs in the third chord of another key and, designated as such, the following A and F are properly seen as being in the ruling chord in F major, and preceded by the corresponding third chord. But here the B-flat is an anticipation. The first half of it should still be a B-natural, as was the previous tone, but the B-flat enters early. This setting is justified by the similarity of the C-major chord and [51] the third chord in F major which contains the minor seventh, [C to] B-flat. The second voice and the bass also attest to the presence of this chord. The reason is that the ruling chord in C major and this third chord in F major, as was said, are rather similar to one another. Therefore the melody could quite properly sound this B-flat even though the other two voices were set according to the harmony of the first chord in C major. The three motions of harmony are alternated throughout this short example. A deceptive cadence is presented in the eighth measure.

The entire difference between this and the authentic cadence is that after the third chord with the seventh, the bass, instead of going to the root of its ruling chord, goes to another tone which does not belong in this chord at all, just as happens here, where the bass goes to A instead of C. After this unfamiliar harmony, however, the first chord in C major immediately reappears, and the succession of the proper three chords in the original key continues from here to the end.

The harmony is made more difficult for a beginner if still more chords which belong in other keys are found in the upper voice, even though nothing other than the natural succession of the three chords occurs. We also want to show an example of this [Example 61].

Ex. 61

This example has been drawn up merely as an exercise in harmony. The first chord, which begins with the complete harmony, is followed directly in the upper voice by a G-sharp, which is an indication of A minor, and the harmony is arranged accordingly. The bass descends in contrary motion to B, the sixth [below]. Next, according to the natural succession, must come the first chord in A minor. This occurs and is immediately followed by F-sharp which, since it does not belong in A minor, indicates here the key of G major, in which it is the major third of the third chord. Meanwhile the bass sounds the proper root, and because the seventh, which is C in this case, is always present in the third chord, the previous C can conveniently remain stationary here also. The ruling chord follows. Another modulation occurs with the following E in the upper voice. This E tells us that the harmony of the ruling chord in C major could accompany it, all the more since the preceding G-major chord bears a great resemblance to the third chord in C major, and because the minor seventh, F, appears in the upper voice. The harmony has been arranged accordingly. However, since E, as well as the following F, are retained in the upper voice, the composer here has an opportunity to introduce chords foreign to the key, in order to show that it is possible to go through other keys by means of the inner voices. This also effects a change, so that the harmony might not continually remain in the same key, and that all the more, since at the very beginning the upper voice provided the opportunity for key changes of this kind. Now to construct foreign harmonies to an upper voice, one simply looks through the related keys to see whether the tones in the upper voice might not be found there also, and one is guided accordingly. [53] Here the E remains stationary and the first half is already harmonized. The other half of the E is also found in the second chord in G major, but because the harmony of the third chord does not follow, one must look elsewhere for this tone. It is the third chord in the key of D minor which could be used here, because an F follows as the third of its first chord. Thus the second half of the E in the upper voice is given C-sharp in the bass, as the indication of this new key. The second voice sounds G and then A, as the other tones of this chord. Thereupon it resolves into its ruling chord. The situation is similar with the second half of the tone F which remains in the upper voice. Here one again must determine which closely related key contains F in the second or third chord. An F is found in the second and third chords of C major, but since it is much too soon to return to the original key, and there are certainly several other keys in which this tone is found, it is preferable to choose the extension instead. It is the compound diminished seventh chord in A minor which is suitable here, with G-sharp in the bass and the third, B, in the second voice. The following E in the upper voice [m. 6] assumes the harmony of the ruling chord in A minor. Hereupon the upper voice has G, which is not found in A minor (except in passing), and thereby obliges one to search anew for his accompaniment in another key. Although the proper indicative tone[45] is not present, the key nevertheless is apparent from the subsequent F, which is from either the first chord in F major or D minor. That it belongs in the latter key can be perceived from the fact that the third

---

[45] Daube's term is "der anzeigende Ton," the note which indicates the key (i.e., leading tone). He consistently uses words related to "anzeigen" (to indicate) for this purpose. Other examples are "der Hauptanzeiger" (main indication), p. 60, and "der Anzeige" (indication), p. 193.

chord in D minor bears a considerable resemblance to the first chord in A minor. Thus C-sharp is put in the bass and E in the second voice. This then resolves into its ruling chord, whereupon the corresponding third chord reappears. The C in measure [eight] then provides another opportunity for modulation. If F-sharp is set with it in the bass, and A in the second voice, they produce the harmony of the third chord in G minor, just as was done here. The corresponding first chord follows, and the second half [of the measure] allows another modulation. The B-flat is found in the third chord of F major. The following A, which quite reasonably can be the third of the ruling chord in F, indicates that this harmony may also be chosen. Thus the bass for the sustained B-flat can be C or E, while the second voice takes G. The similarity of the ruling chord in F major to the third chord in B-flat major shows that the following E-flat[46] [54] in the upper voice belongs in this harmony. The bass can have F or A, and the second voice the remaining note of this third. After the ensuing first chord in B-flat major, the partially similar third chord in C major can return, because the D remains stationary. The bass ascends a half step to B, and the second voice goes to F or G. Measure [twelve] contains E and B-flat, the first tone of which belongs to the harmony of the ruling chord in C major, while the other is part of the third chord in F major. The two chords have a considerable similarity, thus this modulation also occurs easily. This seventh, and the following A in the upper voice, cause the bass to ascend one tone in contrary motion, thereby giving rise to a deceptive cadence. Then the proper bass tone, F, appears, and the second voice sounds A and F consecutively while the upper voice has D, which now outlines the second chord in C major. This is followed by a formal cadence in the upper voice, for which the bass is given G, as the second inversion of the ruling chord. The second voice goes to E, and the first to C. This bass G is repeated once again with its own harmony of the third chord. The root C with its octaves closes this example without other accompaniment.

The three preceding examples, together with the explanations of them, will suffice to give the amateurs an idea of composition in three parts. They serve for practice in major keys and, although this exercise can also be done in minor keys in exactly the same manner, we do believe that the repetition of a good thing, or an abundance of examples, does not impair the clarity. We would like to give another example in the key of A minor [Example 62].

---

[46] "D-sharp" in the original. Subsequent usages of D-sharp also have been rendered as E-flat where appropriate, in accordance with modern usage. Daube's use of "D-sharp" (*Dis*) to indicate both D-sharp and E-flat is a vestige of fifteenth-century German organ tablature notation, in which all chromatic pitches, except B-flat (b) and B-natural (h), were indicated as raised rather than lowered notes, regardless of the key. In his *General-Baß* of 1756, Daube uses this old nomenclature consistently, in his *Dilettant* of 1770/71 he applies it inconsistently (partially adopting the newer designation for lowered pitches, i.e., C-sharp is *Cis*, D-flat is *Des*), in the present *Dilettante* of 1773 he applies the old system only to D-sharp/E-flat, and in his *Erfindung der Melodie* of 1797/98 he consistently uses the newer terminology (Wallace, "Daube's *General-Baß*," pp. 20–23). See Daube's *General-Baß*, Chapters 1 and 9. In 1755 Riepel treats the nomenclature for E-flat as a matter of controversy. "Is it possible that we should say *Dis* [when E-flat is notated], for the designation *Dis* takes its name not from E but from D. . . . This clearly introduces a profitless confusion. Accordingly, a few clever German composers have (just recently) devised an adroit nomenclature: works, and all notes prefixed by a sharp end in -is; . . . all notes prefixed by a flat end in -es" (*Anfangsgründe*, vol. II (1755), p. 2).

Ex. 62

This example begins with the complete harmony of the ruling chord in A minor. However, since E appears two more times in the upper voice, one can, for variety, follow this harmony immediately with the third chord, of which this E is actually the root. For this reason, the bass is given G-sharp, and the second voice has B, the third above, and then D, the fifth above, which completes the harmony of this chord. Now, according to the order of succession, the harmony of the ruling chord must follow, which likewise happens here. The tone F in the upper voice can be included either in the harmony of the second chord, or in the diminished seventh chord which occurs in minor keys, as we have done here. The bass has G-sharp, and the second voice again the third and fifth above it, B and D, whereupon it resolves into the ruling chord [m. 3]. With regard to the harmony, the B which comes next is divided into two parts, the first of which is harmonized by the second chord, and the other by the third chord. Now since A is also in the second chord, the preceding [bass] A remains stationary, the second voice takes D, and then [56] E which belongs in the next chord, while the bass sounds G-sharp. Then the ruling chord is heard twice, after which [m. 5] the second and third chords appear in order. Now the bass ascends a tone, causing a deceptive cadence. Instead of the harmony of the first chord, a partially similar harmony follows, namely the inversion of the third chord in D minor. The bass descends a tone to E, in contrary motion to the upper voice. The second voice has G, its third, and A, thereby completing the chord. The natural resolution into the ruling chord of D minor follows [m. 7]. Now even D-sharp appears in the upper voice. Which harmony should one furnish here? This foreign D-sharp indicates the third chord in E minor, which requires either B, A, or F-sharp in the bass. But since this tone ascends a half step to E, and the preceding bass F likewise is situated a half step above the lower octave E, contrary motion permits the harmony of the chromatic chord in E minor here, all the more because F can then remain stationary in the bass with only its third, A, in the second voice. The resolution takes place as with the third chord in this key, namely into the ruling chord [m. 8] in E minor. The upper voice and the bass go to E, and the second voice to G, the third. Because of the similarity of this chord to the third chord in A minor, the second voice may also go to G-sharp here. The E remains stationary in the upper voice, but its harmony is partially changed. The bass descends a whole tone to D, indicating that the key of E minor has now been left behind. The second voice goes to G-sharp, thereby indicating A minor, and this accordingly is followed by its ruling chord. However, since the upper E lasts even longer, one again has the opportunity to sound another harmony which bears some resemblance to the preceding one. This is the inversion of the third chord in D minor. The bass goes to C-sharp, which indicates the key of D minor, while the second voice sounds G. This is followed by the first chord [m. 10], which is designated for resolution in this key. Now C appears in the upper voice, but its correct accompaniment cannot be discerned from this, since it cannot indicate the key. In such a case one must have recourse to the following tone, which here is B-flat, the harmony of which can be either the ruling chord in G minor or B-flat major. But since, until now, all examples have shown that similar chords follow one another very well, [57] one must look for a harmony similar to that of the previous chord even if no indicative tone is found in the melody. Therefore, since this C was preceded by the ruling chord in D minor, it can be part of the third chord in G minor. Moreover, it can be followed quite well by the first chord in G minor, of which the [soprano] B-flat is the third. For this reason the bass goes to F-sharp, the second voice to the third, A, and this is followed by G in the bass, and in the second voice also, in order to move in contrary motion to the bass and still avoid leaping to the fifth, D. With the B-flat which remains stationary in the upper voice [m. 11], another new harmony can be employed. This may be drawn from either the third chord in F major, or from the diminished seventh chord in D minor. The following A [m. 12] indicates the resolution to its ruling chord. Either of these would be correct. We have put C-sharp in the bass, and its third, E, in the second voice, whereby the diminished seventh chord is heard, and the indication of the key of D minor is given by the bass. The natural resolution occurs when D appears in the bass, and its third, F, in the second voice. The upper tone again remains stationary, and the second half of it is given another foreign harmony. This tone, A, is found in the third chord in E minor, for which the bass may merely rise a half step, and the second voice may be moved up to its third, F-sharp, whereupon most of the intervals of this third chord are present. It resolves as usual into the harmony of its ruling chord, with the bass taking E, and the second voice the octave above it. Now a tone indicative [of the original key] appears in the upper voice, namely G-sharp, while the second voice stays on E and the bass descends a tone to D in order to show that a new key may be at hand, particularly since this tone D is also found in the third chord in A minor. The inversion of its ruling chord follows [m. 14], with the bass taking C, and the E in the second voice remaining stationary. The next two tones in the upper voice, B and D, can reasonably be accounted for in the harmony of the third chord, for which the bass has G-sharp [recte E], and the second voice harmonizes in thirds with the upper voice. Contrary motion now produces a deceptive cadence. Then comes the inversion of the ruling chord, which really should have come in place of the chord which brought about the deceptive cadence. The tone A remains stationary in the second voice during both chords, while the bass states F and then C. Then F appears in the upper voice and is sustained. If one wished, two different harmonies could be used with this tone – the second chord and, instead of the [58] following third chord, the diminished seventh chord, just as happened here. The progression (*Folge*) of chords from here to the end is arranged according to the order of succession (*Rangordnung*). Since A and G-sharp, which occur one after the other, are from the first and third chords [respectively], the E which is common to both chords is set in the bass twice, in order to form the proper cadence.

A FEW REMARKS PERTAINING TO
THREE-PART COMPOSITION

When a beginner has constructed a melody, he should examine it to determine to which chord each tone of the melody belongs, and mark them underneath by the numbers, 1, 2, 3, to signify the first, second, and third chords. He should remember what was said in our thorough-bass method about passing tones, namely that in composing with equal eighth notes in an Allegro movement, usually only the first and third notes are heeded, but that if there are sixteenth notes, only the first note is considered as a tone to be harmonized while the others pass through. If the melody is also intermingled with so-called appoggiaturas, they likewise are handled as passing tones.

Next, in writing the bass, the three motions must be observed. If the upper voice has many running passages, short rests can also occur in the bass. It is well, especially for a beginner, to make certain to give the bass more roots and their thirds than other intervals. However, if a few other bass tones should appear now and then, they must either repeat the directly preceding bass note, or move in sixths or thirds with the upper voice for a change. It is also especially important to remember that the bass line should consist more of stepwise notes than of leaps, since by that means it is made melodic. Wherever the upper voice has long tones, the bass can be assigned rapid notes mixed with passing tones in such a way as to always promote the singing style. After this, if one wanted to, it would be a profitable occupation to figure the bass of one's exercise. In that way all the intervals of the three chords and their inversions are set forth explicitly so that subsequently one does not need to ponder a long time before writing down a harmony to go with the upper voice. After this is done, one writes the second voice. We have said above that two equal voices go well together in thirds or sixths. When the melody of the upper voice has even stepwise [59] tones, the second voice may be set in thirds or sixths with it. Which of the two intervals it should be is shown by the harmony of the bass with the upper voice. On the other hand, if there is no place for these successions of thirds and sixths between the first and second voices, the third of the bass is usually set in the second voice. It quite often happens that this voice proceeds in thirds with the bass, especially when the upper voice sustains a tone. If a succession of thirds or sixths is impeded by the previously composed bass, even the bass may be altered in that place. Diversity of movement can be arranged by giving one voice rapid notes while the other two voices sound long tones, perhaps also mixed with short rests. Two voices may proceed quickly at the same pace while the third has slowly moving, or even sustained tones. Also, two voices may have slow or rapid tones while the bass rests. Each voice may also move at its own separate rate of motion. For example, one may have nothing but sixteenths, and another eighth notes, while the third can sustain a tone. All three voices can proceed at an equally slow rate of motion, but this never should happen, or at least certainly very seldom, at a faster speed. Why? Because the main melody, which indeed always must remain the center of attention, would be hindered or entirely obscured. The melody should rule and the harmony should serve.[47] In places where the melody has modulated into another key, the harmony immediately must be reoriented according to the three chords proper to this new key, as is demonstrated sufficiently in the foregoing examples.

Ex. 63 Main Example of Everything Discussed So Far

[47] This analogy was used by Mattheson in the statement that "the lower voice has to be governed by the higher melody, as the servant by the master . . ." ("die Grund=Stimme nach der Ober=Melodie, der Knecht nach dem Herrn . . . zu richten habe.") (*Capellmeister* (1739), vol. II, p. 186, Eng. trans., p. 388). Daube observed earlier that the harmony is expected to reinforce the affect of the melody (p. 41), and to "forfeit an interval" in deference to good, melodic, voice-leading (p. 73). Incomplete harmonies often occurred in the popular progressions of parallel thirds or sixths with bass (described above), which often were identified with rustic or pastoral topics, as in the "Pastoral Symphony" of Handel's *Messiah* (1742). Later it will be seen that melodic layout also governs compositional structure. See n. 51. Ex. 63: m. 12, middle voice, appoggiatura was *f♯"* in original.

Ex. 63 (*cont.*)

Ex. 63 (*cont.*)

This example [Example 63] in the natural unbound style of three-part composition is written in such a way that a beginning composer [63] could easily imitate it. In this piece we paid little attention to constructing a beautiful melody or an artificial harmony. Our aim was a natural, light, and flowing manner. The purpose of the piece was to combine these qualities with the preceding short examples, observations, and explanations of the separate elements, and to present all of this for review.

We still want to make a few comments about this example. The four sixteenth notes in the first measure should, for melodic reasons, be written this way [Example 64]:

Ex. 64

It would be clear to set a bass to this, since both [large] notes are from the third chord and may very well be harmonized by a bass F-sharp and D. Therefore, since appoggiaturas are never represented by a three-part harmony, but can well occur in two voices at once, as here, their status remains unchanged even when they are written as large notes and incorporated into the rhythm along with the other tones, as one sees here. We have already mentioned how appoggiaturas are to be recognized, but let us state it once more. An appoggiatura usually repeats the tone which preceded it in the same voice, or at least repeats a tone which is found in the preceding chord. Sometimes they even take the place of passing tones. In both voices the first of these four sixteenth notes is found in the previous chord and consequently can be regarded here as an appoggiatura. The second note of both voices belongs in the third chord, from which the bass is taken. The third note is inserted here for the formation of the melody and again occurs in the position of an appoggiatura or a passing tone. The fourth note in the first and second voices again belongs in the third chord. It would be written like the first half of the second beat if the small appoggiaturas were represented by ordinary notes. In the fourth measure, where a rest occurs in both [upper] voices, the bass moves rapidly, so that there might never be a lack of motion. This also occurs in the seventh and thirteenth measures. On the other hand, when the upper voice has rapid passages, the bass has long tones interspersed with rests. The second voice likewise sustains tones wherever [64] it either is preferable to have the upper voice proceed alone, or where the second voice cannot accompany it in thirds or sixths. Sometimes this voice also goes in thirds with the bass. Modulations always occur by means of the similarity of two chords, after which the natural progression (*Fortschreitung*) of the three chords in order is observed throughout. Seeing that we have treated the natural and unartificial style of three-part composition sufficiently, we now want to describe the other style also.

At the very beginning of this discussion we said that the artificial style of composing three parts is that in which art and nature are combined. This means that outside of the already discussed first style, all kinds of artificial ties, unusual resolutions, imitations, etc., etc. should also be included in it. We want to explain each piece separately, so that the ambitious amateur might be able to understand it more easily.

Ex. 65

This example [Example 65] seems to be comprised of more art than nature, although it does show the natural succession of the three chords, especially in the first four measures. In the first measure the melody of the upper voice clearly indicates the second and third chords, and the bass is arranged accordingly. In places such as this, where a long note in the melody is preceded by fast tones, one investigates to see whether the second voice or the bass might not also be able to sound fast tones against the sustained tone. In doing this it is not necessary to contrive an imitation of the fast passage introduced in the upper voice. It is enough for the rapid motion to be alternated between the two voices. To increase the clarity of the upper voice, we have begun the second voice with a rest and later supplied the necessary third above the bass. Since this third is still sounding at the beginning of the slow tone in the upper voice, it forms a retardation that is disregarded by the bass, because a bound tone is usually treated like an appoggiatura. With the indicative tone, F-sharp [m. 1, beat 3], the bass takes D, the corresponding root, and since the second voice makes a passage in the third chord, the bass moves very slowly so as to increase the clarity of the melody in the two [upper] voices. The running passage of the second voice belongs in the third chord, as is certainly implied by the tones which appear therein. There are four tones, namely D, A, and twice C, which belong in the third chord, whereas only three passing tones are among them, namely E, and twice B. The larger number prevails here. In this measure [m. 1] we also find the true source of the ninth, which is represented by a figure in the bass. It is this same upper third, E, from the preceding second chord which, as mentioned before, remains stationary until the entrance of the third chord, [66] and by means of its retention a ninth is formed [with the bass]. Then, so that the ruling chord will not be heard at once, despite the fact that it is designated by the melody of the upper voice, the bass ascends a tone, thereby producing a deceptive cadence. The second and third measures contain nothing new, in that the melody of the first measure is repeated twice more, each time a tone lower. The second voice does likewise. The bass makes a slight variation. The tone E, which presented the deceptive cadence, is moved down to D in the following measure [m. 3]. Instead of the half notes of the first measure, quarter notes are introduced because of the necessary descent from E to B in the bass. From the [fifth and] sixth measure[s] on, various artificial resolutions occur. The tone G-sharp [m. 5] gives an indication of A minor. Since the bass for the sustained G in the upper voice is B, its third, and since the second voice also has G for the sake of the melody, we have, for variety, let the second voice then go to F, thereby forming an inversion of the third chord in C major. Its ruling chord would naturally have to follow, but this does not happen, since the bass remains on B, and the F is taken a half tone lower to E. These two voices, together with the upper G-sharp, make up the harmony of the third chord in A minor, the ruling chord of which also follows. During the soprano F-sharp [m. 6] the bass remains on C, and the second voice likewise on E, which gives rise to an inversion of the second chord in E minor. With this same bass and upper voice, the second voice then goes to D-sharp, which produces the third inversion of the diminished seventh chord in E minor. The soprano G indicates the third of its ruling chord. The bass, by reason of contrary motion, goes to B, and the second voice goes to E, but exchanges this

tone immediately for D, the third above the bass. This entire measure also could have
been arranged in the key of G major, simply by giving the second voice D-natural (*simple*)
instead of D-sharp, and then D instead of E. In this case it would have come out as a
transposition of the previous measure and therefore would have been more natural.
But since we wanted to demonstrate other modulations etc. in this example also, we have
chosen the other alternative. The seventh measure has been made to conform to the one
before it, because it simply recurs a tone lower. The harmony of the eighth measure,
except for the fourth quarter, has likewise been transposed down another step. In this
measure the harmony of the second chord in G major appears, whereupon the two upper
voices move to A and F-sharp from the third chord in this key. Now the bass remains
stationary on G until the end, confirming the rule that with oblique motion it is permissible [67] to use different harmonies with a sustained tone, provided only that the first
and last of them are five–three chords. This rule has already been cited before, but since
a repetition is not superfluous at an opportune time, especially when examples are
present, we have demonstrated it in this way. After the ruling harmony, the second
and third chords occur,[48] and then the ruling chord reappears and one similar to it. Then
the harmony proceeds again in the order of succession until it ends with the alternation
of the second and first chords. This example shows us a possible application of artificial
techniques. It still contains no imitations etc., but is produced by the natural progression
of the three chords in conjunction with oblique motion. Only from the fifth measure
on does anything out of the ordinary take place, namely a few unexpected keys appear
which, in any case, do have their natural resolution. This class of three-part composition
always requires a fine judgement, which certainly cannot be acquired without an understanding of most chords and their resolution, generally not before one has perused and
comprehended the thorough-bass method. When this has been accomplished, and
a mastery of harmony acquired, one will be able to combine nature and art well in this
style. The latter then must be applied so that it seems to be the more prominent in a
certain piece, although, after all, it is merely subservient to nature. To the listener
the melody appears in its utmost simplicity and sounds entirely spontaneous, but it
nevertheless has been made to comply here and there with the design of the harmony,
so as to also benefit its members, that is, its voices. And these voices themselves have
a melody which, in places where the upper voice is in the brilliant style, still has a
naturally flowing line. In arranging this, the instruments themselves are to be taken into
consideration. The melody for a harpsichord etc. can be intermingled with more half-step
appoggiaturas and contain fewer ties, than one which is to be performed by violins,
wind instruments, etc. The reason is that the former instrument does not sustain,
whereas the latter instruments can prolong their tone at length, and so the half steps
produce a different effect, depending on whether they are heard on one or the other
instrument. Therefore, the nature of every instrument must be thoroughly explored,
provided that one wants to write some pleasing music for them in which art and nature
are combined.

[48] Ex. 65: apparently a measure containing these three chords was omitted after m. 8. "The ruling chord reappears and
one similar to it" (with f'-natural) describes m. 9.

The imitation of a melodic motif in all three voices might be contrived in the following manner [Example 66].

Ex. 66

This example already combines more art with nature than did the previous one. Yet the melody of the first voice always does remain in its range, without the second voice disturbing it or endeavoring to take its place. The harmony for the most part is arranged according to the order of the three main chords. No irregular resolutions are used here either. A few retardations have been introduced in the proper place. In the very first measure D and B from the third chord are retarded, since they are retained during the root of the ruling chord, which then gives rise to a four–nine chord. But since the bass goes to its third, C, instead of waiting for the resolution of the ninth as it should have, the resolution then occurs to a sixth, namely C in the bass and A in the middle voice. At the beginning of the second measure the bass ascends a half step, which produces the harmony of the deceptive [70] cadence. This is followed by the second chord, and so on according to the order. An eighth rest occurs in the bass, and then the previous bass E recurs and is even retarded at the beginning of the third measure, as is the C in the second voice, despite the fact that the second chord is indicated by the upper voice. The tone D follows and once again remains stationary with the harmony of the third chord, which likewise happens just at the entrance of the harmony of the first chord. Here it is dislodged by the proper bass, C. The retardation now occurs in the upper voice. The proper tone at the commencement of the fourth measure would be B, the sixth of the second chord, but the preceding C remains stationary and becomes an appoggiatura. The bass, however, takes no part in this, but rather accommodates the previously mentioned B and its order of succession. The second voice does likewise in stating A, the fifth of the second chord. Now the bass should remain stationary, since the harmony of the third chord follows, but because there is another half step between D and E the bass also passes through this tone, D-sharp, in order to include somewhat extraneous elements in the harmony; besides, two closes, namely A to G-sharp in the upper voice and D-sharp to E in the bass, produce a good effect. The rest in both upper voices provides an opportunity for the bass to move through the intervals of the third chord in a short melodic motif which subsequently is imitated by the upper voice in the intervals of the first chord [m. 5]. Because of the similarity of this chord to the third chord in D minor, the second voice imitates this motif in the first chord in D minor. And because of this same resemblance to the third chord in G major, the melodic motif can be carried out in both voices until after the first chord in F major [m. 7] where, by merely transposing it down a third, the first voice leads it into the third chord in A minor. Here [m. 8] the bass again takes it over and the second voice repeats it in the first chord. The bass imitates it once again, namely in the first chord in D minor. After this [m. 10], the upper voice sounds it in the first chord in G major. Because of the similarity of this chord to the third chord in C major, the C-major harmony can follow. And by means of the similarity of this setting to the third chord in D minor, it happens that this chord comes next. After this, its ruling chord appears [m. 11], and then the third chord in E minor, which may be used here because the third chord in A minor which follows bears some resemblance to the ruling chord in E minor. Then, in accordance with the order, the first chord appears. The A and C of this chord are heard once more, but the bass is given F [m. 12]. [71] One takes this freedom in making a deceptive cadence. Here, however, it is done because both upper voices remain stationary and the intermediate rest does not interfere. Thus, this bass F can be introduced by means of oblique motion. Yet, at the option of the composer, the bass could also have been taken to C instead of F. The progression from here to the end takes place in accordance with the course of the three chords.

This type of imitation can be used in all musical pieces. It is even allowed in the menuet. But, as we already mentioned above, it must be used carefully, so that the main melody is not obscured or made indistinct, as would happen especially if the second voice were taken a little higher than the first voice, as is certainly done very often by inexperienced composers. Later we will also show how to write this type of alternation for two voices.

Ex. 67 Example of Imitation in Triple Meter

Ex. 67 (*cont.*)

Throughout this example [Example 67] there is the most precise succession of the three chords and their assigned harmonies. The essential content of this piece is the above-considered retention of a tone in the second voice and the bass, the three different motions, and the fact that the second voice never ascends above the first voice. In the ninth measure the second voice begins to present the melodic motif taken from the first measure, and this occurs in the third chord in A major. The first voice imitates in the first chord. But since this motif is comprised of an ascending octave leap and then a descending step, the first voice must imitate it in like manner, which, instead of G-sharp, gives rise to the tone G, which actually belongs to the third chord in D major and can very well be used here because the other intervals all appear in the ruling chord in A major. In this way, the melody is now situated in the first chord of D major, which [73] gives the bass an opportunity to imitate the melodic motif in this key [m. 11]. This chord, as the one which preceded it, has two aspects, in that it presents here the ruling chord in D major, but at the same time, due to the inclusion of C, also displays the intervals of the third chord in G major. Actually the first chord in G major, or rather its first inversion does follow [m. 12]. Once again, the similarity of this chord to the harmony of the second chord in D major facilitates the subsequent use of the third chord in this key as well. And since, in the natural course of events, the first chord must follow, the bass then can remain on the root, D, while the harmony of the third chord in A major is heard above it, as has been done here [m. 13]. Now the harmony proceeds in order to the cadence. The rest which follows provides an opportunity for the bass to have a running passage [m. 16], which then is imitated by the other voices and is carried out until the end. No further cadence occurs, because the bass passages were derived from the intervals of the first chord, and therefore the other two voices could not include any other tones either, provided that the aim is to bring the entire piece to a conclusion.

This is one of the easiest pieces which could be imitated. The melody is completely natural and flowing, and the artificial style has been incorporated in such a way that one hardly notices it. When using such pieces as models, an amateur will do well to depend on his imagination and judgement more than on the keyboard. If it is necessary, the first two or four measures may be searched out at the harpsichord, but the rest should be decided upon by reflection and the writing of trial versions. In the course of this work, we also intend to be mindful of facilitating this process.

Furthermore, concerting passages are also introduced in three-part composition. These consist of an alternation [of motives] between the two voices, so that sometimes this one and sometimes that one occupies the first place. It is also necessary to handle this style carefully. The entire melody must be arranged so that it is never interrupted by the other voice. It must be divided between the two voices, so that in listening to such a piece, one would believe that a single voice were carrying out the main melody. It is known that a passage is often heard twice during one piece, which commonly happens when the passage contains something distinctive, pleasant, [74] and singable, or else presents the brilliant style. In this case one gladly hears it twice. Therefore, this style originates in [the principle of] repetition.

Ex. 68 Example with Concerting Passage

Ex. 68 (cont.)

We purposely have chosen a melody [in Example 68] which will strike the amateurs as very easy, and one which is simply flowing and contains no intervals other than those inherent in the key. Anyone who has a good grasp of something easy, can quite soon proceed to something difficult. Our aim is to demonstrate how to construct a harmony pleasing to the ear, which gives approval whenever nature has a greater share in the harmony than does art. At the beginning of the melody a few bound tones are introduced, which can be divided into two parts, so that the first half is properly harmonized, whereas the other half is, in effect, not present. The first half of the G in the first measure belongs in the preceding ruling chord. The second half is not realized, but rather the bass harmonizes with [the soprano] F, which in this case has been taken from the third chord, [77] because it is followed directly by the first chord again. The second voice begins with the third, E, and is retarded along with the upper voice. The tone F likewise remains stationary into the beginning of the second measure, where it, too, is disregarded, since the bass is directed toward the following tone, which is from the first chord and requires the root C in the bass. This E is also bound, and the second half of it is abandoned, because the bass, conforming to the following D, goes to G, the root of the third chord. Now since, at the very beginning, the second voice commenced in thirds with the upper voice, it can also continue this progression without the bass paying attention to it. The rest of the harmony proceeds in order. The initial four-measure melody is now repeated in the second voice, while the first voice appears in its place. The ninth measure begins with brilliant passages, which likewise are four measures long and are repeated in the second voice. Therefore, in order to make this very clear, the second voice has been given only simple struck tones interspersed with rests[49] while the bass has a steady, supporting motion. At the end of this passage the first voice again takes up the melodic line and carries it to the cadence in G major [m. 20]. Then a measure-long figure appears and is repeated three times. The upper voice and the second voice each sound it twice. This figure, in somewhat varied form, is then continued [m. 25], while the bass has a few slow tones mixed with rests. At the end, the previous close is repeated. Further explanation will not be necessary, since this style (*Manier*) is quite easy to imitate. But still, it should be said that not all passages are suitable for repetition. A melodic motif designed for this purpose must deserve to be heard twice in succession. It must be carefully chosen, appealing to the ear, and include nothing dull or tedious. Any bright, lively passages, any singing, playful, and skipping figures can be repeated. Good judgement is best in determining these matters also.

The alternation of the brilliant and the singing styles should also appear in this type of three-part composition. The alternation of these two styles, together with a good execution of *forte* and *piano*, contributes much to the enhancement of a piece. The effect is remarkably distinctive.

Ex. 69 Example Alternating the Brilliant and the Singing Styles

---

[49] Daube's repeated recommendation of rests is reflective of the varied, transparent textures of *galant* music. He uses rests to clarify phrasing, create characteristic rhythms for each voice, ensure that moving parts will be heard clearly, allow wind players to breathe, and create textural diversity by temporarily reducing the size of the ensemble, often in correlation with stylistic contrasts. See, for instance, pp. 108–9, 123, and 126–7. Also see the comments on general rests, p. 104 Ex. 69: mm. 5 and 7, second voice had eighth notes in original.

Ex. 69 (cont.)

The alternation of the singing and the brilliant styles has been brought about very naturally [in Example 69], and one sees that the harmony has been gauged accordingly. The former has a thin accompaniment. It begins without any harmony. The second measure contains three tones of equal duration and the following three-part texture likewise exhibits no particular change of movement or harmony. Now if this piece is begun with a very delicate *piano* which continues until the unexpected intense *forte*, what change does such a sudden *forte* make on the ears of the listeners? The harmonization of this *forte* [m. 5] is carried on with vigorous movement in the accompanying voices,[50] and when the upper voices subsequently rest [m. 8], the bass repeats the passage-work once again while the upper voice prepares for another expression of the singing style. The second voice must rest two measures while the bass progresses slowly with the upper voice. This slow bass movement continues, even though the second voice joins in again with the very same movement. Here [m. 13] the brilliant style reappears, in the second measure of which all three voices reach a unison and go in parallel motion for a single measure. When this procedure occurs unexpectedly in a brilliant Allegro, and does not last long, it sometimes wins approval. After the cadence [m. 16], the two lower voices proceed in sixths, while immediately after that the upper voice again sounds two short *piano* phrases with intermittent *forte* exchanges. The subsequent very intense *forte* [passage] then hastens to the cadence, where it is heard once more with the full harmony of the first chord.

[81] In large scores such as symphonies, concertos, etc., this alternation of the singing and the brilliant styles can be introduced very beneficially. In opera arias also it is quite often heard and wins much approval. Moreover, the ear likes something new and unexpected. Therefore the melody must necessarily possess a beautiful continuity, but it certainly also ought to be constructed so that the listener could not tell what to expect from one passage to the next. And thus it is with the harmony also, in which multifarious changes and surprises must be introduced. Another characteristic of the second type of three-part composition is beautiful symmetry, or good division of the main melody, and similarly a harmony which fluctuates between full and thin. The former has to do with the rules for the invention of melody,[51] as we will try to demonstrate in the proper place. The principles of beauty in nature which are sought for everywhere – in all the arts and sciences, in languages and styles of writing – have been found to a great extent in music also. One branch of knowledge supports the other. It is certain that these principles, which have been taken from the correspondences found in beautiful, charming

[50] For use of texture and dynamics to emphasize stylistic contrast and create surprise, see pp. 108–9 and pp. 115–17, where Daube recommends proportions of styles for a complete movement. See also pp. 129–30. Quantz advocated a similar alternation of styles in the concerto grosso (*Versuch* (1752), pp. 12, 228, Eng. trans., pp. 23, 311). Riepel distinguishes between four contrasting styles – the *Singer*, *Laufer*, *Rauscher*, and *Springer* – and likewise observes the heightened effect of juxtaposing them (*Anfangsgründe*, vol. I (1752), p. 39).

[51] Here Daube probably refers to the planned fourth volume of the *Dilettant* series, *Anleitung zur Erfindung der Melodie*. A treatise on melody would be "the proper place" to treat "good division of the main melody" (i.e., musical form) since, during the later eighteenth century, large-scale melodic design was becoming associated with developing concepts of form, as in Daube's next paragraph. This relationship can be seen in Riepel's *Anfangsgründe*, vol. II (1755), in which the study of symphonic structure is undertaken with a single melodic line.

nature, and brought to application, are so universal that one even can borrow them from the other sciences and use them in music.[52] Of what does symmetry in architecture consist? Of the beautiful proportions of the various dimensions of the component parts from which the building is constructed. This proportional division is pleasing. Even the uninformed peasant will praise it, although he does not know by what means this beauty is produced. On the other hand, if there is a visible error, it will be criticized repeatedly by everyone. Beautiful symmetry is found today in painting, sculpture, dancing, poetry, literature, etc., in which it always brings forth beauty and edification. It is this which we recognize in music, too, and of which very little was known by our forefathers, many of whom believed that one must give his thoughts free rein and let the idea itself conclude the piece.

Thus, [there are two requirements] for the [proper] division of the main melody. First, it should be constructed so that the caesuras, resting places, and cadences are separated by an equal number of measures. For example, a segment can contain two or four measures, a figure preceding the resting place may be comprised of two, four, six, even eight measures, and a passage lasting until the cadence or the conclusion also may be given an arbitrary but equal number of measures. Secondly, wherever a brilliant passage has been written in the first part, it should reappear in the second part, and likewise with the singing style. No passage may appear in the first part which [82] is not reintroduced in the second, although transposed into another key. However, in case an idea is not to be heard in both parts, it is always better for it to make its first appearance in the second part, although the idea itself still must be repeated. It is very seldom good for a passage to appear only a single time. The repetition also confirms it in its position. However, if one prefers not to have it heard twice, it may be varied the second time, which the ear will certainly retain as something pleasant. In general, the entire musical piece must be divisible into certain main sections, and these again into smaller secondary parts or motives, providing it is to produce a good effect. Also pertinent here is the decreasing and increasing of the harmony, in which variety must be frequently perceived. Continuously full harmony is not pleasing to the ear. Even three-part composition must show an alternation in which one sometimes hears two voices, or indeed, even the unison, and then the three-part settings again. But is it worthwhile to consider which tones should be omitted? We deem it superfluous to give examples here also, since most of the preceding ones contain this changing of the harmony, as well as the division of the melody.

In artificial three-part composition it also quite often happens that the bass part must be altered so that more beautiful ties, imitations, or countermelodies might be arranged in the second voice. Sometimes a rest is set in the bass in order to accomplish this. The same thing is done with the second voice also, indeed, even with the first voice, when they are concerting together and the first voice assumes the secondary position. Both must likewise be altered for the sake of the bass, especially if this can improve

[52] In his *Erfindung der Melodie* (1797/98), p. 5, Daube alludes to the idea of the relationship of the arts through principles of nature as demonstrated by "the famed Abbé Batteux." Compare Batteux, *Les beaux arts* (1746).

the melodic quality of the bass line. All of this occurs particularly in the so-called sonatas *a tre*,[53] in which all three voices should be very melodic, and also where the bass often plays a melodic motif from the upper voice so that it might not constantly remain in its steady, supportive role and move along slowly, all of which has been pointed out already. Nature and art must be united if the work is to please the greatest number of listeners. This discussion is to be concluded by another elaborate example in which we want to review everything which has thus far been illustrated by separate examples [Example 70].[54]

Ex. 70

[53] The sonata *a tre* or trio sonata, a standard genre of early to mid-eighteenth-century chamber music, featured a concerting texture of two trebles and bass plus continuo. J. A. P. Schulz considered the chamber-style trio sonata one of the most difficult genres of composition and one of the most pleasant types of chamber music (Sulzer, "Trio. (Musik.)," *Allgemeine Theorie*, vol. II (1774), pp. 1180–81). See also Türk, *Klavierschule* (1789), p. 398, Eng. trans., p. 387.

[54] While many of Daube's melodies are in the expansive Italian cantabile style or exhibit the rapid passagework of the concerto tradition, Ex. 70 seems to draw on his North German heritage of small, rhythmically diversified melodic figures.

Ex. 70 (*cont.*)

Ex. 70 (*cont.*)

Ex. 70 (*cont.*)

[89] Because all of the foregoing examples were Allegro movements, we have chosen a slow tempo for this one. This piece will not be displeasing in performance, although the only consideration in writing it has been practical instruction. In performing it, however, remember that the bass line is to be played by a violoncello, so that, in view of the short melodic motives, the three voices acquire an equality which cannot be obtained on the harpsichord. Bowings, slurs, and the so-called *forzando*, etc. are best expressed by a violoncello. The second voice begins the melody and continues it, accompanied by the steadily moving bass, until the sixth measure. The main content of the entire piece is proposed by this initial melody. In it we find a mixture of accidentals which, especially the sharps, are used as appoggiaturas. However, they constitute something extraneous and unexpected, since this short statement modulates into three different keys which, however, on account of their brevity, are not at all detrimental to the main key. In the second measure the melody modulates into the key of B-flat major, but since the third chord in this key bears a great resemblance to the first chord in F major, and since the following B-flat-major chord itself likewise resembles the second chord in F major and immediately returns to this key, the melody is enhanced by this very short excursion and the ear hears something unusual which, however, disappears again the next moment. The same short encroachments [of the tonal boundary] are found in the fourth measure. In the [fifth][55] measure the return route is indicated already. In the [sixth] measure the E-flat is presented again, which gives rise to the aforementioned

---

[55] "sixth measure" in the original, "seventh measure" in the following sentence and paragraph. Ex. 70; m. 28, "$\frac{9}{3}$" over second *Bb* in original.

resemblance of two chords. Then a formal cadence is made in F major. The melody, however, immediately modulates again, since at the entrance of the first voice it prepares for the first modulation from F major, which is likewise accomplished by the bass. The three-part harmony now makes its appearance. The melodic motif taken from the first half of the following measure [m. 7] is played beforehand [m. 6] by the second voice almost as if it appeared unintentionally. Then it is repeated an octave higher by the first voice, in fact, it appears here in the same [rhythmic] position in which it was originally played by the second voice. The bass repeats it, which is quite unexpected, since the initial bass line was not imitative. The second voice also participates in the imitation.

The third melodic motif is now imitated by the second voice while the bass continues its steady gait as before [m. 10]. At the beginning of the eleventh measure, the two voices join and proceed together until the cadence. Now [m. 12, beat 3] the upper voice introduces a [90] very short melodic motif, consisting of only five rapid tones, which then is imitated at once by the second voice so that the two voices repeat it in thirds and lead to a short caesura where the second voice takes it up anew, now in the third chord in B-flat major. The first and second voices change places and arrange the same repetition in thirds [m. 13, beat 4]. This melodic motif, with a slight change, is played once again by both voices in succession, whereupon it is continued, mixed [with other figures], until the entrance of the second melodic motif [m. 17]. This motif now appears in the key of D minor and is repeated three times by the two voices alternating in thirds, while the bass causes oblique motion and does not proceed as it did above in the seventh [recte eighth] measure where it, too, imitated this melodic motif. The upper voice sounds a few slow tones, which again provide opportunity for imitation, at the same time giving rise to two chromatic chords. The first of these is the augmented sixth chord in A minor, which here goes to the third chord in D minor [m. 19] on account of a certain resemblance, and the second chromatic chord is the augmented sixth chord in E minor, which here, however, moves back into the harmony of the third chord in A minor [m. 19, beat 3]. It is not followed by the ruling chord, but rather by the third chord in D minor, whereupon a formal cadence is made in this key [m. 20]. Now the first theme reappears. The second motif is repeated by the bass, taken over by the second voice, and introduced once more by the upper voice. The first voice now [m. 23] presents the third melodic motif anew, specifically with the same tones which the second voice had in the tenth measure, while the second voice now plays this melodic motif a fifth lower and then repeats it. In the next measure [m. 25] the bass takes up the imitation of part of this motif which, however, must appear somewhat altered, since at the same time the upper voices are also sounding rapid tones. The second melodic motif comes forth once more, that is, as it was ornamented in D minor. This motif is repeated several times in alternation between the two upper voices, whereupon the very short motif which occurred in the twelfth measure appears [m. 28, beat 3] for the formation of the close, this time with a repetition of the first tone which, however, the bass disregards, realizing the note in the first voice. And since this tone subsequently remains stationary also, the same fate befalls it, that is, the bass harmonizes with the tone in the second voice [m. 28, beat 4]. This alternation of retained tones between the two voices is continued several more times, while the bass proceeds in the said manner. If this is to be expressed in figures [91] the adjacent ninth, octave, and seventh must be divided into two bass notes, the first of which is given two figures together. Now, due to the presence of the third chord of this key, in which the seventh is heard, and to contrary or opposite motion, the deceptive cadence appears [m. 30]. Then all three voices have a rest in preparation for the formal cadence. Moreover, these general rests often improve the melody and harmony when they are introduced quite unexpectedly. The listener is taken aback, as it were, and is thereby once again made eager to hear the continuation [of the piece]. The formal cadence is heard, but the final very short melodic motif is repeated several more times, while the simultaneous imitation in thirds and sixths by the second voice turns out quite well. Then all three voices hasten at an equally rapid pace to the final cadence.

We hope by now to have discussed three-part composition to the satisfaction of every amateur. To our knowledge, at least, it has never before been explained so clearly, though so extensively also. According to this description, an amateur can know to which class any three-part score belongs, and whether it possesses the features which have been pointed out here. Whoever has the patience, from the very beginning of each discussion, to work from the accompanying examples, and to construct their own test pieces and imitations according to the successive chords of each example, and to proceed in that way, step by step, to the end of the discussion, has our promise of much progress in the knowledge of composition, in theory as well as practice. Everyone can come to know this truth. Even those with moderate talent will certainly learn so much that they can be satisfied with it.

5

COMBINING FOUR VOICES

This discussion is based on the preceding one. All that was explained there can be applied here. Indeed, one can almost say that four-part composition is the easiest of all, in so far as the four voices do not concert among themselves, [92] but rather are to be regarded as four simple voices. What is essential here is the knowledge of the three chords, of their order, of the three motions, of the retardation, and of the relationship of the keys. All this and much more is to be observed in an artificial two- or three-part piece. But [in natural four-part writing] the main concern is simply to distribute the voices well, taking special care that the two outer voices, namely the upper voice and the bass, carry no irregular harmony (the inner voices can tolerate fifths and octaves more readily), and that the other two voices remain in their proper position. The viola in particular should be kept in its appointed place, where it sometimes appears as a middle voice and sometimes as a higher bass.[56] Furthermore, care is to be taken that this voice may never ascend above the first voice and thereby alter the main melody. And since it is tuned in unison with the violins, it is quite easy, in view of the preceding, to understand why it should not rise above the first voice. We have found these mistakes even in the scores of skilled people. But, with most music it is best for the viola part to have the least number of players,[57] in which case, of course, such an error of voice-crossing will be less noticeable. However, the nature of this instrument requires that it would always proceed [in a range] lower than the violins. Only there is it allowed to concert with the other voices. Now which intervals should the viola properly have? Those which are still left after three voices have been composed. In the first chord it is usually the octave above the bass, but if the third chord has preceded, it also can be the fifth, G. The other two chords are naturally four-part and therefore only the previous directions need to be followed. First the three-part settings must be written out, namely two upper voices and the bass. Then whatever is still left is given to the viola. However, this is to be understood only of four-part composition without the alternation of full and thin harmonies, but not of the artificial construction of this number of voices. We will give a few examples of both types. For the sake of beginners we again want to start with an explanation and analysis of each chord [Example 71].

Ex. 71 Various Types of Four-Part Writing in the First Chord

The two upper voices move together here in a constant alternation of thirds and sixths. The bass proceeds with its principal tones (*Grund*). What still remains of this harmony is given to the viola. In the first measure E and G are assigned to this instrument, since these two tones are missing in the other voices. This also happens in the next two measures where the viola has G. Toward the end it is given another tone which the other voices do not have, namely B.

---

[56] "The higher bass," used fairly frequently in the transparent textures of this era, came to be called "das Bassetchen" (little bass). It was defined as "that voice which provides the lowest voice as long as the real bass voice is silent. This usually happens in a higher octave; for example when the viola plays the bass part while the bass rests" (Koch, "Basset," *Lexicon* (1802), col. 222). See Ex. 74 and p. 109.

[57] "The least number of players" and similar phrases, indicate that Daube may have imagined his "four-part scores" for either string quartet or four-part string orchestra. At this time there was little distinction between quartets and symphonies; either might be heard with one or more players per part, depending upon available performers.

Ex. 72 The Second Chord

[94] [In Example 72] the two upper voices move in thirds and sixths until the fourth measure where they come together on a second which, however, is converted into a sixth again, since the [second voice] remains stationary. A third appears, changes to a sixth again, and then to the concluding octave. For the first two measures the bass has the root, which remains stationary when the third chord enters and then goes to the third above the ruling root. Now comes the root and its third from the second chord, and then the root once again followed by the root of the third chord and the close. The viola has nothing but the missing tones, or else perhaps the octave of another part.

Ex. 73 The Third Chord

[95] A greater variety is already to be found in this example [Example 73]. The second violin does not always proceed in thirds or sixths, but goes to the nearest adjacent tones in either similar motion or contrary motion with the upper voice. The bass does the same. With contrary motion it is allowed to go to the tones adjacent to the previous bass note, even though they are not roots or their thirds. At the beginning of the sixth measure two tones from the preceding third chord are retained and become, in this case, the fourth and ninth [above the bass]. Strictly speaking, both are simply appoggiaturas, of which we have spoken several times already concerning their definition, origin, and various designations. Now if one were to inquire into the intervals which still remain, they would be exactly those that are in the viola part. However it certainly is not good, and seldom has a pleasing effect, for a piece to be set in four parts throughout. Remember that the fourth tone of the second and third chords is written only when it repeats the preceding tone. For example, with the second chord it is C which can be retained from the first chord if another voice already has D, and with the third chord it is F which is in the preceding second chord and thus may remain here if G is already situated in another voice. The fourth tone in the first chord is an octave which is never detrimental to the good effect. To encourage a good melodic line within every voice it is helpful for the voices to resolve properly among themselves as well, that is, according to the rules of harmony. The first voice should be set with the second in such a way that their intervals are resolved correctly. For example, the F in the second measure is subsequently resolved as if it actually had been situated in the bass, that is to say, the voice descends a half step, instead of ascending a tone to G and therefore possibly relinquishing this E to another voice. The relationship of the second voice to the viola is the same. These two [voices] begin with a sixth changing to a seventh, whereupon the viola moves to another seventh, which likewise is resolved to a sixth by the downward [motion] of the second voice, and so on. Even the bass must maintain a good relationship with the viola, although in the natural style of four-part composition this is not always necessary. A good relationship between the parts themselves is favorable to the melody of each voice, and the harmony also benefits greatly from it, especially in artificial composition in which the retention of one or two voices produces unusual chords.

Ex. 74 Large Example in which the Three Chords Alternate

Ex. 74 (cont.)

[mm. 11–12, 12–13, the second voice has tie marks in the original]

After writing the first voice, a prospective composer might well consider carefully how he wants to arrange the other three voices, and at which point the composition could be four-, three-, or even two-part. These are things which should be looked into well beforehand. We have said something about this already in our thorough-bass method and also in this work, and now the opportunity arises to speak of it yet once again. Everything in the brilliant style should be expressed through full-voicing. An exception is the serious style in rapid pieces, in which all the voices can be used in unison. Pieces of a delicate, singing, or playful nature may well be represented by three, two, and even by a single voice, when followed at once by something in the brilliant or rushing style.

The use of *piano* and interspersed rests also has a good effect. The expression of the affects will be explained more clearly later.[58]

The initial melody of this present example [Example 74] is of a serious nature, for which the full harmony is suitable. The following change to the playful or singing style already permits a modification. For that reason we have given the bass line to the viola, in order that this higher bass might increase the effect of the change. In the ninth measure, the bass re-enters unexpectedly, whereupon the full harmony continues until the end. The E-flat in the twelfth and following [99] measures also has a good effect because the first voice meanwhile sustains F. In the fifteenth and following measures, the tones B-flat, C, and E-flat in the first voice are merely appoggiaturas which are written as regular notes. The intervals of each voice are kept as close together as possible. And whenever a tone can remain stationary, it is also good that it be sustained longer, unless the melody of this voice should call for the opposite. Even with an accompanying voice the melody remains the main object. For melodic reasons it is sometimes even necessary for an incomplete chord to be heard at times. In order to produce a good melody small mistakes are often permitted in the inner voices, indeed, one even finds them in the outer voices of [works by] great masters, who preferred to concede a little mistake for the sake of a good bass line. But this already requires a vast [amount of] experience and judgement, without which it is better to refrain from taking such freedom. Since this example is based on the natural style of composition, in that no artificial ties, imitations, modulations, etc. are to be found in it, we also want to give a few examples which include artificial techniques.

Ex. 75 Example of Imitation

[58] In the projected third *Dilettant* Ex. 75: b. 4, viola, first note *e'* in original.

Ex. 75 (cont.)

The initial theme [of Example 75] consists of only two measures, and yet it is capable of being employed in various ways and of providing the opportunity for an extensive treatment. At the beginning it is imitated by the second voice while the other two voices each carry on a separate melody. It is worked out this way for eight measures. Next [m. 9] a short, playful motif is introduced, which is followed by a general pause. Then [m. 13], in order to show the amateurs how the theme also could be distributed among four voices, we have repeated it once more. The viola begins and is answered by the first voice. The bass takes over the theme and the first voice accompanies it in thirds. Then [m. 16] comes the second voice, followed again by a repetition in the viola, while the second voice accompanies it in thirds. Now [m. 18] the first violin commences the theme once more and the bass makes the imitation. Then a repetition occurs in the first chord, [played] by the second voice [m. 20]. The first voice then makes a literal imitation, and the second voice accompanies in thirds, resulting in a transposition down by thirds. Finally the melody presses toward the formal cadence and the close. This imitation is contrived merely from the chords of the first eight measures, and consequently is indeed very different from the fugal style or canonic procedure. The first two measures, as was said above, have the main content. The other measures owe their existence solely to the transposition of these two measures. [103] We still want to draw up another example with modulations into other keys, in which the two upper voices carry out the imitation, while the others each play their own separate lines [Example 76].

Ex. 76

We have continued with the previous theme for the purpose of demonstrating that even the smallest initial melody, or a part taken from the middle of a piece, might be used in many different ways, of which more is to be said below.[59] Here the bass has this theme all alone, while the second voice introduces an unexpected theme which includes

[59] See p. 152

tones foreign to the key and is imitated by the first voice. The transposition is then carried along to the diminished seventh chord, which thereupon is resolved into the third chord in D minor. The entire harmony consists of the constant alternation of the first and third chords. The latter directs the modulation into another key and the former provides the corresponding resolution. The viola has the most simple accompaniment of all, but it does have its own distinct movement.

We have already said that all the special alternations etc. which are to be encountered in artificial three-part composition, could be used here also. There are so-called quartets in which only the first voice is in the brilliant style and the other voices merely carry on the simple harmony.[60] One finds a few in which the melody is divided between two voices, and the other two merely accompany. There are also those in which all four voices concert among themselves [Example 77].

Ex. 77 Example of a Four-Part *Allegro* Movement

---

[60] The first of these types, which flourished toward the end of the eighteenth century and beyond, probably corresponds to the virtuosic "*quatuor brilliant*, which features brilliant soloistic performance . . ." (Levy, *Quatuor Concertant*, p. 327, n. 2); the second type represents an intermediate stage between the trio sonata (with the viola replacing the harpsichord in the middle range) and the more democratic concertante quartet; the third type corresponds to the *quatuor-concertant* style, popular in France between 1770 and 1800 (ibid., p. 46). Many of Daube's "four-part scores" contain the stylistic traits of the latter type, as analyzed by Levy. See Hanning, "Conversation," pp. 512–28 and, regarding "a style which sought to blend the popular elements of Paris with the intellectual traditions of Vienna," see Hickman, "Leopold Kozeluch," pp. 42–54.

Ex. 77 (cont.)

Ex. 77 (cont.)

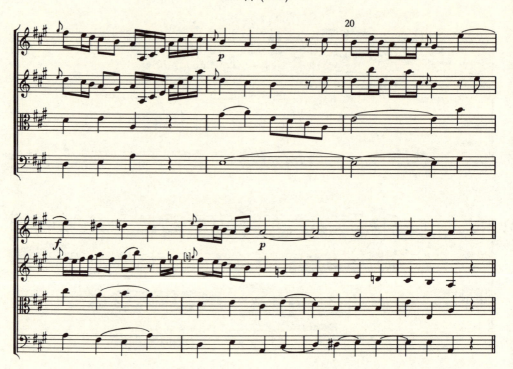

The bass takes up the initial theme at the end of the first measure while the other voices continue their own lines. At the end of the fourth measure the two violins have a very short melodic motif without any other accompaniment. In the sixth measure all four voices rejoin. At the beginning of the seventh measure the short melodic motif is stated several more times, with a strong *forte* heard each time in between. Now, for a change from the singing style, a very strong rushing motif appears in all four voices and, with a slight variation, continues for six measures. After this, another short singing motif appears [m. 15] and is repeated with some variation. Then come two measures [mm. 17–18] which contain a mixed melody, that is to say, they are composed of both the singing and the brilliant styles. The melody seems to remain in the key of E major, since the second and third chords of this key are there, but the D which accompanies it introduces the third chord in A major, the harmony of which very suitably serves to resolve the preceding chord. After this harmony follows the third chord in D major which, because of its great similarity to the ruling chord in A major, can perform both of these roles. Now the cadence in A major ensues and, by means of a rapid ascending passage, the melody arrives [m. 19] at the first tone of the short singing melody of a few measures previous, which is accompanied by sustained tones in the bass and viola. This and what follows is [110] merely a repetition. After this the first violin has three sustained tones, during which the other voices modulate into several keys, namely into

D major through the harmony of its third chord, and then into E major, likewise through its third chord [m. 23, beat 2]. The third chord in A major now appears and the formal cadence follows.

This example could be pursued much further if one wanted to show the proper arrangement of the melody and harmony, but since we have resolved to present everything easily and clearly but not copiously, any further continuation must be omitted. It will be sufficient if an amateur has this much knowledge and has imitated a few examples. Then it will not seem difficult to him to extend each piece further, especially since we really have prepared the way in the thorough-bass method, as well as in this work. Still, we will continue to do everything possible to facilitate the acquisition of this knowledge.

A FEW REMARKS PERTAINING TO FOUR-PART COMPOSITION

First an amateur should consider carefully which type of four-part scores he wants to construct; whether he wishes them to be in the manner of symphonies, or in the style of concertos, and whether they are to be composed like the simple or the artificial three-part sonatas. The first type is based on the alternation of the rushing and brilliant style with the singing style. Here the first Allegro can consist of three parts rushing style and one part singing style.[61] The second type is that in which the first voice has various solos, which are lightly accompanied at times by one or two voices. This accompaniment, moreover, incorporates various rests. The third type is distinguished by nothing other than the alternation of four-part and two-part harmony. The melody of the first violin continues practically from beginning to end with singing passages in the style of the Italian arias, though without ritornello. The harmony here serves only the melody, without having many different changes of motion. We pointed out the fourth type a short time ago, and sought to illustrate it by means of examples.

When an amateur has chosen one of these four styles, he should try to find a melody which is suitable for it. Then, after a melody has been found [111] and written from the beginning to the end of the piece, it must be analyzed harmonically. As was recommended for three-part composition, the chords can be indicated simply by the numbers 1, 2, 3, written underneath. Then one determines which melodic motif may be set in four, three, or even two parts. We have given instructions for this also in the preceding discussion of three-part composition. One must also carefully consider whether these melodic motives are to be divided between the first two voices. Then one should begin to write a bass for the melody, employing mainly the roots and their thirds. The other intervals

[61] These stylistic proportions, when combined with remarks about the "proper division of the main melody," hint at Daube's ideas on form. See pp. 97–8. In this case, the proportions would correspond approximately to a sonata form with the second-key area in the singing style. Daube's advice for a slow movement reverses these proportions. See p. 116. In Ex. 77, and in a proposed continuation for Ex. 84, Daube even correlates style and formal function, suggesting that the modulation to the first new key take place during a rushing and brilliant passage – presumably corresponding to the transition of a sonata form. See p. 132. Compare the four main types of phrases or periods mentioned by Momigny (*Cours complet*, vol. II (1803–06), 397–8).

are brought into the bass only when it is supposed to carry out a particular melody, or when it moves in thirds or sixths with the upper voice. They also may be set in the bass if they repeat the directly preceding tone, all of which has been cited at various times. When the bass is also finished, the second voice is written. The preceding examples show that this voice might sometimes move in thirds or sixths with the upper voice, but it is permitted to make such passages with the bass as well, especially when this is suggested by the chords. The bass may also be altered, or even omitted entirely, if the second voice can thereby achieve a good or better effect for the main melody. Many times the full harmony cannot elicit the same effect as that produced by an incomplete harmony. The ear is simply far too accustomed to variety. A melodic motif comprised of only two voices more often seems exceptionally beautiful when preceded or followed by the complete harmony in the rushing style. The viola is the last part to be composed. It sometimes moves in octaves with the bass,[62] or else is given whatever tones are still missing from the full harmony. Often it may have the tones which remain stationary. When it plays the role of a high bass, the regular bass rests or joins in only occasionally, since the viola makes a good impression too. The viola can contribute greatly to the enhancement of the harmony of a piece if it is written by a skillful master.

This, to some extent, is the procedure an amateur might follow in constructing a four-part Allegro movement. To write down each and every instruction here would result in prolixity, and certainly we must omit much more of which experience itself is the teacher. Composition, the setting or distribution of the voices, the continuation of the [112] melody, etc. are things which, without good talent, time, and practical experience, are learned in only a mediocre way, despite the best introductory method. The slow pieces in a four-part score can be composed in a different way. The preceding description is taken as a basis for this one. The alternation of the brilliant and the singing styles may occur in slow movements also, but the former must contain more running than skipping passages. The proportion advised here is three parts in the singing style to one part in the brilliant style. To the previously described four styles of melody and harmony, can also be added that in which the melody of the upper voice is very song-like, while the second voice proceeds with a steady, moderate movement, and the bass joins in only occasionally. The accompanying voices also can carry on a continuous or intermittent pizzicato. The melody of the upper voice can also be repeated alternately in the second voice by muted violins. When the accompanying voices are to play *piano* continuously, the attentiveness [of the listeners] is increased if the *piano* passage is interrupted occasionally by a single *forzando* tone.[63] The melody can also incorporate very brief

---

[62] Early quartets and symphonies are full of passages in which the viola doubles the bass line. This practice strengthens the bass at strategic points and provides textural variety. In his examples, Daube couples the viola with the bass at the beginnings and ends of phrases (thus shaping them texturally), on leading tone–tonic progressions, and in passages of parallel thirds and sixths in alternation with two violins. See n. 21. Although two-part orchestral writing declined after the transition period, a three-part texture of one bass line and two trebles remained an acceptable variant throughout the century. See Carse, *XVIIIth Century*, pp. 146, 193.

[63] It was this very technique which so delighted the London audience in the Andante of Haydn's Symphony No. 94 that the entire work became known as the "Surprise Symphony." Daube's remark preceded the Haydn symphony by eighteen years! It is possible that Haydn knew the *Dilettante*, since he did own Daube's *General-Baß* (1756). (See the Introduction, p. 9) More probably, however, in an era when dynamic contrasts were increasingly in vogue, Haydn simply epitomized a common stylistic trait by using it in an especially effective way. See p. 130.

rapid passages which, however, must be played vigorously. For variety, the accompanying voices may sustain quite long tones, specifically those that can remain stationary throughout two or three chords. This oblique (*einseitig*) motion produces a good effect if it does not appear too often. The last Allegro is like the first, in that the same things can occur or be observed in both, except that the last Allegro is usually in triple meter.[64] Yet it is to be said here that one is not obliged to display the art of diversified harmony in this movement to the same extent as is customarily shown in the first Allegro. It suffices for the melody to be fluent and gay, and for the harmony to be varied occasionally.

Ex. 78 Example of a Four-Part *Andante* Movement

[64] Daube obviously has in mind the three-movement format derived from the Italian sinfonia, rather than the four-movement format often used in Vienna at this time (LaRue, "Symphony, I," *The New Grove*, vol. XVIII, pp. 439, 444).

Ex. 78 (cont.)

We did not intend to introduce many modulations or foreign harmonies here, but rather merely to show the amateur the easiest alternative, that of an altogether simple harmony. But nevertheless, we hope that after a beginner can construct three different motions to a melody he might be able to go further on his own. At any event, in the discussion of five-part harmony we will have another opportunity to present more of this. The melody of this slow piece [Example 78], especially the first part, is supported by the most simple alternation of the three chords. The second violin has only a single kind of movement, which usually is assigned to the viola and to the bass. Meanwhile, the viola carries on a separate melodic line which, for the most part however, is based upon broken chords. And since each of these three voices generally has one sort of movement, it is necessary for the bass to move at a very slow pace, as it does, playing pizzicato besides. The second part [m. 9] commences, to be sure, in E major, the first modulation, but it returns again at once. At the beginning of the fifth measure [of the second part] a brief modulation into the key of A minor occurs, but the retention of the two tones, C and A, in the harmony gives rise to a few chords foreign to the key: the first of these is the ruling chord in A minor; the second is the five–three or the first chord in F major; the third can be accounted for as the harmony of the third chord in G major; the fourth is the compound [116] minor seventh chord in E minor, which here, however, is resolved into the third chord of A minor [m. 15].[65] A formal cadence ensues [m. 16]. And after this a few tones with accompanying harmony are played very strongly, followed by a *piano* repetition of the cadence and the conclusion. The bass here generally carries on its slow tones, which are also taken up intermittently by the second voice while the viola stays with its melodic line.

In the performance of such a piece, it is particularly important to make certain that the accompanying parts leave the strength of tone to the first violins, so that the main melody may be heard distinctly throughout. Even in those places where the accompanying parts have a *forte* marking, the main melody must be projected well. If another

[65] Juxtapositions of major and minor modes are rare in Daube's examples, although quite common in the *quatuors concertantes* analyzed by Levy (*Quatuor Concertant*, pp. 135, 146).

part besides the main voice ought to be heard prominently, it is the bass, provided there are not too many players on that part. One knows how effective the balance of the instruments, the expression of *forte* and *piano*, and the clarity of the execution can be. Even if a piece is presented more than once, by different but always qualified people, one will, without thinking about it, receive a different impression [of the piece] each time.

6

COMPOSITION IN FIVE AND MORE PARTS

Scores comprising five voices fall into the same categories as those in four parts which were described previously. The different styles, the imitation of one or several voices, the alternation of the brilliant and the singing styles, etc., can be introduced here also. The only difference is the fifth voice. It may be introduced in a concerting manner, or it may alternate with another voice, or all the voices may concert together, etc. All of this depends on the intention of the composer. Because composition contains no natural chords which comprise five tones, it is quite easy to guess that the voices must take turns doubling the octave or the unison. Even the compound artificial chords, which really do have five different tones, can seldom be introduced, and therefore one must resort to alternating the doubled tones among the voices. An example will show this more clearly [Examples 79–80].[66]

Ex. 79 Example of a Movement in Five Parts

[66] Ex. 79: mm. 3–4, the second part has a tie over the bar line; m. 15, "6" was originally placed over the bass *B*-flat in m. 14.

Ex. 79 (*cont.*)

Ex. 80 Variation of this piece, written in a rapid tempo

Ex. 80 (*cont.*)

[120] These two examples, the second of which springs from the first, are based on nothing but the duplication of the octave, third, and sixth, reckoned from the bass. These intervals are doubled alternately from beginning to end. For that reason we purposely have presented this first five-part example in long notes throughout, so that one might examine this method more clearly. The first chord is the ruling chord, the root and third of which are doubled. The second chord has only the octave doubled. The three upper intervals of the minor seventh chord are retained, but the bass disregards this retardation, going instead to the tone which actually belongs with the following harmony. These three retarded tones are rightfully treated just like real appoggiaturas, and only the bass is doubled here. The proper harmony for this bass tone then has the minor third doubled, as well as the bass itself. Now [m. 3] the bass remains stationary and the harmony of the second chord appears above it, because the bass tone also belongs in that chord. Here the minor sixth is doubled. The retained tone in the second voice occasions the reappearance of the minor seventh chord, the third of which actually should be doubled. But since the fifth is already present in the viola part, it is doubled here, though it immediately

changes to the third.[67] This resolves into the first chord [m. 4] in which the octave and the third are doubled. The retention of the first voice allows the bass to descend a third and indicate the harmony of the ruling chord in E-flat major,[68] because B-flat and G are naturally found in both of these ruling chords. Here the octave and third are doubled. Because the preceding two tones are retained once again, the bass returns to the harmony of the first chord in G minor [m. 5]. The third[69] and octave are doubled. The fourth in the second voice is disregarded, since it was retained from the previous chord, but here immediately moves on. Now the harmony of the third chord in B-flat major appears, in which only the sixth is doubled. The first chord which follows [m. 6] has nothing doubled but the octave.[70] At the beginning of the ninth measure, the upper voice goes into the key of E-flat major. The indicative third chord has a doubled third and octave. The same also occurs in the subsequent ruling chord. Then the soprano E [m. 10] indicates a move into the key of F major. The octave is doubled in this third chord. The first chord, into which it resolves, contains a doubled sixth and octave. The retention of the bass [A, in m. 11] provides the opportunity to return again to the key of B-flat. Here the third is doubled. In the following chord both [121] the third and octave are doubled. The stationary tone in the first voice then [m. 12] assumes the harmony of the third chord in E-flat major, in which the second is doubled. The chord of resolution follows, with the octave and third doubled. Then [m. 13], since the upper voice remains stationary, the bass takes the tone F-sharp, thereby producing the minor seventh chord in G minor, in which only the octave is doubled. The corresponding first chord arrives and then, to the B-flat and G which remain stationary, the bass adds E-flat, and later the seventh, C.[71] Then this resolves into the third chord in G minor and the ensuing cadence.

The second example [Example 80] is nothing but a variation of the first, except that the length of the tones has been halved, and it has been written in 2/4 meter.[72] For variety, the harmony is set in four parts starting in the ninth measure. After several measures the fifth voice again joins in the harmony. We have analyzed the first example so that a beginner might perceive that the basis of composition in five and more parts is merely the doubling of a few intervals, and that the octave, sixth, and third are most suitable for duplication. The ancients also placed great value on these three intervals and based their artificial pieces on them. They could, in fact, write a four-part piece very quickly

[67] Daube omits reference to the *f*-sharp, speaking as if the *c'* were repeated on beat 3.

[68] "D-sharp major" in the original; the three subsequent usages of "D-sharp" in this paragraph have all been rendered as "E-flat." See n. 46.

[69] "sixth" in the original.

[70] Daube overlooks the doubling of the third, *d'*.

[71] Daube's reference to the "the seventh, C" is unclear, especially since he always considers C to be the root of this chord, the second chord in G minor. Perhaps it refers to the interval between the soprano *b'*-flat and the following bass *c* in the penultimate measure.

[72] These two examples represent a microcosm of Daube's approach to, and co-ordination of, the strict and free styles. By recomposing the "long-note," quasi bound-style Adagio as a "poc. Allegro" in the *galant* manner, he demonstrates how the same harmonic structure might serve as the basis for either style, depending upon the degree and type of elaboration. Riepel shows a similar stylistic transformation of a single melodic line (*Anfangsgründe*, vol. IV (1765), p. 31).

if they had constructed but one voice beforehand. The bass was formed by setting in constant alternation the octave, third, and sixth below the upper voice. For example, if the upper voice had D, the bass could have F, B, or D. If the octave were set in the bass, and the next tone in the upper voice were C, then A, the third [below] the upper voice, would have to appear in the bass. But if one did not want to use the third, the sixth, E, might be permitted. If B were then to appear in the upper voice, G or D would be set in the bass. In short, these three intervals were alternated constantly. The addition of a second part to the melody had to be continued in this manner throughout. Next they wrote two more voices, by means of transposition. Each voice was transposed up a third, thus forming four voices which, however, moved at the same speed. In writing the first two voices, only contrary motion was observed. Therefore, if we knew of no better way, but did understand the rules of variation, we then might simply vary the two upper voices, that is to say, provide them with passing tones and skips, in which case some use could certainly still be made of them. [122] Later, in discussing fugue subjects, we will have something more to say about the use of this style of composition.[73] We have inserted this account here only in order to demonstrate the usefulness of doubling these three intervals, and especially to show that they occasion no errors in composing for many voices. It would be very advantageous for a beginner to arrange the following exercises. First he should write two voices and then construct another part to serve either as the first voice or the viola. It could even be tested to determine whether it might be adapted as a bass part by rearranging one or another tone according to the principles of bass writing. After the third voice has been completed, this endeavor might be pursued by setting another voice to these three, and that in whatever position is suitable for it. For example, if the first voice were written neither too high nor too low, another voice, which then could serve as the first voice, might quite conveniently be put above it. The same thing might occur in the low register also. If the bottom voice is not set too low, another bass part can always be added below. Then, when the fourth voice of this exercise has been completed, one investigates the possibility of adding another voice according to the previous directions. In doing this, of course, one sometimes must incorporate short rests, perhaps even whole measures of rest, in order to maintain the diversity of the harmony. One may well be advised to observe the three different motions by which the voices move in relation to one another. After the fifth voice also has been constructed, one could first determine whether or not two horns might be added. Later we will show how to write these parts. Meanwhile, every connoisseur of music knows that this instrument is given sustained tones and frequent rests, and therefore is best used only in brilliant pieces, where it serves to greatly reinforce the harmony. We are sure that such an exercise could contribute to one's knowledge of both melody and harmony, and therefore probably no one would regret having worked through a few examples in this manner. Practice makes the master, and mastery is attained with moderate effort, if one has laid a good foundation in theory beforehand.

---

[73] See Chapter 10, especially the relationship of symphony and fugue, p. 186.

Ex. 81 Another Example with Sustained Tones

[124] Here [in Example 81] the two violin parts are constructed first. One sees that the harmony of these two voices and the bass is arranged from a succession of chords, each of which must be considered from two points of view. Several times in our thorough-bass method we said that the similarity of a ruling chord to the third chord of another key is what gives double significance to such a harmony, which consequently may play the role of the ruling, as well as the subservient, chord. But here the major thirds, which otherwise characterize the third chord, are sometimes omitted. This example shows that the first chord in E minor may, at the same time, also be the third chord in A minor, into which key it is resolved here. The A-minor chord appears, but at the

same time again performs a double role since, on account of its similarity to the third chord in D major, it likewise is resolved into the ruling chord in this key. The harmony continues in this manner by means of transposition, until the E-minor chord eventually appears, whereupon the concerting of the two voices ceases. Meanwhile the two flutes behave quite differently. The second flute commences with the fifth, B, but then remains stationary, despite the harmony of the A-minor chord. The first flute, however, completely disregards this retained tone and begins with the third above the bass, likewise remaining stationary during the next measure, while the second flute descends a tone. This alternation of held-over tones in the two flutes, in combination with the bass, gives rise to an alternation of ninth and seventh chords, the origin of which we have explained.

Sustained tones such as these produce a good effect in large scores. They make the harmony full and easy to perceive. They have been introduced into symphonies in the current taste, where they enliven and strengthen the brilliant passages.[74] We now turn to six-part composition, where we must repeat what we said in regard to five-part composition, namely that four-part composition constitutes the groundwork here also [Example 82].

Ex. 82 Example of a Six-Part Piece

---

[74] Carse considers sustained wind tones a hallmark of the newer, progressive style of orchestration (*Orchestration*, pp. 132–3, 139). Among the composers who effected the transition, he names A. Scarlatti, Rameau, Keiser, Telemann, the Graun brothers, Hasse, Wagenseil, and C. P. E. Bach – most of whom were associated with Daube either geographically or stylistically, if they were not actually known and admired by him.

Ex. 82 (*cont.*)

[m. 1, vn. I, an eighth rest in the original]

This is the easiest way to write six parts. To a great extent it comprises the current taste in symphonies. Bound, artificial harmony should seldom appear in this style, because the brilliant and fleeting melody is not consistent with great artifice.[75] The two horns are preferably in unison with the two upper voices whenever possible, that is, when the melodic motif consists of just those tones which are convenient for this instrument, which otherwise has either sustained, or at least rather slowly moving intervals. However, when very rapid passages occur in the upper voice, the horns usually have the roots of the chords, in which case they often play an octave apart. One sees that various rests occur here and there, so as to avoid always maintaining the harmony at the same level of intensity, and also to provide for the wind instrumentalists to breathe.[76] In six-part

---

[75] In general, the qualities attributed to the symphony by other late eighteenth-century observers likewise center around simplicity of melody and harmony, and breadth of affect. J. A. P. Schulz speaks of its unadorned melody and magnificence of character, and the "sonorous, sparkling, and fiery manner" of the chamber symphony in particular, which may concentrate on displaying the "splendor of the instruments" (Sulzer, "Symphonie. (Musik.)," *Allgemeine Theorie*, vol. II (1774), p. 1122). Kollmann compares the symphony to a large picture to be viewed from a distance, pointing out the need for bold strokes, plain, natural harmony, and "a simpler sort of *Subjects* . . . than what would be proper for the finer sort of Sonatas," since "Symphonies . . . must be more grand and bold than sublime and embellished with graces" (*Essay* (1799), pp. 15, 17, 92–3). Koch quotes extensively from Sulzer, but speaks of the first Allegro as mostly magnificent and grand, the Andante as pleasant, and the last Allegro as cheerful (*Versuch*, vol. III (1793), pp. 301–02, Eng. trans., pp. 197–8).

[76] Daube, a flute player, knew the practical importance of such resting places, as well as their value in varying the texture. Leopold Mozart says that "signs of silence" are often employed "for the sake of elegance," since "a perpetual continuance of all the parts causes nothing but annoyance . . . [while] a charming alternation of many parts and their final union and harmonization give great satisfaction" (*Violinschule* (3/1787), p. 33, Eng. trans., p. 36). See n. 49.

composition [127] the singing, rather slow-moving melodic motives usually are expressed *piano*, while the horns rest. Also, such passages are sometimes set with only three parts. If the horns are to play short solos during these passages, they usually have no other accompaniment, although the bass, particularly a bassoon, might be useful here.[77]

Eight-part composition has the same basis [as six-part composition]. In brilliant passages the four wind instruments have mostly sustained tones. If melodic motives are included, the winds (except the horns, which do not naturally possess all the tones) are usually set in unison [with the strings]. The two oboes or flutes also are given the small solos which are interspersed throughout a long Allegro. These solos consist mostly of short singing passages, in which the two wind instruments usually move in thirds or sixths, except when they are supposed to concert with one another. It is also effective for the melodic motif to be distributed in such a way that the horns take a turn with it, or even concert with the oboes or flutes. Then, if an unexpected loud tutti suddenly interrupts in the fourth or eighth measure, [the effect of] the singing motif is heightened even more. Many symphonies in this beautiful style have already been written, and they are a credit to their masters. We would like to offer a little test-piece of this type, so that the amateurs can study this style from the example itself [Example 83].[78] If they have contrived small imitations even once, it will not seem any more difficult to work them out further.[79] Moreover, at a later time, we will remember to give additional instruction in this technique.

This example, written according to the current taste, contains no extraneous chords whatever, but only those naturally found in each key. The A in the ninth measure might possibly be considered foreign to the key, but it is there merely in order to fill the space between A-flat and B-flat. With its harmony, it can also pass for the compound major seventh chord in B-flat major, in which case the subsequent third chord in E-flat major [80] must simultaneously [131] represent the harmony of the ruling chord in B-flat major. However, this tone A could also be omitted completely, and the preceding tone repeated instead. This would not be an error, since with oblique motion it is permissible for different chords to be sounded successively against a stationary tone.

This symphonic movement begins, to be sure, with eight voices, but by the middle of the measure [1] it is already in three parts, because the oboes and viola proceed alone, a change which also occurs in the next measure. The following four measures have eight-part harmony. After this [m. 7] there is another change from the full harmony.

[77] This is Daube's only mention of a specific bass instrument in this chapter. He assumes that the bassoon would be available to accompany solo horn passages – a suggestion which recalls the use of the bassoon to support wind melody instruments in the traditional trio sonata, but one which also encourages the possibility of an independent bassoon part. J. A. P. Schulz likewise mentions only *Baßinstrumente* without naming them (Sulzer, "Symphonie. (Musik.)," *Allgemeine Theorie*, vol. II (1774), pp. 1121–2).

[78] Ex. 83: vn. I m. 4, beat 2, middle note b'-flat in the original; bass, m. 4, note 3, *f* in the original (noted in *Druckfehler*). Horns, m. 10, the "Mannheim rocket" was presumably intended for the violins.

[79] Note Daube's references to imitation for orchestral instruments throughout (especially in Chapter 8), and to the use of double counterpoint in arias and symphonies, pp. 228–9.

[80] "D-sharp-major" in the original. See n. 46.

Ex. 83 Example of an Eight-Part Symphony Movement

Ex. 83 (cont.)

The two oboes begin a solo, which is answered by the horns. Meanwhile, the viola has sustained tones. Then the harmony becomes six-part again [m. 9], and immediately afterwards the entire complement [of instruments] re-enters. The main melody [in violin I] contains very few passing tones. There are a few at the beginning of measure 5 where they appear as appoggiaturas. Here C is a repetition of the immediately preceding tone, and therefore passes for a retained tone. In view of this, the interval from the bass is judged, not from the C, but from the following B-flat. The other passing tones are in the proper [rhythmic] position, since the first tone is in the harmony and the next one is passing. A little practice makes it easy to recognize them.

In the construction of symphonies it is essential that the rushing and brilliant passages be given the fullest harmony, with rapid movement in both upper voices, and a steadily moving bass. Recurrent passages in the singing style are left to the wind instruments, to which one gives more slow melodic lines than difficult passages, which quite often hinder the beautiful singing style. This would be the case unless one wanted to fashion something especially for two wind instruments, and even then the nature of the instrument must be examined carefully beforehand. Otherwise it would be better to stay with a natural, easy melodic line. While concerting passages for two like instruments may be introduced, it seldom produces a good effect for two different instruments to concert together with the same passages. However, if yet another change is desired, it is preferable to give a different melodic motif to each pair of instruments, which play them by turns, as here. Then, if the interplay of the singing motif in the wind instruments is interrupted by a single *forzando* tone with the complete harmony,[81] the change produces no ill effect, as we may see from the following ten-voice example [Example 84].

Ex. 84 Example of a Ten-Part Symphony Movement

Ex. 84 (*cont.*)

[136] This example, as the preceding one, is written in the unbound style. The entrance of the initial theme has a splendid effect, created by the parallel motion of the main voices. Also, the open-string, free-tone G in the third measure produces a special impression through the intensified unison of the string instruments. The following brilliant passages, the sustaining of the wind instruments, together with the bass melody, provide a very good change from the initial theme. Then, at the commencement of the ninth measure, the full harmony is interrupted by a singing motif. Here all of the wind instruments are heard in various alternations, with each pair of like instruments sounding a short solo, while the violins and viola play a very light accompaniment. Then [m. 12] the two violins also enter, along with the bass, and help to extend the change of melody and harmony. This four-measure singing [passage] can be repeated, and then followed anew by a rushing and brilliant melody, alternately high and low, which should make its way through various chords until the cadence in the first new key. The number of measures of this full harmony is at the discretion of the composer. It is effective for this cadence to be heard once again in the same key, especially if something unexpected appears before the cadence is repeated. A description of the remaining procedure can be reviewed on page 91 of the thorough-bass method, and this subject will be mentioned again in the future.

With the exception of symphonies, one very seldom encounters such fully accompanied scores, unless it would be in a few opera arias, the text of which required an alternation of the full harmony. Ten-part composition is particularly appropriate to the church style,[82] where it can be employed very often. More ties and modulations are also found in this style, although here especially one must observe the expression of the words and the affect. The harmony must be guided by these, rather than by art. Pieces for even more voices are rare because they cannot be performed everywhere for want of qualified people. They are composed, as were these examples, by doubling a few intervals. Anyone who has a good understanding of what has been mentioned so far, and has practiced accordingly, will very easily understand how to write even more voices. Therefore, we consider it unnecessary to continue this discussion further.

7

VARIATION

[137] Strictly speaking, this discussion does not pertain to the [process of] combining the voices, in that it is more concerned with melody. But since the [technique of] variation is also based on harmony, which in turn is bound up with it so closely that neither can exist without the other, we have considered it necessary to insert this [discus-

---

[82] See nn. 13 and 157.

sion] here. It is certain that artificial constructions of all types of fugues, *alla breve*, canons, etc. depend on this [technique].[83] How can one write a melody to a bass theme without a basic knowledge of the art of variation? As has been said already, variations flow from the chords themselves,[84] but with the distinction that the passing tones participate on an equal basis with the proper chord tones. Whereas we also have proposed to describe as clearly as possible the artificial style of composing fugues etc., this discussion will serve simultaneously as a preparation, especially since the proper use of variation has, as yet, very seldom been examined and explained. In the future we will show that even the invention of melody may, in part, be traced to the art of variation.[85] Here we must use the foregoing method, taking up each interval under the instruction in its corresponding harmony. We will take the key of G major as an example. Now if a melody in this key is to be varied, and a G were to occur in it, one would have to determine whether this tone belonged in the first or second chord, which would quickly be discovered under the instruction in the key of G major in the thorough-bass method. If this tone belonged in the first chord, it could be varied with the three intervals of this chord, even without passing tones, for which both harmonizing intervals must be used. The three tones may be situated in the upper or lower [register].[86]

Ex. 85 Variation of the First Chord without Passing Tones

---

[83] J. A. P. Schulz also recognizes the role of variation in both the free and strict styles, as technique and as form (Sulzer, "Veränderungen. Variationen. (Musik.)," *Allgemeine Theorie*, vol. II (1774), p. 1207).

[84] See pp. 185–6.

[85] This is another reference to the projected fourth volume of the series, *Anleitung zur Erfindung der Melodie*.

[86] Daube's variation figures often suggest the progressive rhythms of species counterpoint. See n. 30.

Ex. 85 (*cont.*)

These fifty-one melodic motives [in Example 85] may all be used in varying the single tone, G, and there are still far more to be discovered if the pitch range is adapted to the instrument on which they are to be performed. It is true that one uses the entire chord for these motives, when actually a single tone was to have been varied, and that the other two tones, B and G, are also varied in the process. But it is sufficient that they all belong in the same harmony and [139] are in closest accord with one another. Indeed, owing to their pure blending quality, the ear is left with the impression of a single tone when all three of them are played simultaneously on the organ, harpsichord, or three well-tuned wind instruments. If one were to use passing tones in addition, the three tones of a single chord could be varied even many thousand times.[87] Let us give a few examples of this also [Example 86].

Ex. 86 With Passing Tones

[87] Daube's schematic approach and counting of variation figures recalls the *ars combinatoria*. See n. 9. Also notice Daube's comment that the art of variation "is inexhaustible and no number is capable of defining its value" (p. 143). This statement seems both to assert the qualitative value of variation and to interject an irrational element into the calculation of numerical possibilities. The latter suggests a turning from eighteenth-century schematic codifications toward the Romantic fascination with inspiration and infinity.

Ex. 86 (*cont.*)

[140] To these fifty-two classes of variation we could add many more, if we had not resolved to discuss everything as briefly as possible. Of course, for all that, it sometimes happens that one must write rather extensively in order to express oneself clearly. Readers are dissimilar in reflecting [on these matters]. The first thirty-two of the preceding short examples contain passing tones. The following motives, until number forty-eight, include appoggiaturas. Now, in the thorough-bass method, and here at the very beginning, we said that these tones merely contribute to the formation of the melody, and consequently may not be given a bass.

Therefore, if these three tones are carried through an entire piece with more slow than fast note values, they can give rise to a canon of as many voices as there are variations [on these tones].[88] However, the piece may contain only a single chord. Even if intervals are borrowed from other keys they then are taken for passing tones, as will be shown below.

The second chord is even richer in variations because it has an additional interval. Let us set down the complete chord, and then write a few variations on it [Example 87].

Ex. 87 Variation of the Second Chord without Passing Tones

[88] In Chapter 9 Daube often refers to variation in a limited chordal vocabulary. See pp. 157–8. Ex. 87: motif 31, second note was *g″* in original.

Ex. 87 (*cont.*)

These sixty variations and many more which are derived from an interval of this chord, can all be used in both melody and harmony. For example, one of these variations could be used in an instrumental accompaniment for a very simple church hymn, and likewise a fugue subject could be worked out by this means. In symphonies, in slow pieces, etc., such passages can also be introduced occasionally by the inner voices, while the upper voice plays a slow, singing melody. The art of variation is of no small assistance in embellishing the main melody if it is tastefully employed![89] No voice part can do without it. Yet one must not carry this to excess either, so that the main melody does not become obscured. It is also certain that through this process one can discover many good passages and singing motives which greatly facilitate the invention of melody for a beginning composer. Melodious little arias, menuets, etc. are very suitable for variation. Even the Adagio cannot be left without variation, at least if it is to be completely worked out.[90]

Ex. 88 With Appoggiaturas and Passing Tones

[89] See n. 94.

[90] Daube's comment recalls that the Adagio – originally a cantabile-style Italian aria – was one of the last strongholds of the performers' freedom to improvise, but that by 1773 it, too, was frequently "worked out" in some detail by the composer. "It was formerly more easy to compose than to play an *adagio*, which generally consisted of a few notes that were left to the taste and abilities of the performer; but as the composer seldom found his ideas fulfilled by the player, *adagios* are now made more *chantant* and interesting in themselves, and the performer is less put to the torture for embellishments" (Burney, "Essay on Musical Criticism," *General History*, vol. III (1789), p. x, Mercer, vol. II, p. 10).

Ex. 88 (*cont.*)

The appoggiaturas [in Example 88] begin with number thirty-seven and continue to the end. Anyone who contrives such practice exercises throughout the usual keys will become aware of great progress. If an amateur is thoroughly acquainted with the position of the passing tones and appoggiaturas, he can construct as many variations of a few notes as he might wish. From these he then may select a few which are compatible for one variation of a piece, and others again later for a second variation, and so on. After this he should choose a menuet or short aria, and then use this or that ornamental figure (*Manier*) throughout the entire piece. The only thing to be considered is that the menuet must have a good bass line which moves along quite simply, so that the different variations, some singing, some brilliant, running and skipping, can be fashioned all the more easily, and so that no unnecessary dissonances result from whatever passing tones occur in the bass.

The third chord admits of just as many variations as the second chord, because it has the same number of intervals [Example 89].

Ex. 89 Variations of the Third Chord without Passing Tones

Ex. 89 (*cont.*)

Space does not permit us to list all of the different possibilities here. It will suffice for each quarter [measure] to present a separate variation. Appreciably more variations will result if these are repeated in the high or low register,[91] mixed with rests, dotted, slurred or detached, etc. A little reflection will yield many more. We will be satisfied simply to have given some instruction in variation and shown its value.

Ex. 90 With Appoggiaturas and Passing Tones

[91] This statement seems to presage Beethoven's greater employment of range contrast as a means of varying color and sonority in keyboard works. See p. 141. However, Daube does not include a minor-mode variation, or employ changes of tempo and meter as Mozart and Beethoven later do, and as later theorists suggest. Portmann, citing K. 284, states that if both the melody and the harmony are changed, the result is called a double variation (*Leichtes Lehrbuch* (1789), p. 38). Although Daube encourages expanding the variation to the bass on keyboard instruments and harp, he does not devote the second variation of the theme exclusively to the bass, which Momigny considers customary by 1806 (*Cours complet*, vol. II, p. 607).

These variations [Example 90] of a chord which include appoggiaturas and passing tones can be combined at will. For example, one could take half of the third measure, establish this motif as the variation of a piece, and carry it through all three chords. For a change, one might include half of the fifth measure, and in this way an entire variation on a short aria or menuet could be assembled from these two motives. If one so desired, three or even four motives might feasibly be combined into one variation. It sometimes produces a good effect if quarter notes, which are simply octaves of the intervals in the three chords, are incorporated into these variations. Double stops, arpeggios, short appoggiaturas, and many intermingled trills are also good when introduced at an opportune time.

If a variation is to be written for keyboard or harp, one is guided by these instruments, and so introduces the variation into the bass also. Here it is good if the bass occasionally plays broken chords, then alternates with the upper voice, contrives imitations, etc. And, due to the wide range of these instruments, the variation can expand into the high and low registers, which cannot happen with the other instruments because their ranges [145] are not so large.[92] However, moderate limits must be observed here also. Not all variations are good, even if they have been constructed in accordance with the strictest rules. Melody must never be restrained by art. The rushing style should always be interrupted by something delicate and melodious, [a contrast] which is to be observed here also.

Ex. 91 Example with Variations

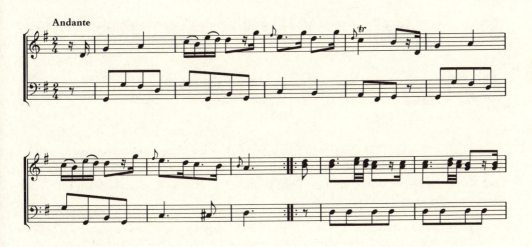

---

[92] Daube's frequent emphasis on idiomatic writing in this chapter is a reminder that the theme and variations form often provided a vehicle for virtuoso finales consisting of variations (originally improvised) on a well-known tune. Also see p. 134. Historically, these late eighteenth-century variation finales can be seen as a link between the improvised ornamentation of a composition by the performer, and the improvised composition of a work by nineteenth-century virtuosos such as Chopin and Liszt.

Ex. 91 *(cont.)*

[m. 9, top part, the first *d"* is not dotted in the original; m. 10, second part, the first *a'* is not dotted in the original]

[146] The first concern in a piece which is to be varied [see Example 91] is to make certain that the bass is well composed. Then one should carefully observe to which chords the tones of the upper voice belong in order to distinguish these from the passing tones. After this one would select from the accompanying examples one or two types of variation and, guided by each tone of the melody and the appropriate chord, continue to write them until the end of the piece. For example:

Ex. 92 First Variation

Here we have taken the thirteenth figure from the second example with passing tones [Example 86].[93] Nothing else appears in the first part, with the exception of the fourth and eighth measures, which are but slightly altered, as are the third and fourth measures in the second part.

---

[93] Kirnberger describes a figure as "a succession of . . . tones, which belong to the same harmony, and in place of which one could have taken a single tone, if one had wanted to sing more simply" (Sulzer, "Figur. (Musik.)," *Allgemeine Theorie*, vol. I (1771), p. 385). This description corroborates Daube's method of inventing figures from the tones of one chord with optional non-chord tones. Türk, like Kirnberger, explains that figures are "notes . . . joined together in various ways, or short embellishments of a simple tone. . . . A melody, in which similar embellishments of simple tones occur, is called a figurated melody and is contrasted with the plainsong melody without embellishment (simple)." He also speaks of some figures having names, such as the half circle (*Halbzirkel*), and similarly describes "ornaments" (*Manieren*) as "those embellishments which are used in place of simple tones" (*Klavierschule*, (1789), pp. 235, 387–8, Eng. trans., pp. 229, 380). See n. 86.

Ex. 93 Second Variation

This variation [Example 93] has been taken from the thirty-first [recta thirtieth] and thirty-eighth figures [of Example 85]. They can also be brought closer together, if one wishes.

In the second part, both figures appear within a single measure. Unless they were to become thirty-second notes, these figures cannot very well be imitated in the third measure, because the third and first chords each occur twice. For variety, both figures have been set an octave higher from the fifth measure on.

Ex. 94 Third Variation

[148] This variation [Example 94] is derived from the twenty-seventh and forty-seventh figures [of Example 85]. The same combining of two figures can take place here, as it did in the preceding example. They may occur in either order.

Ex. 95 Fourth Variation

The twentieth and forty-third figures in the second example [Example 86] characterize this variation [Example 95]. The first two measures incorporate passing tones, while the others consist of appoggiaturas and chord tones.

Ex. 96 Fifth Variation

Even more figures are combined in this variation [Example 96]. The first two measures are derived from the first figure of the first example [Example 85]. The next measure closely resembles the fourth figure [of Example 85], and the fifth [149] measure resembles the forty-fifth figure [of Example 86]. The beginning of the second part has been taken from the thirty-third figure [of Example 86].

Ex. 97 Sixth Variation

This variation [Example 97] is based on the forty-ninth and seventeenth figures [of Example 86]. In this manner one can write as many variations as one might wish. Everyone can draw up some figures of his own and compose his variations from them according to these instructions. Also, for variety, they can be composed of long single or double tones which are sustained throughout etc. If such variations are written for the keyboard, the bass may also contest with the upper voice and alternately sound the rapid passages [Example 98].

Ex. 98 Seventh Variation

Ex. 98 (*cont.*)

This example has been assembled from the twenty-fifth, twenty-ninth, fifty-first, and forty-ninth figures [of Example 86]. The bass makes a short imitation, which could have been lengthened if desired. The harpsichord is very suitable for presenting many variations in the bass.

We now believe that we have given sufficient instruction on varying a short aria or menuet. At the very beginning we mentioned that the art of variation also could be of assistance in the invention and improvement of the melody. How often does it happen that in sketching a melody, one part of it is not pleasing? But if one knows the rules of variation, one can quickly remedy this part of the melody, provided that the symmetry is good, or that the entire melody has been properly divided beforehand, that is to say, the motives and figures at least consist of an equal number of measures. Where have some Italian singers learned the beautiful, melodic, ornamental passages (*Klauseln*) which they introduce everywhere, and by which they are so distinguished? Certainly, nowhere but from the variation [technique] of a great master. How often in the Andante [Example 91] do we hear just the one figure comprising the first half of the second measure, which is borrowed from them? What is it, other than a simple ascending third embellished with appoggiaturas?[94]

It is certainly true that all the music which has been brought into the world until now, and which will ever be composed in the future, is inseparable from the art of variation. Hence, it is inexhaustible and no number is capable of defining its value. We maintain that anyone who has mastered the simple harmonic procedure of alternating the chords according to our instruction in the thorough-bass method, and has gone through this treatise repeatedly and modeled many test-pieces on it, will neither want for the invention of a melody, and good division and continuation of the same, nor have difficulty providing it with a good harmony, and one which is melodious as well.

[94] The correspondence between improvised ornamentation of the mid-eighteenth century and the written variation of c. 1773 may be seen by comparing the present chapter with Quantz's "Of Extempore Variations on Simple Intervals" (*Versuch* (1752), pp. 60–91, Eng. trans., pp. 136–61). Quantz's instructions are directed toward performance, Daube's toward composition, yet the similarities strongly suggest that the elaboration added by the performer in 1752 might have been included by the composer in 1773. The *Figuren* which Daube lists in each chord include some which might be considered written-out ornaments (especially turns and *tiratas*), and he once refers to them as *Manieren*, and once as *Klauseln*. (Compare Türk in n. 93.) Momigny, analyzing the difference between variation and ornamentation, points out that the former generally follows a consistent pattern, while the latter is characterized by flexibility and capricious changes (*Cours complet*, (1803–06), vol. II, p. 614). The substantive effect of Daube's variations may be attributed in part to the regularity and repetition with which the figures are laid out.

8

IMITATION

[151] Imitation has to do with artificial composition. In the discussion of two-part composition we already have demonstrated how one voice could imitate the other, and this has also been done with regard to the second type of three-part writing. The instruction on composition in four, five, and more parts likewise demonstrates its value. Imitation is indispensable in music. Nothing good in either melody or harmony can be accomplished without it. From imitation flows natural beauty. It unites art with nature. One can conveniently divide it into two classes. The first concerns only the initial or main melody of a single voice, and how this should be worked out in a piece by means of imitation.[95] This is not to be spoken of here, however. The second class shows how to arrange the harmony so as to give rise to various imitations which are carried out by a few motives of either the main melody or the inner voices. The present discussion will characterize this class.

Imitation which occurs throughout the harmony is likewise divided into two types, the first of which consists of similar [i.e., real] imitation. This takes place when a motif from the main melody is either repeated with the same tones in an inner part, or imitated in another key. This type concerns artificial pieces, especially canons and fugues. The other type results when a melodic motif is imitated rather dissimilarly [i.e., tonally], but yet so that the key may not modulate. This little dissimilarity is produced when not all of the intervals are imitated as precisely as possible.

Here one especially must make certain to choose instruments capable of imitation. Likewise, the motives or figures to be imitated must be selected in accordance with the nature of the instruments. For [152] example, a figure from the main melody would be suitable for imitation by the second voice, and probably by the viola, but not by the bass,

[95] In 1722 Rameau scarcely differentiates between imitation and repetition, commenting that "fugue is distinguished from imitation in that the latter may occur only in a single part. . . ." "Imitation . . . consists only of the repetition, at will and in any part we like, of a certain passage of melody, with no other regularity. . . . [and] in any transposition whatsoever" (*Traité*, (1722), pp. 163, 332, Eng. trans., pp. 179, 349). In 1753, however, Marpurg explicitly distinguishes between repetition, transposition, and imitation, the latter signifying "the restatement of a subject through repetition or transposition in different parts. . . ." Further, "the alternating use of one subject in various parts may occur not only at the unison but at all other intervals" (*Abhandlung*, vol. I (1753), pp. 1–2, Eng. trans. in Mann, *Fugue*, pp. 142, 143). J. A. P. Schulz, like Daube, includes both inter- and intra-voice techniques in his comprehensive definition of imitation, and points out the difference between free and strict imitation (Sulzer, "Nachahmungen. (Musik.)," *Allgemeine Theorie*, vol. II (1774), p. 798). Kirnberger also includes both techniques, calling imitation "the observation of the similarity of the elaboration," a definition which points up the fact that the notes being imitated usually are figures elaborated from a basic progression in what Schulz terms "figural pieces." Moreover, his free imitations, which require only a similarity of shape and rhythm, bear a strong resemblance to Daube's variation figures in the three chords (*Kunst*, vol. I (1771), pp. 203–04, Eng. trans, pp. 217–18). Koch, writing in 1802, seems to have dropped the older application of the term "imitation" to a single-melody technique, although he still speaks of the decorative value of imitation in free-style works ("Nachahmung," *Lexicon*, (1802), cols. 1029–30).

that is, in the lower tones of this voice. Here one must give special consideration to the peculiarity of the tones. The low tones are the basis of the harmony. The entire musical structure rests on them, as it were, and therefore its movement should be fairly steady, but also lively according to the character of the piece. But [for the bass] to imitate hopping, playful, and gay passages of the main melody, and to give its foundation to the upper voice in exchange, is against the nature of the music and greatly hinders its effectiveness. However, we are speaking only of the low bass register, and not of the high tones of a violoncello or bassoon.

Ex. 99 A Few Examples of These Two Types

[153] This imitation [in Example 99] is the most strict, since the second voice contrives it, not only in all the intervals, but even in the same tones. A piece in which one voice exactly imitates the melody of the other from beginning to end is called a canon. The value of imitation is greater, however, if only one motif from a melody is imitated. In doing this, the composer still has the freedom to continue his melody spontaneously, which is not the case with the former, since the continuation of the piece relies on the most strict imitation in the second voice from beginning to end. With two like instruments one must take care to contrive the melodic motif in such a way that it may be repeated by means of imitation, or so that the melodic line is not hindered even if one voice ascends above the other, as at the beginning here. The melody of the first four measures really sounds thus [Example 100]:

Ex. 100

Here the high tones of both voices are combined into one voice. In a piece comprised of two concerting voices, one does not perceive the melody as played separately by each voice, but rather from the upper tones that are heard. Therefore the main melody can be disturbed by another, accompanying voice ascending above it, which does occur quite often in the scores of capable men. However, if two like instruments are to concert together, it is always better for the melody to be arranged so that it is compatible with its repetition in the other voice. And this melody distributed between two voices, when taken as a whole, nevertheless constitutes one interdependent melodic line, as shown here by the second melodic motif from the fifth measure on.

However, if the instruments are unlike, so that one is tuned an octave lower, as a violoncello and a violin, for example, it is not necessary to follow these instructions. The violoncello may imitate the violin and ascend above it into the violin clef as often as desired. This will not interfere with the main melody at all because the violoncello moves an octave lower, as does also the viola da gamba, the lute, the bassoon, and the horn, etc. In combining unlike [154] instruments, one nevertheless must also direct one's attention toward the distance of the intervals between the two instruments, provided that the harmony is to have an effect equal to that of the melody – a matter heeded by very few composers, but which is particularly necessary if the music is to be effective. This observation pertains to imitation above all. Thus the inner parts also are included. Only the bass, in so far as it does not imitate, is excepted. Let us set down another example of two unlike instruments here, so that an amateur might be able to remember these comments better [Example 101].

Ex. 101

The beginning is again set up by imitation. For the entrance of the second voice, the first voice moves down a fifth, which would have severely impeded the continuation of the melody with two like instruments. But in this case the descent is not at all detrimental, since the bass is a whole octave lower than the upper voice. Thus the two voices begin close together in the second measure, but the bass nevertheless is still a fourth lower. The imitation ends in the fifth measure. From there on the bass proceeds as usual, and can be just as low as the instrument permits. The bass melody must merely be good and flowing, and at the same time be compatible with the imitative motif.

[155] Strict imitation can also be arranged in another key. This is beautiful if the imitation of a melodic motif occurs as if it came about unintentionally. But even here it is to be remembered that the melodic motives should fit together well and constitute a well-arranged whole, so that no voice interrupts the continuity of the melody in the other voice.

Ex. 102

This imitation [Example 102] first begins in the fourth measure, where it occurs in the first-related key, while the upper voice carries out its line without heeding the initial melody. We have already cited such examples here and there near the beginning, [while discussing] composition in three and more parts. This example can also be arranged so that the second voice commences with this same melody and the first voice then imitates the melody of its predecessor in the higher octave [Example 103].[96]

Ex. 103

[96] Ex. 103: double bar line at end of m. 9 in the original.

Ex. 103 (cont.)

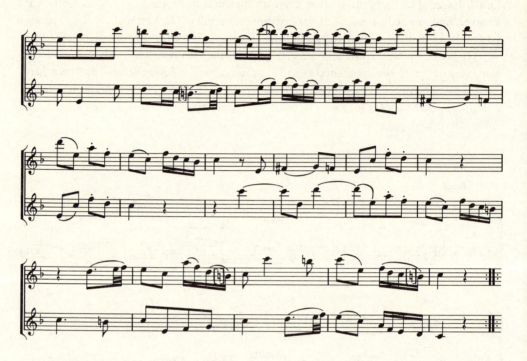

In the eighth measure a new motif is introduced, which subsequently goes into
C major, and then is repeated by the second voice at the same [pitch] while the accompanying voice acts partly as a bass and partly as a second voice.[97] Toward the end
another figure appears which likewise is imitated by the second voice at the same [pitch].
The [157] entire piece is organized so that each motif may reasonably be heard twice,
especially since the initial theme is imitated in the related key (and the other motives
likewise in this same key), a change which is not displeasing.

This type of imitation can also occur with two unlike instruments [Example 104].

Ex. 104

---

[97] Quantz, speaking of duets, likewise says that even with two voices, there must always be a proper fundamental part,
either in one voice or the other (*Sechs Duette für zwei Flöten* (c. 1760), vol. I, Preface).

Ex. 104 (cont.)

The imitation begins already in the second measure, but it lasts only one measure, since the lower voice then continues as a thorough-bass until the actual imitation of the entire theme follows in the ninth measure. The imitation lasts five measures, whereupon [m. 14] the bass resumes its usual role. After the cadence in B-flat major [m. 16] a new motif commences and is imitated at the fifth. This alternation of the violin and the bassoon continues until the end. Running passages are very good to introduce with two concerting instruments, especially when they alternately play long tones against [the passages].

The other type of imitation is that in which the second voice is not obliged to imitate the intervals of the first voice so strictly, and therefore does not modulate out of the key either. This type is found in both melody and harmony. The three chords form the basis for it. If a melodic motif occurs in the first chord, the other voice imitates it in the second or third chord [Example 105].

Ex. 105

The running passage commences on the fifth, E, and leaps down to the ending tone [i.e., tonic note], A, from where it ascends stepwise to the upper third, C-sharp, and again descends two thirds where it then must sustain the third of the second chord. The second voice should imitate these leaps and steps. Consequently it begins on the fifth above D, then leaps down to D and climbs stepwise to the third. In short, it imitates all the leaps and steps of the first voice, but a dissimilarity results nevertheless. This occurs in ascending to the fourth [tone above the root of the chord]. In the first voice this tone is D, the ordinary fourth in the key of A major, but in ascending [four tones] in the second voice one finds G-sharp, which is an augmented fourth above D. If this interval were to be the same as in the passage in the first voice, it would have to be G [natural], in which case the melody of the second measure would no longer belong in the key of A major, but rather in the key of D major. At the beginning of the third measure there is a retarded tone, which occurs in order to prevent a similar descent in both voices. The imitation of the running passage should now take place in the third chord. Therefore one must first investigate how to arrange the downward leap and stepwise ascent of this running passagework. Now in this case it is best [for the line] to leap down to the root of the third chord, because the downward leap was to the root in the first measure, and likewise in the second measure. What follows, with the ascent and final descent of two thirds, is like the foregoing, except that the seventh, which in the two previous measures was major, now suddenly becomes minor. The reason for this is the same as before. Here one is not concerned with E major, which includes D-sharp, but rather with the retention of the initial key. Then, in accordance with the natural progression of the three chords, the ruling chord must appear, which likewise occurs here in the fourth measure. The second voice is retarded in keeping with the pattern established by the first voice. And since the downward leap has previously been made into the root of each chord, the same must happen here. The retarded tone descends [160] to A, and then commences the stepwise ascent. Here once again a dissimilarity appears. Initially, in the first two measures, a downward leap of a fifth took place; in the third measure a descent of a ninth had to occur. Now the retarding tone descends only one tone before it commences the ascending running passagework, whereupon the two voices then come together for the cadence.

This imitation is a little more difficult to contrive than that of the previous examples. The continuity of the key should not be broken, but rather the beginning and end should be made in the same key. The melody likewise must not be subjected to the slightest constraint, but must be arranged as if the two concerting voices constituted a single voice with regard to the upper melody. The dissimilar intervals must be placed so that they are hardly noticeable. We have shown and taught the entire art of this imitation in the present examples. For further reinforcement let us draw up another example with two unlike instruments [Example 106].

Ex. 106

The arrangement of this example should be given special notice. The opening melodic motif is already imitated in the second measure, while the upper voice harmonizes in thirds. In the third measure, however, it deviates from this and has a stepwise ascending passage which produces contrary motion. In the fifth measure the upper voice takes up just a portion of the melodic motif, and that in a different [rhythmic] position, since it enters after an eighth rest, whereas at the beginning it commenced with the very first beat. This partial melodic motif is then immediately imitated in the intervals of the third and first chords. This imitation is repeated, and then the voices move in a parallel or joint progression to the eighth measure. From here on this short figure is introduced again, and is [162] imitated by the bass until the two voices quickly move together to the cadence a few measures later [m. 12]. Then the upper voice introduces a new running passage which is repeated a fifth lower by the bass while the upper voice sustains the third of the second chord. This repetition, which alternates [between the two voices], is continued until the main cadence.

Such modification and dismemberment of a melodic motif are of great assistance in the continuation of an entire melody, and create a very good effect when handled well. If the melodic motif is long, one can break it up several times and develop each part separately. A suitable portion can even be interpolated as a short solo or duo, if this motif has been presented before in the entire context and with the full harmony. The main theme of a symphony or a concerto may be contrived in such a way that the subsequent dismemberment could produce all kinds of changes in the melody as well as the harmony, which may sometimes appear in two, three, and more parts. Much of beauty can be effected by the interspersion [of different textures], especially when this is accompanied by a definite alternation of *forte* and *piano*. This style (*Manier*) thus provides a possible method by which one could dispense with the search for different ideas in [the process of] composing, and yet be able to arrange pleasing alternations of the melody and harmony which will increase the effectiveness of the music. Indeed, if one were only to go through those pieces which have won general approval, one would surely find that their fame rests not on the diversity of many thoughts, but rather much more on a good arrangement of a few melodic motives, and the way they are fragmented and used in the appropriate place.[98]

In discussing composition in three and more parts, we have shown that imitation could also occur with more voices. However we still want to add this brief consideration. If the imitation is distributed among three voices, they must be arranged in such a way that the continuity of a good melodic line in the upper voice is not interrupted, and so that the third voice, for example the bass, would occur as if unintentionally. One must be able to hear it distinctly, but yet so that the upper voice is prominent also. An agreeable

---

[98] In this early, perceptive description of "classic" motivic fragmentation and development procedures, it is significant that Daube mentions orchestral writing – where motivic development was becoming a hallmark of the style, especially in the instrumental works of Haydn. In 1773 this technique may still be seen to represent a Rococo dissolution of the long, imitative lines of the older style, which, during this era, were freely broken into motivic fragments before being worked out by various means.

change may be provided by four wind instruments engaging in imitation among themselves. But this cannot very well occur except when the first imitation occurs a fifth lower or a fourth higher. The second pair of instruments then repeats these two previously heard measures in the same key, or else contrives the imitation in another key. This concerting [163] works very well between two flutes and two oboes. Two horns may also play the imitation or repetition, if the melody is selected [with this in mind]. Let us give another short example of both types [Example 107].

Ex. 107

[164] The imitation in this example occurs unexpectedly. The two sustained tones in the first and second voices provide an opportunity for the bass to sound a moving passage against it. The first voice imitates and changes it a little in the third measure. The melodic motif of the fifth measure is imitated by the second voice and then by the bass, but then is abandoned unexpectedly, and the regular accompaniment continued. Such short imitations are to be used in the church, opera, and chamber styles. They make an especially good impression if they do not last too long.

Ex. 108 Four-Part Example for Two Flutes and Two Oboes

The first four measures [of Example 108] are based merely upon a division of the melody, which is successfully accomplished by the alternation of instruments. The fifth measure contains a motif which is imitated immediately at the beginning of the sixth measure. The oboes also have a little imitation here. The first oboe takes the second half of the melodic motif and moves in sixths [with the flute] into the next measure where [the line] drops a third. These five tones are imitated at once by the second oboe. This imitation is not detrimental to the main melody, since it remains in the lower register only, and never ascends above the flutes. This imitative section comprises four measures, after which a change occurs [m. 9]: the first oboe takes over the melodic motif from the flutes and the second oboe imitates it, while the flutes accompany with the partial melodic motif. But since the melody already is in the key of C major at this point, it must return to either the key of G major or E minor. In the second measure of the melodic motif an F-sharp is heard, and in the next measure [m. 11] the second oboe has D-sharp, which then presses back into E minor. Then the two oboes have a sustained tone, which is interrupted immediately by the second flute and proceeds to the ruling chord in the following measure, where the first flute joins them. Then the two flutes move in thirds to the caesura (*Einschnitt*), while the first oboe proceeds an octave below [the second flute], and the second oboe sustains a tone.

Ex. 109 Four-Part Example for Two Horns and Two Bassoons

Melodic motives for two horns are hard to find [Example 109]. The difficulty is that some tones are naturally lacking on this instrument. And although a way of supplying this deficiency through art is now known, this [remedy], after all, is feasible only for slow passages and sustained tones, and even then such a piece is not to be written for everyone. Therefore, it is certainly better to try to write these artificial tones only for exceptional masters [of the instrument].[99] The entrance of the second horn occurs in the second measure, where it is given G in preference to the proper tone, B, so that at least no tone is missing. Meanwhile the bassoons sustain long tones until the third measure, where the first bassoon takes up the melodic motif and the second bassoon imitates it. In the fifth measure the second horn and second bassoon sustain a tone while the other two instruments proceed in thirds. The next little motif, which is played by both bassoons, is then imitated at once by the horns.

Although this subject is one of the most important in the entire [study of] composition, and well deserves to be discussed still more, we nevertheless imagine that even the present discourse might already seem too long to the reader, and that it might be time to discontinue it, since a change would be pleasant here also. In the following chapters there will still be opportunities to mention whatever is necessary in this regard.

9

CANON

[169] In the preceding discussion we spoke of the imitation of a musical motif. The present discussion has to do with the entire piece. The canon is a melody which has been contrived in such a way that the second voice might be able to enter at a chosen distance after the first, and to imitate most strictly all the previously heard tones of this melody throughout the entire piece. When pieces of this kind have a spontaneous melody they are always worthy of praise, but as soon as even the slightest constraint is evident, it is better that one choose the free style of writing.

The canon is divided into many different classes, of which we want to point out the most important.[100] The simplest type of all is that in which the second voice imitates

---

[99] Also see Daube's discussion of horn writing, pp. 126–7. The natural, valveless horn of Daube's time was limited to the pitches of the overtone series, which, in the mellow middle register suitable for symphonic writing, meant only triadic pitches. The gaps in the scale sometimes were filled in by "stopping" (i.e., inserting the hand into the bell to change the natural pitches). These "artificial" tones sounded muffled and were often out of tune unless played by "exceptional masters [of the instrument]."

[100] Daube's list of "most important" types rivals those in the more academic treatises of the time. It includes: (1) simple canon for two voices (a) of like range at the unison, (b) of unlike range at the unison, (c) of like range at other intervals; (2) simple canon for three voices (a) of like range at the unison, (b) of two trebles and bass at the upper fifth/lower fourth, (c) of two, three, or four trebles and basses in double canon at the unison; (3) artificial canon for

all the tones of the first voice, and the entire piece consists of only two voices. This type is very easy to construct. One writes down an initial melody of only one measure. After this one writes this measure in the second voice, and again invents a first voice to go with it. This in turn is written in the second voice, for which one again seeks out a harmonizing upper voice, which then once more is set in the second voice. One proceeds with the continuation of the first voice and the repetition in the second voice in such a way for as long as desired. In doing this one merely makes certain that the melody of each measure is well fitted for the preceding measure. However, if this initial melody is sometimes to appear in the second voice as a first [or higher] voice also, the second measure in the proper first voice must be written lower than the initial melody, as often as this [procedure] will allow the melodic line to be continued naturally.

Ex. 110 Example of the Beginning of a Canon

The first two measures [of Example 110] show how to begin. One should proceed in this manner until the end, always writing the measure set in the first voice, into the following measure of the second voice as well. Above this measure a new melody or accompanying voice must be set at once in the first voice. We see this accomplished in the fourth measure. The upper voice carries on the melody according to its role. The third step indicates that the imitation in the second voice may also be accompanied by lower tones in the upper voice.

The singing style which already has been praised so often in the preceding discussions is to be recommended for the artificial treatment of the canon. A piece in which art exists alone, without nature, is scarcely created for the ear. The canonic melody must be singable and flowing, or all art will be employed in vain. The three chords must form the basis for this as well as for other kinds of composition. But it is true that the more voices a canon has, the more likely it will be necessary to dispense with the succession of chords. There are many canons which are constructed of only the first and third chords. Why? Because the fifth of the first chord is also present in the third chord. Therefore, if this tone remains stationary, the other voice can sound two different kinds of intervals against it. But if one wanted to write a canon based entirely on one chord, [171] the

two voices (a) in augmentation, (b) in diminution, (c) in double augmentation (three voices), (d) in inverted retrograde, (e) as a crab canon (retrograde), (f) with different clefs (two or four voices), (g) as a climax canon ascending or descending; and (4) artificial canon for three or four voices (a) with different clefs, (b) in inverted retrograde with different clefs, (c) as a crab canon with different clefs, (d) as a climax canon descending or ascending.

first measure might simply be varied as often as possible, in the course of which sustained tones, rests, and rapid and moderately moving passages can appear. Anything is correct as long as it is a variation of the first chord.[101] In this way many measures are produced by means of variation, and just as many entrances of accompanying voices are present, which all can commence in turn at the beginning, and sing around in that way until they seek for a conclusion of their own liking. The ancients applied themselves to creating much with this device.

Ex. III The Preceding Example Concluded

The first canon [in Example III] consists of only four measures, and the first and third chords. The second canon, on the other hand, goes directly to the second chord in the second measure, and even to the minor seventh chord, which is repeated in the third measure also. This canon can only be played by two voices, whereas the first one can be played equally well by three voices. The reason is the same as that mentioned before. The second measure of the second canon originates in the first measure. In writing this, only intervals which are in the three chords and which harmonize with the first measure have been selected. The third measure is an accompaniment of the second, and the fourth stands in exactly the same relationship to the third measure. In the fifth measure the first voice is on top again. In the sixth measure the melody again ascends by leap above

[101] See p. 135.

the fifth measure. The seventh measure is an accompanying part again, while the upper voice leads in the eighth measure. The da capo ensues, and there the first measure is now an accompanying part, since the last measure is also imitated by the second voice. The canon can be terminated at the beginning of any measure.

When a canon is finished it is not written in two voices, as here, but in only one voice, in which the entrance of the second voice is marked with a sign. However, if the canon is constructed in an overly artificial manner, the sign of the entrance of the second voice is not marked, so that those who want to rehearse or hear it have trouble guessing the proper entrance. These overly artificial pieces, however, frequently do not reward the effort of such a search, because nature very seldom plays a part in them, and therefore the melody is deficient and the effect of the music is lost.

This two-part type also permits the melody to modulate into other keys. This is done by writing a tone which also is found in a chord of a different key, but this must usually be the third chord of the other key [Example 112].

Ex. 112 Example of a Canon in which the Melody Modulates into Another Key

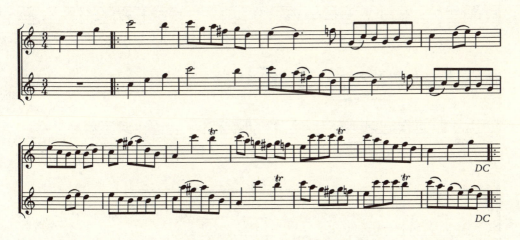

[174] The third measure of this canon already introduces F-sharp which, as is known, belongs in the key of G major. At the end of the fourth measure F reappears, which takes the melodic line back to C major. The seventh measure even brings in G-sharp, and provides the opportunity to go into A minor. This key lasts until the tenth measure, where G-sharp suddenly disappears and F-sharp appears instead, which again belongs in G major. The ruling chord likewise follows it immediately. In the twelfth measure the melody is in the initial key again, whereupon the repetition also takes place. This piece can end in the first measure. In modulating into other keys, as was mentioned before, one merely must concern oneself with that tone which is found in two different keys. In the third measure C remains stationary in the second voice, and thereby prepares for the key of G major, since this tone, C, is found in the third chord of G major as well. The second D in the seventh measure lends itself very well to modulation, since it is

also present in the third chord of A minor. A and C from the ruling chord follow. The tenth measure demonstrates that since A and C also are found in the third chord of G major, one voice might very well sound F-sharp against them, which occasions the movement into G major. The method of returning to C major is commonly known. Therefore, whoever takes the trouble to invent a good melodic line of this kind will do well.

Since each measure is heard twice, one can easily imagine that the melodic line must be arranged accordingly, and must include some motives which may be heard twice, in alternation with others composed of accompanying passages. They have the best effect when one voice can be played an octave lower [Example 113].

Ex. 113 Canon in which the Bass Imitates the Upper Voice

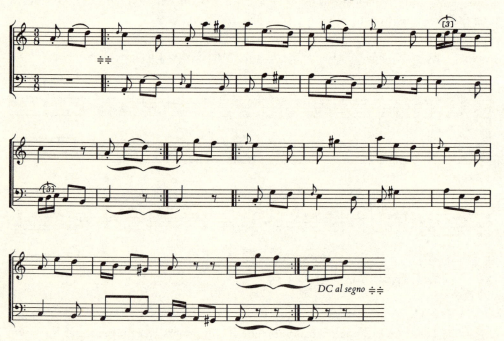

Since, for the most part, the entire science of canon is based on the variation of the previous measure, it can be extremely useful to a prospective composer. But unnatural, anxious searching must be avoided. Instead, one should proceed according to the foregoing discussion, trying to vary a single measure as often as possible, without restricting oneself to the guiding principle of canon.

The two-part canon also may be handled in another way. The imitation can be contrived at the second, third, fourth, fifth, etc., either above or below. The process of construction is the same. The only difference is that the position of the half step cannot always be preserved in the imitation. A few examples will make this clearer [Example 114a–f].

Ex. 114

Ex. 114 (cont.)

[178] In the first example the second voice begins with the minor third, although the first voice began with the major third. The reason is that the key of D major contains C-sharp rather than C[-natural]. Between the first and second measures of the first voice the interval D to E is a major second, whereas the second voice has a minor second. The same thing is to be observed in the second example also. In the third and fourth examples the intervals of both voices are alike. In the third example a C-sharp has had to occur in the second voice because the imitation commences in the nearest-related key, D major; it is also quite easy to effect the return. The fifth and sixth examples, on the other hand, do not contain this similarity [of the voices], since the half step in the second voice is not imitated, and vice versa.

Those canons in which the imitation occurs a second, third, etc. higher must always be arranged so that the second voice commences [Example 115a–f]. Then each measure in the upper voice is set higher at will, and an accompaniment or continuation of the canon is written for it again in the second voice. As has been said already, the principle of varying each measure applies similarly to every kind of canon.

Ex. 115

All of these types are comprised of variation and are constructed in the manner which was described at the very beginning of this discussion. The half step which appears in one voice therefore must be treated freely in the other voice. The melody can seldom turn out as well as in the unbound style of writing. Yet, if a single characteristic figure with tones of diverse time values can be introduced, it becomes tolerable. Brevity is especially to be favored here, and then one can use canons in the church, and also in the theater and chamber, where they are included as short solos within the melody of a large piece. Two-part canons particularly should be kept in mind for this purpose.

[181] Regular three-part writing is helpful in the construction of canons in three and more parts. One can use any short melody for them. As soon as the first voice reaches the end of this short melody, it is begun by the second voice, and when it is concluded by the second voice, the bass, which concurs with these two voices, is written in the violin clef, and then the three-part canon is ready. The entrance marks then are set in each voice. To increase the clarity it is good if one voice forms a running bass when the other two voices enter.[102]

Ex. 116 Example of a Canon with Three Voices

[m. 6, middle voice, the quarter note *a'* is not dotted in the original]

[102] A running bass is just one of Daube's methods of increasing clarity. Others include scoring each of three parts for a different instrument p. 166, and the use of rests, pp. 167, 175, 183. Ex. 117: m. 6, lower voice, trill over *e″* in original.

Ex. 117

Ex. 118

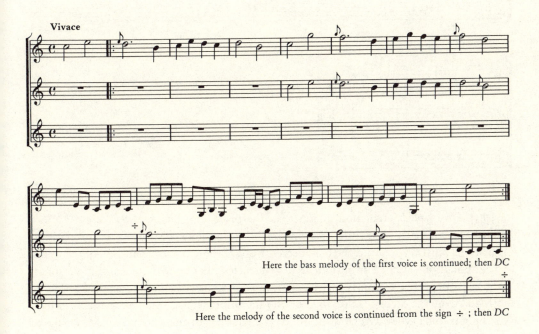

Here the bass melody of the first voice is continued; then *DC*

Here the melody of the second voice is continued from the sign ÷ ; then *DC*

[184] The first canon [Example 116] involves a bass [-like part] only in the fourth measure, after which the melody quickly returns to the beginning again. In this canon the
entrance [of the second voice] occurs immediately after the first measure. In the second
canon [Example 117] the second voice enters after the second measure, and in the third
canon [Example 118] it first enters after the fourth measure. With the entrance of the third
voice, this canon presents the bass part, which also is differentiated from the others by its
rapid movement. All the types of canon which have been described can be included
between the rushing or brilliant passages in a large Allegro, with a violoncello or a viola
playing the third part in a three-part canon. In this case canonic composition is still used
to advantage, but otherwise not. If each of the three parts is also played by a different
instrument, the effect can be even better.

Another type of three-part canonic composition is that in which the second voice
commences a fifth higher or a fourth lower, whereas the third voice follows at the octave
in the initial key [Example 119].

Ex. 119

[185] This type is even more useful than the preceding, but it also is slightly more
difficult to construct. The little that one can say to facilitate this three-part composition
is that one must try to avoid the major seventh above the root in the melody of the upper
voice. But if one wanted to introduce it nevertheless, it might occur amid rapid tones,
as if in passing. The reason is that if one wanted it to be sustained, it would have to be
introduced in the second voice also, or the imitation would suffer very much, which
certainly is to be avoided as far as possible. The entrance of the third voice also would be

made difficult. The melody must consist of an alternation of the first and third chords. The intervals of the second chord should appear only in passing. Short rests also can be interspersed. This canon, as those previous, is written on a single staff, and the entrances are marked by a sign. If it is to be a riddle canon, no entrance is marked, as we already have said above. One likewise does not indicate whether the second voice is to commence at the unison or at another interval. However, we can see no reason why our ancients tried so hard to conceal this art. However thoroughly one understands composition, one still must search through all of the possible species of a riddle canon until the entries etc. have been found. And then this effort is often poorly rewarded if the harmony and melody do not have a pleasant effect.

There is another pertinent type which may be sung or played by three, or even four voices.

Ex. 120

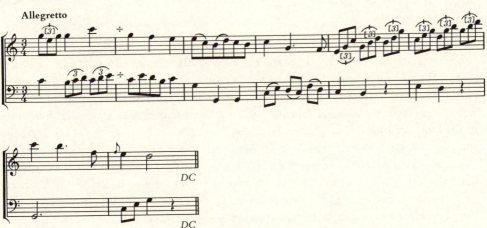

This example [Example 120] can be played with the upper voice and the bass simultaneously; as a canon between two soprano voices or two bass voices alone; or even as a three-part piece with the incorporation of the existing bass part, and then finally with four voices, namely two upper voices and two bass voices. The [process of] invention is quite similar to the foregoing.

Our intention here was not to carefully seek out the melody for all of these different types, but rather only to clarify them. Accordingly, in order to show the amateurs of composition as many kinds as possible, we now want to present the other artificial canons, which the ancients held in such great esteem that no one could pass for a master without knowing how to construct them. It is indeed true, that someone who knows how to write them correctly can also construct most fugues, for this [ability] proceeds from the knowledge of canon.

The so-called augmentation canon is included among the artificial types. It consists of the second voice imitating the melody of the first voice in tones which move twice as slowly. The diminution canon is the opposite.

Ex. 121 Example of an Augmentation Canon

DC

The intervals of the first chord are the most essential ingredient of such a canon [Example 121]. This canon is constructed in the same manner as the preceding ones, in that the first measure in the second voice is made to enter with notes twice as long, and then a new melody is continued above it in the first voice. The shorter such a canon is, the more useful it is also.[103] Indeed, a melody of only a single measure is good. At the end the voices can be exchanged, as one sees here, if the first voice then takes over the augmented melody of the canon. Such a canon may still be employed in a church piece, but a few other voices would have to accompany it and serve to complete the harmony here and there. Something of value could be produced especially if such a canon were sung by two voices and supported by accompanying instruments. However, an appropriate text must be selected for it.[104]

The diminution canon is the opposite of this [Example 122]. Perhaps we can please our readers by mentioning this remnant of antiquity. Much time lavished on it in order to produce something good would be time poorly spent, since the design of such pieces is too artificial and forced. However, in order to demonstrate that in which the ancients excelled, we want to present an example of each species, and to indicate how it might be employed.

---

[103] Daube considers brevity a virtue, because it permits the incorporation of canonic passages into *galant* works, where it provides another source of variety.

[104] Daube's recommendation of free, instrumental parts to accompany a two-voice, vocal augmentation canon is another practical suggestion for the current use of a strict-style technique. The instruments would provide a clarifying backdrop from the canonic lines, and "an appropriate text" would justify the fact that this canon is not as easily perceived as some types. This concept recalls Daube's *Beweis, daß die gottesdienstliche Musik* (1782), in which he advocates the use of different texts to stimulate composers (tired of setting the Mass text) to create appropriate, expressive church music. See the Introduction, pp. 15–16.

Ex. 122 Example of a Diminution Canon

If, when the second voice ends, it exchanges with the first voice and takes up its part, the resulting alternation can lend itself to the concerting of two voices. Here, too, one might be able to use a measure-long canon better than a longer one.[105] The bass may present the second voice, as might occur in a solo, for example, but such a canon must not last long.

The ancients also created the canon in double augmentation. To the previously explained augmentation canon they added a voice in which the length of the already extended tones of the second voice was doubled [Example 123].

Ex. 123 Example of a Canon in Double Augmentation

[105] The difference in rhythmic motion suggests concerting with two distinct motives, another way of looking at brief canonic passages – even of this artificial type – as a resource for variety in the *galant* style. See nn. 102, 103. See Horsley, *Fugue* p. 32.

This three-part type is comparable to the wheels of a clock, in which one wheel moves so slowly that another goes around twice while the former goes around only once. Another wheel moves so quickly that it goes around four times during this period.[106] Anyone who perhaps wishes to imitate this type is advised to use only one chord from beginning to end, varying it until a tolerable melody is formed. The intervals not belonging in this chord must be omitted completely. Then it is ready. However, if one wanted to include another chord nevertheless, it would have to first appear at the end of each measure, as was done here, where the tone G concludes the first measure. The usefulness of this type is still unknown. It might be, then, that such a canon is merely a curiosity.[107]

[190] Now we present another type, which is dedicated only to the friendship of two persons. This is the inverted retrograde canon, which is written in such a way that the person seated opposite sings the notes as they appear from his point of view [Example 124].

Ex. 124 Example of an Inverted Retrograde Canon

Briefly, the construction of this type consists of writing a melody of several measures. At the end, after the last note, one sets down a tone which will harmonize with this last note when the paper is turned around, namely, as it then will be viewed. And in this way one works backwards, one note after the other, to the beginning. Stationary tones and ties can be introduced here. However, one must arrange the melody so that no accidental sharp occurs in it, because, from the other point of view, it would apply to an entirely different tone. One also can draw an even number of bar lines and again divide

[106] Daube's analogy bespeaks the fascination with clockwork held during this mechanically minded age – a fascination evident in the popularity of music boxes and musical clocks. Even Haydn wrote pieces for them. (See Hill, "Haydn's Musical Clocks.") It also recalls Kirnberger's analogy of unity in art with the cogs and mechanical parts of a clock (Sulzer, "Einheit. (Schöne Künste.)," *Allgemeine Theorie*, vol. I (1771), p. 302). See n. 41.

[107] Daube apparently included this canon for the entertainment of his readers. The same can be said for the following "friendship" canons, the crab or retrograde canon, which "serves only for amusement or novelty," and the canon in several different clefs, which might be used "in intelligent society." Kollmann says that canon "affords a great variety of practice and amusement, by making us acquainted with combinations of sounds, different from those in all other sorts of musical pieces" (*Essay* (1799), p. 56) – a comment that recalls Daube's valuation of canon for providing textural variety. Canon was a traditional musical plaything, popular with the Viennese dilettantes for whom Daube was writing. Professionals also enjoyed this diversion. Mozart wrote a number of social canons (*Neue Mozart-Ausgabe*, vol. III/10 (1974)), and Haydn and Albrechtsberger exchanged canonic greetings (Mann, *Fugue*, pp. 260–62). Even Riepel, who refers to canons as "childish inventions and curiosities," nevertheless gives his students two "friendship" canons in parting (*Anfangsgründe*, vol. II (1755), pp. 129–30). See n. 110.

this same number into two parts on the staff. Then one begins to write the melody in the first measure, and the accompaniment for it in the last measure of the second section upside down. Then the melody is continued into the second, third, fourth, etc. measure from the beginning, and immediately afterward the accompaniment of each one likewise is continued into the second, third, fourth, etc. measure from the last measure on, counting backwards. One proceeds in this manner until the end which, in this case, means the middle.

Now when the piece is finished, one checks to see that the whole melody is there when the paper is turned around, because, since one must always set the accompaniment of each measure upside down in the same measure back from the end, a mistake in writing can be made very easily.

Ex. 125 Another such Example

The minor keys are not as easy to use for this as the major keys, unless the major seventh were avoided. Among the major keys, A major is particularly good, because its third represents the root or the octave when the page is turned around [Example 125].

When such a canon is filled with all kinds of alternating passages, and consists chiefly of the singing and brilliant styles, it can very well be used as a duet. In doing this one has all freedom to write in any key and to combine the melody with the harmony as desired, but one must proceed according to the foregoing instruction that when the entire piece is complete, one should set down in the following measure a note which, when viewed upside down, harmonizes with the last note, and continue to write in this way until the end. An equally artificial type is the so-called crab canon of the ancients, in which the second voice commences at the end, and proceeds backwards to the beginning [Example 126].

Ex. 126 Example of a Crab Canon

[192] This type is constructed like the foregoing, except that the notes are not viewed upside down. One writes down a melody and then additionally blocks out on the staff the same number of measures as it contains. After this the note which harmonizes with the first tone is put in the last measure. In fact, since that note begins the canon, it must be the harmonic interval which will end it. In this way also the second, third, and fourth notes from the last note are written down to go with the second, third, and fourth notes from the beginning. And by this means one proceeds steadily to the middle of the entire piece.

This retrograde harmonizing voice also can be constructed by setting down an accompanying tone immediately next to the last tone of the melody which was written first. One holds this last tone, so to speak, with the forefinger of the left hand, moving it back continually, tone by tone, while the accompanying voice is written forward, until one finally has arrived at the beginning of the piece.

The third way consists of setting the second voice under the written melody in accordance with the instructions for composition, as [in Example 127].

Ex. 127 Another Example

This example really is composed of only four measures, to which a second voice has been set. The second voice subsequently has been written backwards, [193] so that the fourth measure of the second voice has become the fifth measure of the first voice; and then the third has become the sixth, the second has become the seventh, and finally the first measure of the second voice has become the eighth measure of the first voice.

One can say that the construction of this kind of canon is as easy nowadays as it was difficult for the ancients, since any melody, however artificial, is suitable for that purpose, provided only that one follows the instructions given here. Its effect can be good, even though it serves only for amusement or novelty. Here one is compelled only to try to arrange the rapid passages so that they are equally melodic both forward and backward, that is to say, that they contain no awkward leaps. This rule pertains to every melodic line. The descent of a diminished fifth, and the leap of an augmented fourth, etc. are included among these intervals.

Another artificial type is that in which a canon for two different voices, for example, soprano and bass, is written so that each voice reads the notes according to its own clef as indicated at the beginning [Example 128].

Ex. 128 Example of a Canon with Two Clefs

The soprano begins. The bass rests three measures and a quarter, whereupon it also commences, playing the notes according to its clef. The end is determined arbitrarily. To construct such a canon [194] one writes a melody of optional length, and then determines with which second clef these same notes might be used, and especially whether this new key is adaptable to the initial key. The second voice is constructed for it in the manner originally described, namely, by using simple harmony and variation, which also has been illustrated in the above example, where the second voice proceeds a fourth lower or a fifth higher. If the melody were arranged so that the bass could be played an octave higher, one might very easily construct four voices in this manner, the third and fourth of which would move an octave lower than the first and second voices [Example 129].

Ex. 129 This Example Distributed among Four Voices

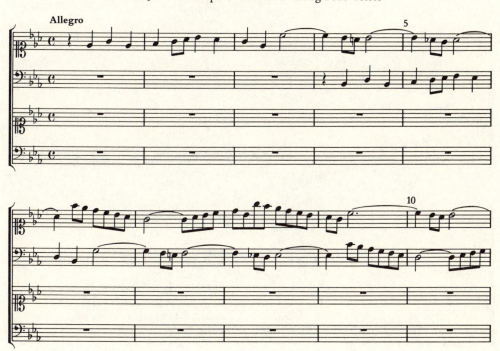

Ex. 129 (cont.)

[198] With the entrance of the third and fourth voices, a separate melody is given to the two upper voices, but one which at least is interrupted now and then by short rests, so that the canon is heard distinctly. In this way such a canon can be put to good use. And although it is basically only two-part, the variation produced by the low voices, along with the melody written above it does, after all, make a four-part score, which can well produce a good effect, depending on the main melody.

The so-called climax canon also should be included here. In this type, when one voice reaches the end, it begins to repeat the same canon a tone higher, while the second voice still continues in the initial key [Example 130].

Ex. 130 Example of a Climax Canon

[199] The construction of this kind of canon is based on the following [premises]. It is known that the first voice begins alone in all canons, and that the measures which it plays alone initially must be accompanied during the repetition. The clue lies in this accompaniment. It must be arranged so as to harmonize eventually with the preceding two measures of the [same] upper voice and also with the entrance of the transposed initial theme. This canon has eight measures. The repetition of the seventh and eighth measures[108] forms an accompaniment which is contrived so that it also must agree with the following transposed initial theme. A beginner may well be advised to set the last two measures of such a canon, with both the initial theme and the accompaniment, below one another, in order to see at once which harmony is possible [Example 131].

Ex. 131

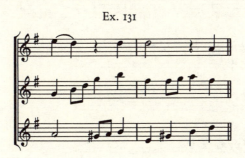

[108] "fifth and sixth measures" in the original: correct only if counting from repetition marks.

Here one sees that the first measure of the first voice harmonizes with the entrance of the key of A major, as well as with G major. The E makes a fifth with the A, and a sixth with the G. The following D in this case is an anticipation in A, and a proper harmony in G. The following D belongs in the third chord of A major, just as in G major. The last A again is an anticipation of the chord in the third measure of the transposed repetition of the beginning, and in G major it is the fifth of the third chord. After such a canon has been constructed in two parts it is written in one part, and the entrance marked with a sign.

One proceeds in the same way in writing a canon in which the repetition occurs a tone lower [Example 132].

Ex. 132 Another Type with the Same Name

If such a canon is long, short modulations into different keys can also occur, just as in the example given at the very beginning. But one must not modulate at the close, because it would be detrimental afterwards, at the entrance of the transposed repetition of the theme.

Now we come to three-part artificial canons. These are written with three kinds of clefs. When each voice enters it performs the notes as they are read according to its own clef. To make this more clear, we want to give an example in three voices [Example 133].

Ex. 133 Example of a Canon with Three Clefs

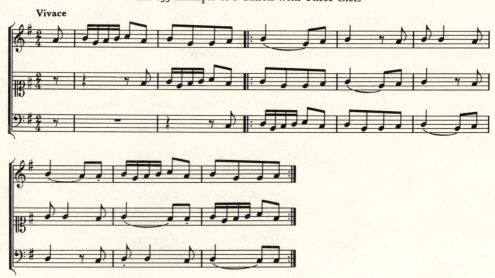

This canon appears to be artificial, but the process of construction is easily identified. It consists of writing an initial melody of one measure, as here for example, then transferring it into the second voice and, after this entrance, into the third voice, as if all three voices were meant to commence in succession at the unison. After this one sets the clef of each voice in the signature and then arranges the accompaniment accordingly. This is the way such a canon is constructed.

All clefs are not to be used here. The choice must be made according to the nature of the initial theme and the entrance of each voice. For example, if the bass, the tenor, or a higher voice were to begin, different clefs would likewise be required for the accompanying voices, or else the entire harmony would certainly cause considerable difficulties. Here we have employed the violin and piano clefs, along with the bass clef. The two soprano clefs are separated by a third, whereas the bass clef constitutes a sixth when calculated from the violin clef. Equally important is which voice begins. The alternation of the sixth, third, and octave determines most of the harmony in this canon. Here the violin clef begins, the piano clef answers, and the bass clef follows. One cannot concern oneself so carefully here with the succession of the three chords, nor with the thorough-bass and the complete harmony. The bass enters with a six–four accompaniment which results from the inversion of the third chord in G major. This canon, when reduced into one voice, looks like this [Example 134]:

Ex. 134

Now, although both entrance signs are there, it is certainly rather difficult for a person inexperienced in this work to solve, since one does not yet know which voice is to begin first. The following example [Example 135] is written in three other clefs.

Ex. 135

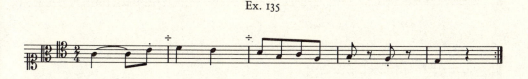

Here the soprano appears first, followed by the alto and then the tenor. Such kinds are to be used in intelligent society,[109] but even there they must also contain a good melody, without which all musical art amounts to nothing. Indeed, all types of canons

---

[109] See n. 107. In the following four-voice examples, Exx. 136–7, the clefs are arranged according to the order of entrance; in the following example "of this type," Ex. 138, however, the order of clefs was exactly reversed from Daube's instructions for resolution and no rest is indicated at the end in the original. Perhaps these were misprints, perhaps intentional enigmas to be solved by "intelligent society." Compare n. 112.

furnish strong evidence that harmony may be used in many different ways by means of the art of variation.

Experience teaches that four voices could also be arranged in this way. The procedure is the same. One must find a very short melodic motif, which is made to enter repeatedly with the very same notes, and then, as was said before, one writes the clefs in the signature, and then arranges the accompanying voices so that they harmonize in all four clefs during the repetition. One will understand this canon easily if one already knows the preceding types, but here one must take care to introduce more sustained tones. This canon, reduced into one voice, appears thus [Example 136]:

Ex. 136

[203] To please the amateurs, we also want to write out this example in the usual four parts [Example 137].

Ex. 137

[204] We have just indicated how this type of four-part canon should be constructed. Here we want to reveal another device of art. One should construct a short melody, the first half of which consists of intervals from the ruling chord and contains no leaps other than those in the chord. Should other tones occur, however, they must appear in passing. The second part of the first half can be a long tone, as here, or else this tone is repeated, during which a second above or below it also may very well appear as a passing tone. The second half of this short melody also must consist of slowly moving intervals from the third chord. These tones must be long in order that the main entrance of each voice might be heard more clearly. The entire preceding example is arranged as prescribed here, and consequently every amateur can easily comprehend both theory and practice, which might be very difficult to learn in any other way.

Ex. 138 Another Canon of This Type

In this canon [Example 138] the bass begins, followed by the tenor, the alto, and finally the soprano. At the end every voice rests for one measure before starting again from the beginning. The ending of a canon is always left to the discretion of the performers.

From such monuments of antiquity one sees how hard they strove to increase the greatness of art in those days. These artificial types of canons, fugues, etc. were already in vogue 200 years ago.

In another artificial species of four-part canons, the second pair of voices inverts the melody of the first pair. We have given an example of this type above, but with only two voices sung by two persons sitting opposite one another, each of whom sings the notes as they appear from his point of view. The present canon consists of four voices. A further difference is that the persons who sit opposite us must sing the notes from the right to the [205] left hand, that is, at the correct starting point. The clefs for it are the soprano, alto, tenor, and bass clefs, of which the soprano begins, and the other three voices follow one at a time. This example appears here as it should look with its actual four-part harmony, but not as it is written in a single voice [Example 139].

Ex. 139 Example of a Four-Part Canon in which Two Persons Sing the Notes Inverted

Ex. 139 (*cont.*)

[206] In the process of construction one writes down a single measure of a melody and then places this same melody on another staff, but in the second measure, whereupon one sets the optional clefs in the signature and turns the page around. Then the notes as they appear in this position are written on the other two empty staves (now returned to an upright position), in such a way that the voices always enter a measure apart. After this an accompanying voice, which must harmonize with the entrance of the three voices, is added for the continuation of the initial melody. This accompanying voice, however, should be arranged so that subsequently, even when the paper is turned around, it would come out so that it harmonizes precisely with the repetition of the initial melody. Then, when the empty measures are filled and the canon has been completed in this manner, it is written in one voice and the entrance signs are added [Example 140].

Ex. 140

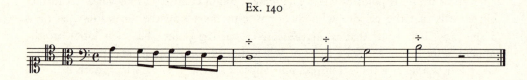

Whoever wants to solve such a musical riddle must be patient in trying out all of the types, and still many people will not find the solution. It is rarely used. Yet, if words were written underneath, there might be an occasion to use it among good friends.[110]

This next canon [Example 141] also deserves to be included in the artificial class because it, like the preceding one, is written on only one staff, even though it has four parts. In this canon two voices enter consecutively at the beginning, and two voices enter consecutively at the end and proceed backwards. We already have cited a similar type above, which differs from this one in that it is two-part and has but one kind of clef. The two-part type already was known to the ancients by the name crab canon. But we cannot really say whether the four-part type also was known to them.

---

[110] Most social canons contained words, messages, or greetings. See n. 107.

Ex. 141 Example of a Four-Part Crab Canon

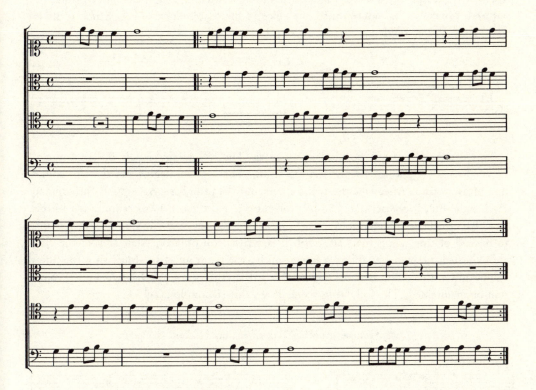

In this canon two voices, the soprano and tenor, enter one after the other at the beginning. The other two voices, on the contrary, begin at the end and sing backward, after
the alto rests two measures and the bass rests three measures. Now when these voices
have reached the beginning, they then take up the proper initial melody, while the first
two voices are obliged to sing backwards. The full score given here shows that if one
wanted to compose such a canon, it would first have to be written in the usual voices.
What one necessarily must know about composing it is to make very few leaps, to avoid
the major seventh of the key, and to include sustained tones. The three chords certainly
do appear in it, but their complete harmony cannot always be heard, and since each voice
carries the melody, no particular voice acts as the fundamental or bass part, unless one
wanted to construct an additional part especially for this purpose. For this reason it very
often happens that a fourth and sixth occur above the bass. Still, we want to explain
how the chords follow one another in this example. The first chord begins. The second
and third chords appear in the second measure. The third measure again contains the
harmony of the ruling chord. The fourth measure has the second chord. Then the first
chord follows in contrary motion and in this way the chords alternate among one
another.

[209] The canon analyzed here is fairly unknown. It, as all the preceding ones, arises from the [principle of] variation. After it has been written in four voices and constructed without mistakes, it is reduced into one voice in the customary manner, which really is the correct way to represent it [Example 142].

Ex. 142

This canon also might be difficult to solve. The following kind is different again. Each voice enters a tone lower at the repetition. The soprano begins and the alto comes in a measure later. After this the tenor enters and then the bass. As soon as the soprano reaches the end, it repeats the melody a tone lower, and the other voices imitate it in this way. Eventually the conclusion is made in whichever key one chooses. It still remains to be said of this canon that, although it is written on only one staff and all the clefs are indicated, nevertheless the two lower voices, the tenor and bass, must sing the notes a tone lower than indicated by their clefs, so that the octave of the two upper voices will be maintained. The following score shows this [Example 143].

Ex. 143 Another Type of Artificial Canon

[211] This canon is still useful. It can be used in the church and chamber. The alto enters a fifth lower, which gives it a rather fugue-like character. Even more freedom may be allowed here,[111] but contrary motion must be observed carefully and the ending of each voice must be arranged so as to accommodate the change of key. The melody also may be interspersed with short rests, as seen here, which are especially useful for insuring that the initial melody may be heard distinctly, even when it enters in the second voice. Such canons can be arranged in different ways. It is not necessary that the soprano always commence and the alto follow. The [entrance positions of the] voices may be exchanged here, just as in the regular fugue. When this canon has been arranged in four parts and is completely finished, it is written on one staff, as were the preceding ones [Example 144].

Ex. 144

The following canon does the opposite [Examples 145–6]. The four voices move one tone higher at the end, when the repetition occurs. Here the tenor takes the lead and the alto follows a fourth higher. Then comes the soprano which enters an octave higher than the tenor, while the bass follows an octave lower than the alto. Each voice enters a measure later than its predecessor. Both this canon and the preceding one have already been described above under the name of climax canon, where two-part examples have been given.

Ex. 145 Another Type of Artificial Canon Written Out in Four Voices

[111] See pp. 186 and 186–7.

Ex. 145 (cont.)

Ex. 146 As it is Actually Written

In constructing these two types, one also should remember to employ more long than short notes, and to try to avoid leaps as much as possible. Since every canon of this type is written on only one staff, all four voices must also have the half steps which are introduced by the leading voice. For example, the tenor begins, and has [E to] F in the second measure. This half step is imitated accordingly in the alto part, which therefore must go to B-flat instead of B-natural. The construction of these two types generally requires that the fourth, fifth, or sixth measure of the melody be arranged so that it could later harmonize with the entrance of the [214] second voice (which is a fifth lower or a fourth higher) in such a way that the voice which is repeated first also may begin a tone higher or lower.

In the first example one sees that the fifth measure, when transposed down a fifth (which is where the alto and bass enter), contains the harmony which the soprano needs in order to institute the repetition a tone lower. The second example demonstrates that the fourth measure, transposed down a fifth, is adapted so that the voice which first repeats could re-enter a tone higher. The suggestions given before are recommended here also.

Now, in concluding this discussion, we want to cite two more four-part canons which are constructed in the same way as those already explained as climax canons [Examples 147–8]. The first consists of two voices moving up a tone when the repetition occurs. [In both examples], however, the alto and tenor do not sing the notes according to their clefs, but rather must transpose them, the alto a tone higher, and the tenor a tone lower. At the end they repeat the melody a tone higher, in the same way as the other two principal voices, and so it continues as often as the repetition occurs. In the second canon, on the other hand, the repetition is instituted a tone lower. To save space, we want to show it only as it is written in one voice.

Ex. 147 Another Canon of the Climax Type, in which, at the End, Two Voices Repeat the Beginning a Tone Higher

Ex. 148 Another, in which, at the End, Two Voices Begin Again a Tone Lower

[215] The voices enter in the same manner in both examples. The tenor follows the soprano at the octave after a rest of two measures. The alto has four measures of rest, whereas the bass has six. In the first example the alto enters a fourth lower, and in the second example [also a fourth][112] lower [than the soprano]. This type of canon closely resembles the foregoing examples. Whoever is well experienced in counterpoint at the twelfth, may be able to imitate this unusual type easily despite the difficulties. The rules pertaining to the construction are the same as for the foregoing types.

We now have discussed most canons and taught their construction. We hope that every amateur who has talent and patience will be able to imitate them very soon. The canons which appear here, as all the examples in this treatise on composition, are intended more as a basis for the instruction and clear explanation of this knowledge than for [the illustration of] a good melody. If an amateur, even at the beginning, should simply vary the canons sketched here, and write them down according to their proper chords, he would certainly notice that in doing so he would come to know the entrances of every voice, the alternation of the few chords, and the style of the melody. Indeed, everything is to

---

[112] Exx. 147–8: the clefs were not in order of entrance; they read soprano, alto, tenor, bass in the original. Ex. 148: m. 8 appeared to be a breve rest (or possibly a half rest above a whole rest) with a "2" above in the original. This does not work out. The text "[also a fourth]" originally read "a fifth." This conflicts with the transposition instructions in the preceding paragraph and with the bass voice in this canon. The alto and bass must be in octaves in this canon involving "Two Voices."

be gained by this. One will see that variation is the basis of melody, just as harmony is the basis of variation,[113] and also discover that one may profit greatly from the study of canon. After careful consideration we have taken up the discussions of variation and canon consecutively, because one proceeds from the other. The following explanation of fugues and double counterpoints, etc. is also based entirely on them. Most fugues are even easier to write than canons, because more freedom is allowed, with which the melody can likewise be further extended.

10

SIMPLE FUGUE

The discussion of imitation provides the basis for the construction of fugues. Just as we have said in the foregoing pages, that variation is the basis of melody, which arises from it, so we can say here that when a melodic motif is invented, the art of imitation teaches how it [216] might be repeated. A piece in which such a repetition [i.e., answer] is instituted, continued, and carried out to the conclusion according to certain rules is called a fugue.[114]

The main characteristic of a fugue should be that the initial theme is melodic and animated, and that the secondary motives fit together well with the main motif or initial theme, so that it would seem as if it were a single voice proceeding from beginning to end.[115] Even if the upper voice does rest now and then, the melodic line still must be arranged so that there might be a continuity between the main theme in the low register and the upper voice which just ceased, and likewise when it joins in again. In the treatise on musical style we intend to tell how this might be achieved.[116]

If a fugue has these characteristics, it can be called excellent, and accordingly can be used everywhere. What are all our good current pieces – symphonies, opera arias, concertos, etc. – other than unbound or approximate fugues?[117] This means, above all, the imitation of one or two main motives. A regular fugue requires a far greater restriction,

---

[113] This statement sums up Daube's treatment of variation as central to his reconciliation of the free and strict styles. See the Introduction, pp. 25–6.

[114] Compare Kirnberger's similar preliminary definition in Sulzer, "Fuge. (Musik.)," *Allgemeine Theorie*, vol. I (1771), p. 407.

[115] Even in fugue, Daube merged the homophonic preference of his era with the older, strict-style techniques. Compare p. 231 and pp. 255–6. The "repeated theme," however, should be "clearly perceived" (p. 204).

[116] i.e., Vol. III of Daube's *Dilettant* series, planned but apparently not carried out. See the Introduction, pp. 11–15.

[117] Compare Kirnberger: "Today composers also write purely instrumental fugues. Actually all pieces with several concerting voices, be they duos, trios, or quartets, fall into the fugal [category], because the voices always must imitate one another, provided a true melodic unity is to be maintained. Only in this case the imitations are not carried out as strictly as in fugue proper. But whoever wants to construct such pieces must necessarily have experience in fugal composition" (Sulzer, "Fuge. (Musik.)," *Allgemeine Theorie*, vol. I (1771), p. 410).

but nevertheless it should certainly be worked out with greater freedom even today, since we are not lacking in melody.[118] Let us endeavor to give some instruction in this.

The initial fugue theme which one constructs is of an optional length. If we should state our thoughts on the standard, we would prefer the middle path between brevity and great length.[119] In a brevity of several notes no good melody can be produced and the much too frequent repetition cannot have a pleasant effect. Length forfeits clarity when an overly long theme occurs in the bass or tenor while the upper voice is sounding another melody because it may not rest that long.

The imitation [i.e., answer] is instituted in the key in which the initial theme closes. But it does happen sometimes that not all the intervals of the initial theme can occur in the repetition, and therefore an amateur must mainly know which intervals may be altered in such a case. They are the whole steps in every key. But the half steps [217] must be retained unaltered throughout.[120] In this rule, therefore, lies the only clue, which is easy in itself, but causes many people difficulties.

With an initial theme which commences and closes on the ending tone [i.e., tonic note], the repetition imitates the entire theme, either at the unison or at the octave. If it happens, on the other hand, that the initial theme commences on the fifth of the key and closes on the ending tone, the repetition, of course, must begin on this tone, but it must finish in the first-related key, because this new ending tone bears the greatest resemblance to the first tone of the initial theme. Here one must take care that the half steps in both keys are heard as immovable. The accompanying example will show this clearly [Example 149].

---

[118] Theorists often distinguished between regular or proper fugues, constructed according to certain rules, and irregular or improper fugues, which departed from the rules. Rameau was the first to formulate rules which deal systematically with both the beginning and ending of thematic entrances (*Traité* (1722), pp. 332–7; Eng. trans., pp. 349–53). From Marpurg onwards, the regular fugue included, in addition to the correct form of subject and answer and their proper order in the exposition, good countermelodies and episodes (*Abhandlung*, vol. I (1753), pp. 17–18, Eng. trans. in Mann, *Fugue*, pp. 155–6). Scheibe considered irregular fugue the middle step between free imitation – short fragments of melody imitated within a piece of any type – and the formal regular fugue (*Der Critische Musicus* (1739), pp. 451–3). Also see Mann, *Fugue*, pp. 50–51 and Horsley, *Fugue*, pp. 122, 289.

[119] Compare Rameau, *Traité* (1722), p. 338, Eng. trans., p. 355; Marpurg, *Abhandlung*, vol. I (1753), pp. 27–8, Eng. trans. in Mann, *Fugue*, pp. 161–2; Kirnberger, "Führer. (Musik)," in Sulzer, *Allgemeine Theorie*, vol. I (1771), p. 410; Kollmann, *Essay* (1799), p. 31. Compare Padre Martini's use of *soggetto*, *andamento*, and *attacco* to designate medium-length (one-and-a-half to three measures), longer, and shorter subjects (*Esemplare*, vol. II (1775), pp. viii–ix).

[120] Daube never speaks of transposing the subject up or down a fourth or fifth to find the proper half steps for the "repetition" [answer], but suggests thinking of the 3–4 and 7–8 half steps of the subject as specific chord members and half steps in the corresponding key. (He discusses only major-key fugue themes.) Thus Daube seems to view tones of a subject – especially first and last tones and those which form half steps – as chord members in a certain key. The chord membership of the last tone partly determines whether the imitation (answer) may begin in the third chord (dominant level) or the second chord (subdominant level). See the next three paragraphs and p. 196. Since the second and third chords appear to be of nearly equal importance in Daube's harmonic system, it is consistent for dominant and subdominant level "imitations" (answers) to be considered nearly equally legitimate. This chordal, functional orientation may explain the apparent contradiction between Daube's strongly tonal, half-step, key-oriented approach on the one hand, and his frequent allowance of the modal-referent, subdominant answer on the other.

Ex. 149 Example of a Four-Part Fugue

Ex. 149 (*cont.*)

Ex. 149 (*cont.*)

In the second measure the initial theme already has the half step F-sharp, which is the third of the ruling chord in D major. Therefore, this third also must be present in the imitation, and since this must occur in the related key of A major, one immediately discerns the reason why the first downward leap of a third from A to F-sharp in the initial theme does not take place in the following related key of A major, but rather becomes a second in the imitation [mm. 7–8]. The imitation must begin in the key in which the initial theme closes, but the next tone is already adjusted to its key and proper conclusion. Here the second violin begins with D, in order to agree with the conclusion of the first

voice. The second note, or second measure, is already transposed, since the remainder of
the initial theme is set in the key of A major. The same thing occurs in the second repetition [i.e., third entry, m. 16]; the first tone enters on the unison A, whereas the second
tone already is readjusted to the original key.

But when the initial theme commences on the octave of its ending tone and closes
in the next-related key, no change occurs at the beginning of the repetition, but does near
the end. In this case the repetition must return to the initial key. [225] Thus, one puts the
half step which belongs in this next-related key in the same place in which the half step
appears in the initial theme, and then the preceding or succeeding whole tones are very
easily adjusted accordingly.

Ex. 150 Another Example of a Fugue

Ex. 150 (*cont.*)

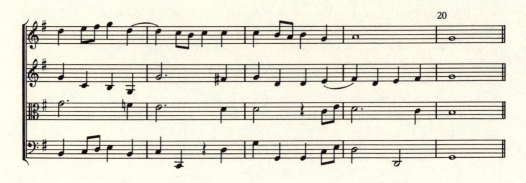

Here [in Example 150] one sees that the new key of D major returns to G major in exactly the same place where the key of G major changed, for C-sharp [m. 2] is the major seventh in D major, and F-sharp [m. 4] is the major seventh in G major. The same situation exists here as in the previous example. The second measure of the initial theme contains two thirds in the melody – the first is B and G, the second is G and B – the first of which is retained in the repetition, while only the latter had to be changed to a second. Why? It was a third without the half step and consequently this could be done more conveniently. So we see here again, that the half step in both types must be observed very precisely. If this is not done, the repetition will very seldom be without mistakes. The three types described here are called regular fugue subjects.

Now there are also several types of fugue which can be called irregular. These do not begin on the octave or the fifth of the key, but rather on another degree. Here again the previous explanation applies: when a fugue theme begins on the second of the key and concludes in the same key, the repetition also begins on the second of the new key and, near the end, again adjusts the half step to end in that key.

The theme [in Example 151] begins on the second above the ending tone. Thus, the repetition is likewise instituted on this same interval of the next-related key. One sees that the repetition also occurs completely unaltered in the new key, because the rest at the beginning makes it possible to start with A after the C, especially since this tone [229] also is in the second chord in G major, which does have a considerable similarity to the ruling chord in C major.[121] The ending tone in the ninth measure provides an opportunity for the theme to be heard anew in the initial key.

---

[121] Rests were customarily recommended before a re-entry, in order, as Marpurg puts it, "to state the theme again with renewed freshness" (*Abhandlung*, vol. I (1753), pp. 128–9, Eng. trans. in Mann, *Fugue*, p. 185). According to Padre Martini, "the great masters made it a carefully observed rule that . . . a rest . . . had to be followed immediately with an entrance of the theme . . ." (*Esemplare*, vol. II (1775), p. 33, Eng. trans. in Mann, *Fugue*, p. 274). See also Fux, *Gradus* (1725), Ger. trans., Mizler (1742), p. 125, Eng. trans. in Mann, *Fugue*, p. 83; and Mattheson, *Capellmeister* (1739), vol. III, p. 435, Eng. trans., p. 798. Compare, pp. 196 and 198. See also pp. 204, 206, and 243, and n. 49.

Ex. 151 A Fugue Theme which Begins on the Second of the Key

However, if the initial theme is intended to end in the next-related key, the melody nevertheless must contain an accurate indication of the key in which the entire fugue is to be concluded.[122] The repetition, of course, is begun in the new key, but it is readjusted at once according to the old key, in order to sound a close there also [Example 152].[123]

---

[122] Compare. p. 235, rule 6.

[123] In this case Daube's answer is exact, but occurs at the subdominant level (upper fourth or lower fifth), thereby outlining the basic fifth of the tonic key (i.e., 2–5 answered by 5–1 of the key). Compare Marpurg, who says that if the subject (*Führer*) begins with 2 in the tonic, the reply (*Gefährte*) may begin with the dominant itself or 2 in the dominant (i.e., 5 or 6 of the key), depending upon which makes the better melody or the closest likeness to the subject (*Abhandlung*, vol. I (1753), pp. 53–4; see Horsley, *Fugue*, p. 100). The subdominant answer – either at the subdominant level or in the subdominant key – though more prevalent in the preceding era, was not as rare in eighteenth-century practice as some theory texts would seem to indicate, nor did all such answers simply represent lingering modal traditions. Nalden states that a subdominant answer frequently is used when a subject begins on the dominant, and is necessarily answered tonally (i.e., at the subdominant level), and the "subject's melodic line does not present opportunity for subsequent adjustment." Subdominant answers also frequently are used "when it is necessary to redress tonal balance." In a French overture . . . for instance, when the first section ends in the dominant, the following fugue

Ex. 152 Another Type

This repetition likewise has no change of intervals. The rest makes it possible for the initial theme to be repeated. If a fugue theme commences on the third and ends in the next-related key, [230] the repetition likewise begins on the third of the new key in which the theme ended.[124] Toward the end of the repetition the intervals must be adjusted according to the half step of the initial key [Example 153].[125]

often "sets out in that key, and a subdominant . . . [level] answer is given in order to achieve a tonal balance between the two main tonalities of the piece, tonic and dominant" (*Fugal Answer*, pp. 98–112). Seen in this light, Daube's acceptance of subdominant answers, liberal by comparison with other theorists, may be seen as a reflection of valid compositional practices not often recorded in theoretical treatises, and reinterpreted in the context of his three-chord harmonic system.

[124] Daube does not discuss the solution for a non-modulating fugue theme which begins on the third of the key, perhaps because if the final tone of the subject were the tonic, it would not be found in the same chord as the first one of the answer. But the fact that Daube treats a theme beginning on the mediant at all is interesting historically. While Fux maintained that "the voices of a fugue cannot start at intervals other than those that constitute a mode, that is, intervals other than the unison, octave, and fifth" (*Gradus* (1725), Ger. trans., Mizler, (1742), p. 124, Eng. trans. in Mann, *Fugue*, p. 81), Rameau expressed the opinion that the fugue subject should begin and end "only on the tonic note, its dominant, or its mediant" (*Traité* (1722), p. 337, Eng. trans., p. 353). Marpurg was the first theorist to treat the formulation of answers to subjects beginning on all degrees of the scale (*Abhandlung*, vol. I (1753), pp. 31–56), by which time the effect of the major-minor key system is becoming visible. Thus, while Daube's classification of subjects which begin on the third degree as "irregular" may at first come across as mildly reminiscent of the older modal tradition, his inclusion of subjects which begin and end on all scale degrees is in keeping with the more progressive stream of theory and practice.

[125] Whereas Daube adjusts the answer to the original key near the end (i.e., 3–5 modulating subject answered by 7–1 at the dominant level), Marpurg says that for a non-modulating subject beginning on 3, the answer will start with 3 in the dominant, but if the subject moves to the dominant, 2 in the dominant will usually answer 3 in the subject (*Abhandlung*, vol. I (1753), p. 47; see Horsley, *Fugue*, p. 98). Marpurg recommends 3–1 answered by 7–5 (non-modulating) or 3–5 answered by 6–1 (modulating), thus contriving the answer to the non-modulating subject at the dominant, and to the modulating subject at the subdominant level throughout. Rameau also provides a choice in answering the third degree. But since French theorists of the time analyze all fugue themes as non-modulating, he explains it in terms of chords: "Either the sixth or seventh note should . . . answer the mediant . . . . By observing what follows rather than what precedes and by conforming to one another those chords found above the bass used for the melodies answering in fugue, we shall usually avoid mistakes" (*Traité* (1722), p. 337, Eng. trans., p. 353; see also Horsley, *Fugue*, p. 92).

Ex. 153 A Fugue Theme which Begins on the Third of the Key

[231] This theme lasts only to the beginning of the third measure. The following E already is directed toward the new key of A major, of which it is the fifth. Thus, the repetition does not continue beyond the first A of the sixth measure. The second A already is regarded as the fifth of the initial key. An initial theme always must be considered in this way, and the repetition adjusted accordingly, something which seems difficult to many able composers using another method, but which becomes very easy through a clear explanation. When the fugue subject commences on the fourth, it preferably ends on the root, on which the repetition begins [Example 154a–b].[126]

126 Note the *alla breve* in Ex. 154b. Throughout the treatise, even in examples of canon, fugue, and double counterpoint, Daube avoids the "proper" *alla breve* meter associated with the strict style, perhaps because it was considered old-fashioned. Petri says that this meter is "grandfatherly" (*altvaterisch*), and today is used "merely in fugues, and is played as rapidly as a faster 4/4 meter (*Anleitung* (2/1782), p. 144). Riepel, however, comments that common time sounds "livelier" than *alla breve* (*Anfangsgründe*, vol. II (1755), p. 87), which would account for the increasing popularity of the former among those of progressive taste. Scheibe mentions that *alla breve* belongs in the stately old church style, but says that it also occurs in *galant* chamber and orchestral music (*Composition*, p. 203). However, the "old-fashioned," strict-style association of *alla breve* meter was fading gradually into history. Schubart wrote that "*alla breve* is equally suited to the church and to the secular style" (*Ideen* (1806), p. 357).

Ex. 154 A Fugue Theme which Begins on the Fourth of the Key

Neither repetition tolerates any alteration of its intervals. The rest facilitates the entrance of the third voice. If one wanted to arrange the repetition in the key of F, this also would be feasible (*füglich*) [Example 155].

Ex. 155 The Previous Fugue Theme, but with the Repetition in F Major

The second note of the initial theme is the third of the ruling chord in C major, and the third note is the half step in this key. The same [half step] must appear in the repetition also. The second note must be the third of the first chord in F major, and the third note must be the half step which belongs in this key. This is the reason why there must be a descending third at the beginning of the repetition.[127] When a theme commences on the sixth of a key and closes on the root, the repetition once again must be instituted on the sixth of the new key, and conclude in that key [Example 156].

Ex. 156 Another Type which Commences on the Sixth of the Key

The repetition could also be transposed to F in this example. But if this were to happen, the half step in the first measure, namely F, the fourth of C major, would have to be observed in the imitation also, and the fourth of F, namely B-flat, then would be put in that position. The preceding passage could be arranged accordingly. It would be best if the half step F in the repetition were introduced again in the place where the half step C is located at the beginning. If this is done, the second, A to B, with which it commences must be changed to the third, C to E, in the repetition. After this the repetition may continue and finish in F. If one would like to write a fugue which is to commence on the seventh [Example 157]:

Ex. 157 Fugue Theme which Commences on the Seventh of the Key

---

[127] In Exxs. 154a and b, the subject moves from 4 to 1 (tonic) and the answer from 1 to 5, giving the effect of moving to the dominant key. In Ex. 155 the subject moves from 4 to 1 and the answer from 1 to 4, the visual effect being I (subject)–IV (answer), whereas retrospectively the aural effect is I–V (subject)–I (answer), yielding a modulating subject beginning in, as well as on, F. Dominant and subdominant alternatives also are allowed for answering a subject beginning on 6. (See Ex. 156 and the following text.) However, in these cases the aural effect corresponds with the visual: I–V and I–IV. (See also n. 123.) Marpurg, by contrast, states unequivocally that fugue subjects which start on the fourth and sixth degrees of the scale are answered by the fourth and sixth degrees, respectively, in the dominant (*Abhandlung*, vol. I (1753), p. 52; see Horsley, *Fugue*, p. 98).

Ex. 157 (cont.)

The imitation permits no modification of the intervals, even if the repetition is arranged a tone lower. On the other hand, if this theme were not to conclude in the same key, but rather in the next-related key, a slight modification would then have to take place in the repetition. Here it is [Example 158].[128]

Ex. 158

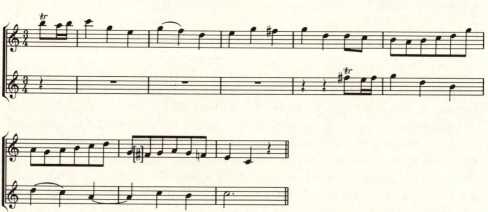

If the imitation is to be adjusted according to the intervals of the key, it must commence with the seventh, F-sharp and, because it is to return to C again, the A which appears in the sixth measure must remain stationary so that in the seventh measure it will become the sixth in C, just as the E in the third measure of the initial theme is the sixth of G. The rest justifies the entrance of the repetition here also, which is correct in itself, but the last tone, G, in the upper voice may not be sustained.

[128] For a non-modulating theme commencing on the seventh degree, Daube again permits either a dominant or subdominant answer (i.e., 7–1 answered by #4–5, or 7–1 answered by 3–4). See n. 127. If the theme modulates, however, it is adjusted to return to the original key near the end. Compare Marpurg, who states that if 7 is treated as the leading tone to the tonic in a non-modulating subject, it must be answered by the leading tone to the dominant (i.e., 7–1 answered by #4–5), but, under other circumstances, an answer of 6 in the dominant (i.e., 3 in the tonic) to 7 in the tonic is more appropriate (i.e., 7–1 answered by 3–5), with an adjustment after the 3–4, as in Daube's subdominant version (*Abhandlung*, vol. I (1753), pp. 54–6; see Horsley, *Fugue*, pp. 98–9). Both, however, think in terms of the answer being a parallel of the subject in the dominant key and refer to the seventh scale degree as the third of the dominant key (Marpurg) or the third of the "third [dominant] chord" (Daube).

[235] This discussion of fugue subjects which are called irregular on account of their beginning, will now be followed by a discussion of fugue subjects which can be called irregular on account of their conclusion. We still want to touch briefly upon this species. The first type of these subjects reasonably includes those which end on the second of the key. The chord for this second note is the third chord, as is easily understood, and therefore the repetition also is initiated in this key [Example 159].[129]

Ex. 159 Example of a Fugue Theme which Ends on the Second of the Key

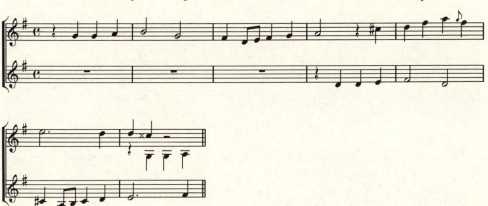

The melody begins on the ending tone and closes on the second. Here we mean only the close of the initial theme. The imitation occurs in the third chord, to which the last note, A, belongs. Therefore, since the second voice also ends on the second of the new key, the third voice can very conveniently repeat the initial theme at the octave above or below, since G is also present in the third chord of D major.

However, if the initial theme commences on the fifth of the key, and still closes on the second, one cannot do other than to initiate the repetition at the octave, [a procedure] which, however, occurs particularly at the beginning. In the middle, and at the termination of such a fugue, the entrance of the second voice, or the repetition in general, may occur at other intervals [Example 160a–c].[130]

Ex. 160 Another Type

(a)

At the beginning of a fugue

---

[129] Most of Daube's answers to subjects which conclude on 2, 4, or 7 entail imitation at the dominant level. Note that Daube puts the scale degree of the final note of the theme into a chordal context to determine the possibilities for the beginning of the "repetition" (answer).

[130] This liberty suggests the *attacco* subject of Padre Martini, which could enter at any pitch interval in relation to the preceding entrance (*Esemplare*, vol. II (1775), pp. viii–ix; see Horsley, *Fugue*, p. 136). See n. 119.

Ex. 160*a–c* (*cont.*)

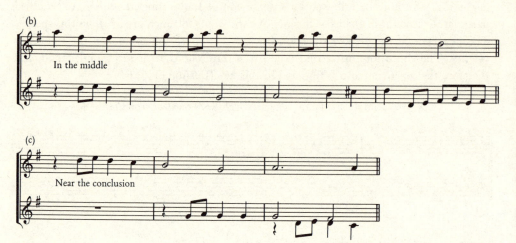

From this example one sees that in constructing a fugue, the repetition is arranged quite exactly at the beginning, to be sure, but a change might very well be permitted during the course [of the fugue], and even more readily at the conclusion, as we subsequently will demonstrate further [Example 161*a–b*].

Ex. 161 Fugue Theme with the Close on the Fourth

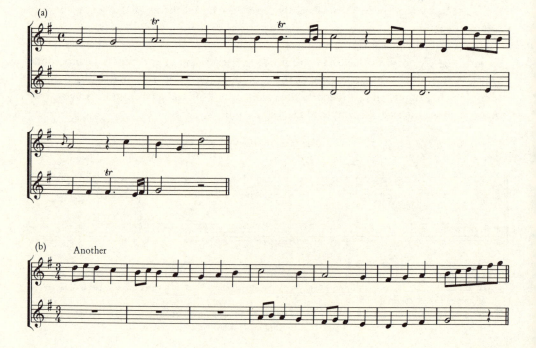

The first example proceeds from the root to the fourth. Therefore, since the latter is to be found in the harmony of the third chord in G major also, the repetition may very easily be instituted on the root of this chord, but with a slight modification, [namely,] that this tone would remain stationary in the second measure and not ascend a tone higher, as it did in the initial theme. The reason is that no other key appears here and the tone E would fit much better in the related key of D major. However, even if the E were not changed, the harmony certainly could be arranged so that the conclusion would occur in G major.[131] The second example begins on the fifth and ends on the fourth. From there, the second voice also enters on the fifth of the next-related key, but returns to the original key again. When the initial theme ends on the third, it must do so in the imitation also, whether it ends in the original or next-related key [Examples 162–3].[132]

Ex. 162 Another Type which Concludes on the Third of the Next Key

Ex. 163 Fugue Theme which Ends on the Third of the Same Key

The first example begins on the ending tone and proceeds to the third of the first chord in the next [-related] key. Here the imitation enters on the root of this new key, but in the second measure the third tone already is changed and oriented toward the initial key. [239] The third tone, F-sharp, in the second measure of the initial theme, belongs in the

---

[131] Even though the fourth degree also belongs to the "second chord," Daube uses it here as the seventh of the "third chord," thus instituting the "repetition" (answer) at the dominant level. The effect of delaying the sixth degree in m. 2 of the "repetition" is to emphasize the dominant and de-emphasize the subdominant harmony. Compare nn. 133 and 134.

[132] Since Daube stresses the position of the half steps in contriving the answer, the third degree, as a member of the 3–4 half-step interval, must be preserved. Compare pp. 196–7.

harmony of the first chord in D major, as well as in the second chord in A major, and therefore the third tone in the second measure of the repetition likewise may be included in the harmony of the second chord in D major.

The second example begins on the fifth and goes to the third of the first chord. Here the imitation, of course, begins on the root of this chord, but immediately adjusts the remainder so that it could end on the third of the first chord in the next-related key.

Another type concludes on the sixth of the key, and the repetition must do likewise [i.e., end on the sixth of the next-related key; Example 164].

Ex. 164 Fugue Theme which Ends on the Sixth of the Key

The conclusion occurs on the third of the second chord, and therefore the repetition must also be arranged on the root of this chord.[133] Although no major seventh, the indication of A major, is to be found in the initial theme, this tone nevertheless must appear in the repetition, whereby it then happens that the half step which occurs at the beginning of the second measure of the initial theme could not be used in the repetition, for otherwise G [-natural] would have had to appear here, which would have led into D major. This may well occur during the continuation of such a theme, about in the middle [of the fugue], but at the beginning it is better to remain in the designated key as

---

[133] Because of the chord membership of the final note of the subject, Daube's answer (Ex. 164) begins on the fourth, rather than the fifth degree of the key. A similar logic is followed for a subject which begins on the tonic and ends on the seventh degree (Ex. 165). Since 7 is "the third of the third chord in G major," the "repetition" (answer) begins on the root of this chord which, in this case, is the normal fifth-degree answer for the initial tonic note.

much as possible.[134] Another irregular ending is that which occurs on the seventh [Example 165].[135]

Ex. 165 Fugue Theme which Ends on the Seventh

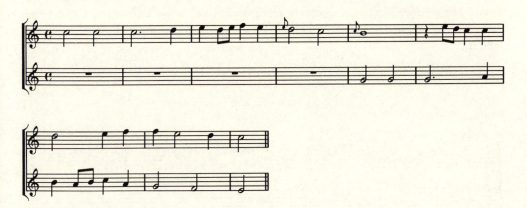

The repetition conforms to the beginning. The fugue subject begins on the root and proceeds to the third of the first chord in G major, where the repetition begins simultaneously on the root.[136] In the seventh measure [241] the last tone, A, already is adjusted according to the following conclusion in C major. To our knowledge, these are all of the types of simple and irregular fugue subjects. We have intentionally selected simple examples. They are there only to give a clear concept. In writing a fugue, it is especially important to arrive at a good first imitation or repetition of the main theme. Therefore, remember that a fugue subject which commences on the octave of its key and closes in the next-related key, returns once again to the initial key during the imitation, in the same place where the original key was changed. And this usually happens on the second or third to last note. On the other hand, a theme which begins on the fifth and proceeds to the ending tone [i.e., tonic key] is altered near the beginning of the repetition. We already have stated this rule at the beginning of this chapter, but it is not superfluous to repeat it here.

---

[134] Although the "repetition" (answer) is instituted on d''-natural, it is adjusted near the end to conclude on c''-sharp, the sixth degree of E major, the "first-related" (dominant) key. The resulting answer is an unusual subdominant-dominant hybrid. Marpurg states that if (the subject) ends on the second, fourth, or sixth of the original key, the answer will end on the second, fourth, or sixth of the dominant key unless this is made impossible by the context (*Abhandlung*, vol. I (1753), pp. 91–3, Eng. trans. in Mann, *Fugue*, p. 167). Daube could have avoided both the violation of his half-step rule and an intervallic adjustment by delaying the entrance of the next voice with a short connecting passage to a normal answer at the dominant level throughout. His reason for the complication – "the conclusion [of the subject] occurs on the third of the second chord, and therefore the repetition also must be arranged on the root of this chord" – again recalls that Daube's harmonic orientation, even in the contrapuntal realm of fugue, is essentially chordal rather than intervallic.

[135] Ex. 165: m. 1, note 1, e'' in the original.

[136] See n. 133.

Now we also want to mention a little something about the continuation of a fugue. We have spoken above of how the theme should be constituted. When the imitation is lower than the main beginning, an accompanying voice is written in the upper register, which is interrupted occasionally by rests so that the repeated theme might be clearly perceived. However, if it happens that the repetition is higher than the beginning of the fugue, the accompaniment accordingly must be written below this voice. Here it can carry on a good melody which is connected with the initial [theme], since this certainly will not be detrimental to the upper voice. We want to give a short example of both, in order to show the amateurs the accompaniment of a fugue as well [Examples 166–7].

Ex. 166 Example of a Three-Part Fugue

Ex. 166 (*cont.*)

Ex. 166 (*cont.*)

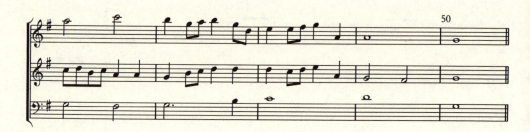

Ex. 167 Another Example of a Fugue Theme

Both examples clearly show how the second voice should be arranged for the imitation of the main theme. First [Example 166] one notices that whenever one voice continues, the other could have a short rest. One must always seek for an accompaniment to the repetition which does not impair the clarity of the main melody, especially when the accompanying voice must occur in a higher register than the repetition of the fugue subject. We see this in the continuation of the first voice [in Example 166]. When the bass enters, this voice has an accompaniment which does not impair the clarity, even though it consists of a rapid figure.[137] Then, since the second voice imitates it with other tones, the first voice sounds a slow melody in the upper register. When the bass commences the theme anew, the first voice is given another running figure which is repeated by the other two voices. The alternation of these figures is continued until the end. Shortly before the end, however, the three voices successively repeat the initial theme before it is completely presented again by the preceding voice [mm. 41, 43, and 45]. This eventual advancement

---

[137] In both the free style and the strict, Daube recommends the achievement of clarity through rests (nn. 49 and 121) and rhythmic differentiation (pp. 71–2 and 83).

of the entrances is an essential part of fugue.[138] In the second example [Example 167], the accompanying voice is arranged so that it presents, as it were, a continuation of the initial theme. The short motif in the first measure is repeated in the fifth and seventh measures, all of which certainly does not detract from the upper voice, but rather heightens [its effect].

Now at the conclusion of the repeating subject [i.e., exposition] it is not necessary to sound the same melody again immediately. Instead, one tries to combine or vary the fugue subject with other passages. If a fugue begins with mostly slow tones, rapid passages can follow, and the reverse.[139] The length of this continuation may be similar to that of the initial theme. But if the theme is short, it also can be twice as long. After this continuation [247] the fugue subject may then re-enter, specifically, in the next-related key. Here, once again, it is not necessary for the repetition to be instituted in the initial key; it can also occur at the octave or at another interval. After this, other rapid passages can be introduced again, which sometimes can be accompanied by the main theme, either in an inner voice or even in the bass. Here it may put in an appearance in various neighboring keys.[140] If the fugue is to be long, this is the [end of the first] half. Something unexpected, pleasant, or playful may certainly be incorporated into these rapid

[138] Stretto, introduced as a new concept in fugal writing by Reinken (*Kompositionsregeln* (1670, in manuscript), in Sweelinck's *Werken*, vol. X, p. 53) and its placement near the end of a fugal composition had been part of a logical tradition since 1673, when Bononcini stated that close entrances of fugal parts should be avoided at the beginning of the composition and postponed to later portions where the listener will more readily understand a complex texture of imitative voices (*Musico prattico* (1673), p. 86; see Horsley, *Fugue*, p. 164 and Mann, *Fugue*, p. 43). Fux and Mattheson also recommend employing the stretto later in a fugue, although Fux and those influenced by him often contrived a series of ever-closer strettos beginning with the second exposition (Fux, *Gradus* (1725), Ger. trans., Mizler (1742), pp. 125–6, Eng. trans. in Mann, *Fugue*, p. 83; Mattheson, *Capellmeister* (1739), vol. III, pp. 382, 388, Eng. trans., pp. 720, 728). Daube refers to this usage two paragraphs later. Many eighteenth-century stretto passages produce the effect of overlapping entries even though considerable freedom is taken with the imitation, and may, when the stretto does not involve all the voices, be accompanied by a free part. See Horsley, *Fugue*, pp. 164, 327, 333.

[139] Daube also recommends contrasting moods, styles, dynamics, articulation, and amount of dissonance between expositions and episodes. See two paragraphs later and p. 212. Also compare. n. 144. Daube's view differs from that of Kirnberger, who states that "episodic passages must always be taken from the main subject" (Sulzer, "Fuge. (Musik.)," *Allgemeine Theorie*, vol. I (1771), p. 408). Marpurg likewise finds *galant* contrasts out of place in fugue. Assuming that the subject, at least, is in the "learned" style (compare Marpurg in n. 141), he writes that "episodes should not contain . . . unusually large intervals, arpeggios . . . , extended runs, accompanimental or highly ornate and florid figures, unison or octave progressions, or melodic lines in arioso style or in the style *galant*, none of which could easily be developed in all voices by transposition or imitation" (*Abhandlung*, vol. I (1753), p. 151, Eng. trans. in Mann, *Fugue*, p. 202). Although Daube's predilection for *galant* contrast represents a minority opinion among German theorists, his opinion reflects "the fugue type cultivated in Vienna in the eighteenth [century] . . . , [which] derived from the Italian tradition, especially from the teachings of Fux," and consisted of an alternation of expositions and episodes (Horsley, *Fugue*, p. 278). Padre Martini's example for beginners contains an episode which serves partly to accomplish a modulation, but also, he says, to avoid the tedium and annoyance of continual statements of the theme (*Esemplare*, vol. II (1775), pp. xxxivff, xxxvii; see Horsley, *Fugue*, p. 269). Later Italian theorists Galeazzi (*Elementi*, vol. II (1796), pp. 232, 234) and Morigi (*Trattato* [1807], pp. 19–21), suggest the possibility of episodes between each series of entries, resulting in fugue in which, like Daube's, the entrances of the theme were relatively sparse and the sections relatively clear. (See Horsley, *Fugue*, p. 270. See also Reicha, *Composition*, vol, II (1826), pp. 222–32 and compare Kirkendale on Reicha's "*fugue phrasée*" in *Fuge*, pp. 231–3; Eng. trans., pp. 195–6.)

[140] Although Daube, like his contemporary Padre Martini, recommends different, closely related keys for each exposition, both dismiss the concept of a set fugal structure or form which was just gaining prominence in the second half of the eighteenth century (*Esemplare*, vol. II (1775), pp. xxxiv–xxxxvii and *passim*; see Mann, *Fugue*, p. 59). See also two paragraphs later.

passages. Also, a general pause may well precede the entrance of the fugue theme in the upper voice.

Now the initial theme re-enters, perhaps in the second-related key. The repetition may occur at the fifth, namely in the next-related key. A short episode (*Zwischenspiel*) of two or four measures allows the fugue theme to enter once more, either in the initial key or that of the related fifth. Here, however, one tries to arrange it so that the repetition could come sooner, especially when it is lower than the upper voice. In this case it does not matter whether the repetition is contrived at the octave, fifth, fourth, or even at another interval. If it can be advanced still further the second time without interfering with the main melody, it is all the better. Short running passages, repetitions of short motives taken from the fugue subject, and likewise the appearance of the short playful passages, etc., all may be heard again before the final cadence.

After the fugue has been formally ended, one can still properly add a beautiful cadential passage, as is customary in symphonies etc. To state each and every thing about the complete construction of a fugue would be attempting too much, and would tend to set limitations where none is possible. However, one always can say that in a fugue, the principal aim should be an equal mixture of nature and art. The ear should hear something pleasant in addition to the artificial. The melody of the fugue subject can be either lively and bright, or serious. If it is the former, the episodic passages must have something serious or pathetic about them. Or, if it is the latter, then they can be lively and bright. Ties, strong dissonances, etc. also might appear in moderation. Their number could counterbalance the consonant subjects. However, if one wants to use them frequently, one should beware of [248] placing them very close together too often. Distance is better here. When the notes of an interval such as the minor, major, and augmented second are adjacent, the effect is not as good as when they are rather far apart. The alternation of *forte* and *piano* is to be recommended in the fugue also, and likewise the staccato and legato of the tones.

At this point, for the sake of the beginners, let us write a fugue which embodies not the strict rules of the ancients, but rather the freedom of the moderns.[141] Here it is [Example 168].[142]

---

[141] A few "freedoms" taken in this example are the "lively and bright" subject, predominant treble, repeated-note motives, varied motivic development, pronounced contrast, free dissonance treatment, and free-voicing. Not all theorists were willing to admit both "serious" and "lively and bright" fugue subjects, despite the great variety of types being written. While Mattheson finds that "a natural, melodic quality . . . with its noble and singable simplicity, generally yields the best fugues" (*Capellmeister* (1739), vol. III, p. 387, Eng. trans., p. 727, and in Mann, *Fugue*, p. 162), and Kirnberger, who mentions the same qualities (Sulzer, "Führer. (Musik.)," *Allgemeine Theorie*, vol. I (1771), p. 410), also finds dance rhythms indispensable for good fugal melodies (*Recueil d'airs de danse caractéristiques*, vol. I [1777], n.p.), Marpurg maintains that "insofar as the melody is concerned, various lively figures and runs . . . have no place in the fugue proper" (*Abhandlung*, vol. I (1753), p. 28, Eng. trans. in Mann, *Fugue*, p. 162). Compare Marpurg in n. 139. Daube, of course, was less interested in "fugue proper" than in incorporating fugal imitation into *galant* chamber music.

[142] This is the only example in the chapter which is not in open score. The keyboard layout, however, is merely a space-saving device. Although free-voicing frequently was used on keyboard instruments, Daube more probably had violin double stops in mind; the orchestral idiom is suggested by his remark that "the most pleasant, singing, or playful figure, as the second figure here, may be given to the wind instruments." (See p. 212.)

Ex. 168 Example of a Fugue

Ex. 168 (*cont.*)

This fugue theme consists of three measures,[143] and from this length the entire fugue, with its different variations, has been constructed. The reason is that we have taken the figures which are found in this theme and subsequently used them for the continuation and connection of the various entrances of the fugue theme. The first measure contains two figures, which sometimes have been introduced separately. The second measure has only one figure which also is heard separately. The third measure likewise has one figure which is imitated alone here and there.[144]

Now we have analyzed this theme and so it is still necessary to point out the places where each figure has been introduced. The repetition of the initial theme occurs on the ending tone. The bass follows, because the upper voice rests to permit the melody of the initial theme to be heard distinctly. At the end of the fourth measure the upper voice comes in again and quotes the third figure in halved values. In the seventh measure the bass imitates the fourth figure, which is repeated by the upper voice. The eighth measure contains the third figure, at the end of which the bass repeats its first entrance [i.e., mm. 4–5], but this time with C-sharp. This episodic melody, or connection with the entire main theme, serves the melody as well as the harmony, since it then is imitated at once by the upper voice. Now [m. 10] the initial theme appears in the bass and is accompanied by both the first and second voices. The bass does not carry this theme all the way to the end, but rather the upper voice unexpectedly takes up the conclusion, and connects it with the repetition of the main theme [m. 13], which it does not pursue once again here, but rather goes into a short running passage, while the bass, after stepping forward with its own initial theme, proceeds very simply. Now [m. 15] the first part of the initial theme is heard again in the second voice at the fifth, that is, in D major, while the upper voice has the third figure. This first part is repeated in the bass, to the last tone of which the upper voice takes the fourth figure and combines it with the third [mm. 17–18], while the bass states the fourth figure with a slight variation.

[252] Now a deceptive cadence occurs unexpectedly [m. 20], and here the second figure is above the bass in an inner voice. This alternation of the upper voice with the bass takes place two more times, to which the inner voice finally adds the second figure [m. 23]. Then the entire [first] half of the initial theme is repeated at the octave, while the upper voice sounds the third figure and, at the end, the fourth also, which then is imitated by the bass and repeated anew in the upper voice. Now the initial theme appears in the bass [m. 26] and continues as far as the third figure. Above this is the bass entrance from

---

[143] Daube's subjects vary from two to six measures, nearly half being three measures long, an asymmetrical length usually avoided in his examples of free-style genres, Chapters 3–6. Presumably Daube thought asymmetrical phrase lengths appropriate to fugue, a genre of "our forefathers," who had not yet discovered symmetry as a principle of nature (pp. 97–8).

[144] Although of moderate length, Daube's subject suggests the *andamento* of Padre Martini, which incorporated several musical ideas (*Esemplare*, vol. II (1775), pp. viii–x; see Horsley, *Fugue*, p. 136). See n. 119. Although he also recommends contrasting episodes (see n. 139), Daube evidently considers motivic development an important "freedom of the moderns" (p. 208), by which "one can lengthen a fugue at will" (p. 212). This procedure suggests Marpurg's "strict fugue," with all thematic material derived from the subject and its counterpoints, as opposed to "free fugue," which may include other thematic material (*Abhandlung*, vol. I (1753), pp. 19–20, Eng. trans., in Mann, *Fugue*, p. 156; Kollmann makes the same distinction (Essay (1799), p. 27). Ex. 168: figure 3 in m. 1, beat 4 in original.

the fourth measure which leads to the repetition of the initial theme presented by the two voices in succession [mm. 27–9]. Finally these two voices are brought together on the second figure, and proceed to the cadence [m. 32] which, however, is not done formally either, since B appears instead of G.[145] Here the first two figures re-enter in the high bass, while the upper voice sounds the third figure twice in succession, [a repetition] which occurs in the bass voice as well. After that, the melody moves quickly to the formal cadence and concludes.

We have analyzed and gone through this entire fugue so that the amateur might see that all the variations, combinations, and the entire continuation of the two voices consist merely of figures from the initial theme. Only brevity has prevented us from pointing out even more. Also, the chords remain in order, and a few retardations have been introduced here and there because they are appropriate to fugue.

Thus, a theme which contains different figures is especially important in the construction of such a fugue. Now when these figures are introduced separately, as here, and each one is worked out, transposed, and extended (for which a few slight variations can also be helpful occasionally), one can lengthen a fugue at will. The serious figure is sometimes given to the bass while the upper voice sounds many running passages, which then can be extended further if the bass allows the serious figure to appear successively in different keys. The most pleasant, singing, or playful figure, as the second figure here, may be given to the wind instruments.[146] If there is yet another figure which is suitable for concerting, as the second and fourth figures here, they can be distributed through all the voices and be presented in a concerting manner. From this one sees that a single [253] very short melody is all that would be required to construct a very long piece, and yet there can be enough variations of the melody. Our forefathers could hardly have been acquainted with this method of analysis, for otherwise they would not have made such an effort to lengthen a piece by means of double counterpoint and the canonic art, in which they gave so much instruction.

Nevertheless, there are also initial themes comprised of only one figure. These either are to be avoided, or else other figures must be added when it is worked out. In any event, at the end of the initial fugue theme it is always better if an episodic figure is heard which, depending on the nature of the initial melody, has something about it that is pleasant, melodious, and gratifying to the ear. This same episodic figure may also be introduced in the middle and before the conclusion. This is no small resource in making a serious fugue theme sound well.[147]

We are pleased [to think that] the art of the simple fugue might now be sufficiently revealed. The art of the ancients still can be used today, provided only that it is combined with the current taste, and that every detail is arranged in just the right place.

Fugal movements can very well be introduced in the church, and also in the theater, whenever there is an opportunity. Choruses, arias for two or three voices, yes, even the

---

[145] See n. 35.
[146] For Daube's discussion of the use of wind instruments, see Chapter 6.
[147] See n. 139.

text itself can provide the best opportunity.[148] However, the initial theme must not be heard constantly, but rather should be intermingled with intervening secondary figures, so as to give the fugue a good melodic continuity, all of which we have said clearly here. Whatever may still be lacking will be acquired through a little practice.

II

DOUBLE COUNTERPOINT

This type of composition also originated during the time when harmony, due to the deficiency of melody, was still held in the greatest esteem. Every effort was made to extend the melodic line, which often was composed of barely two or three measures, [254] and, because the continuation of the melody was lacking, the extension was supposed to be accomplished by means of art.[149] From this, therefore, have sprung canons, fugues, and counterpoint. Double counterpoint is based on the following principle: two different themes are arranged so that either of them could be the upper voice while the other supplies the second voice.[150] But since the first voice is usually higher than the second, it must sound its melody an octave lower when the latter becomes the first voice, or else the second voice must perform its melody an octave higher. If this two-part melodic phrase is four measures long, it is also eight measures long, as soon as the four measures of the second voice are added onto the upper voice. And if these eight measures then are inverted, so that one time the four measures of the upper voice, and the next time the four measures of the second voice, are heard an octave above or below in this same setting, the result is a length of sixteen measures. If this passage is introduced again in neighboring keys, one can very easily hear a piece of thirty-two measures. An example will clarify this [Example 169].

Ex. 169 Example of Double Counterpoint

---

[148] Daube therefore finds fugal movements appropriate for all three functional styles. He elaborates on the importance of a text on pp. 266.

[149] i.e., the voices of the harmonic texture were securely related by the art of double counterpoint, which extended a short segment of upper-line melody with the lower line which had accompanied it. See the following paragraph and pp. 227–8.

[150] Daube defers triple and quadruple counterpoint until Chapter 12, where he discusses triple and quadruple fugue.

Ex. 169 (*cont.*)

One sees that since this four-measure theme is chosen in this way, another equally short melody could serve as the accompaniment for it, and sometimes even be used in place of the upper voice. If the continuation were linked with short episodic melodies as well, an entire piece, which might even serve a different purpose, could be formed. If one wanted to write a formal double fugue, one must carefully ascertain that the two themes are strikingly differentiated, but nevertheless can be heard either in succession or simultaneously. The reason for their difference is that the listener should be able to recognize each theme easily and to distinguish one from the other. The same must be true of the figures of which the themes are composed, and they should be capable of all kinds of inversions.

In this example we see that different intervals also arise through the inversion of the voices. We already have said in our thorough-bass method that thirds become sixths when inverted, and these in turn become thirds. One finds this shown separately here.[151]

[151] The inversion table is a standard tool of contrapuntal instruction.

Example of the Inversion of Intervals
in Counterpoint at the Octave
1.   2.   3.   4.   5.   6.   7.   8.
8.   7.   6.   5.   4.   3.   2.   1.

Here one finds that from the inversion of the unison, the octave results; from the second, the seventh; from the third, the sixth, etc. One sees that the consonant intervals remain consonant in the inversion also, lest one would exclude the perfect fourth, which nevertheless results from the inversion of the perfect fifth.[152] The same is to be understood of the dissonant intervals also. This is the basis of the rule that the quality of every subject can be tested by inverting it so that the upper voice becomes the bass and the [257] bass becomes the upper voice. If the inversion is also good, that is to say the two voices harmonize well, and the dissonances are properly resolved, the subject is well founded. But since the fourth does become a fifth when inverted, one must be careful not to write two perfect fourths in succession.

Double counterpoint is divided into three different classes. The first consists of double counterpoint at the octave, of which we have spoken already. It is called this because its melody may never exceed the boundaries of an octave, provided that each voice is to be heard clearly, and is intended to become an upper voice.[153] If one melody ascends more than an octave [above the lower voice], it will still be above the other voice when the voices change places, because it over-stepped the octave, as [in Example 170].

Ex. 170

Inversion

The melody begins on G, but in the second measure goes to the tenth, B, a high [pitch] which crosses above the melody of the first voice in the inversion, making it unclear. Therefore this is to be avoided.

Double counterpoint at the tenth belongs to the second class, in which one voice may be set a third below the octave in the inversion.

The third class contains double counterpoint at the twelfth, that is to say, the one voice can be written a fifth below the octave in the inversion. The ancients have even more types which, however, have gone completely out of fashion.

All three motions are to be used here, but especially oblique motion, which is prominently employed in all three types of counterpoint, because one melody must consist of

<hr>

[152] Here Daube, remaining practical, sidesteps a hotly debated theoretical issue – that of the consonant or dissonant quality of the fourth.

[153] For further definition see p. 213.

long notes and the other of rapid notes, so that each melody becomes distinct and recognizable. These two different melodies also may not enter at the same time, but rather the slow subject usually must precede [Example 171].[154] It is also good if the [258] two voices are close together before the inversion, because in the subsequent inversion they will move far enough from each other.

Ex. 171 Example of a Counterpoint at the Octave

The two melodies proceed close together, and nevertheless their intervals become widely separated by means of the inversion. It also happens, especially in fugues etc., that double counterpoint is contrived with the bass and an upper voice, in the course of which a cadence sometimes may result which could not very well take place in the inversion. In this case [the solution] depends upon the arrangement of the melody. However, if three voices are available, the cadential passage (*Klausel*) may be given to the voice which has only the accompaniment [Example 172].[155]

Ex. 172 Three-Part Counterpoint at the Octave

[154] Similar advice pertaining to the diversification of rhythmic values, melodies, entrances, and lengths of motives or subjects occurs in almost all eighteenth-century contrapuntal treatises. But because of Fux's long reign as Kapellmeister in Vienna (1704–41) – even despite the wide influence of his *Gradus* (1725) – the species-related contrast of a slow subject with a faster, even-note countersubject might be regarded as a particularly Viennese tradition.

[155] A free, auxiliary voice, by permitting a mitigation of certain rules, allows more freedom of melodic action compatible with the *galant* style, as in Ex. 192. Marpurg and Kirnberger point out that the rules of unaccompanied double counterpoint do not need to be applied as stringently to works involving one or more auxiliary voices which can fill in open intervals or serve as a foundational bass line. Marpurg states that much that is forbidden by his six basic rules may take place when auxiliary voices (*Nebenstimmen*) are present (*Abhandlung*, vol. I (1753), p. 164). Kirnberger likewise specifies that many of the intervallic progressions prohibited in two-part invertible counterpoint would be acceptable in three-part writing, especially if a free underlying voice (*Grundstimme*) were added. Similarly double counterpoint at the octave between the inner voices of a four-part score would require only the avoidance of parallel fourths and fifths, as in Daube's instruction (*Kunst*, vol. II/2 (1777), pp. 12, 70).

Ex. 172 (*cont.*)

[260] Here the upper voice and the bass are in double counterpoint. The latter, which begins, has long tones. In the sixth measure it has the melody of the upper voice, which takes over the bass melody. The [upper] voice sounds the cadence in measure five. In the [tenth and] twelfth measure[s] one likewise finds this cadence in the [bass],[156] until finally the formal close is made through the proper cadence. The various alternations of sharp, flat, and natural signs in the first voice have been contrived for the purpose of showing that even melodies involving accidentals can be introduced in double counterpoint.

Counterpoint at the octave is still frequently used, especially in the church style. It makes a good impression when it occurs in vocal pieces such as choruses and duets etc., where one voice sounds plain, long tones against the other voice.[157] If it should appear in instrumental pieces and sometimes occur in the bass, the violoncello or bassoon is suitable

---

[156] "upper voice" in the original; "middle voice" in preceding sentence. Another interpretation: "The bass . . . measure five. In the [tenth] measure . . . upper voice."

[157] "Long tones" in this context suggests the traditional cantus firmus and the conservative church style. See the second paragraph down, pp. 168, 220, 227 and n. 13.

for playing it, but not the double bass because the tones of the low register are not expressed clearly enough, especially when there are many rapid intervals.[158] The ear is the best judge of these matters. However, a master who understands instruments can disregard this observation, particularly if he also is gifted with good judgement.

These few examples, and the comments made about them, will be sufficient for an amateur to arrive at a clear idea of this type of composition.

Double counterpoint at the tenth will be discussed next. This species can also be used in church pieces. This counterpoint has the peculiarity that, in the construction of two voices, another part arises simply by transposing down a third. This is done in two ways. When the rapid [subject], or countersubject, is transposed down a tenth, both of these voices can still harmonize with the slow theme. When the slow subject is [originally] placed an octave lower, and then rewritten a tenth higher, both of these voices can harmonize with the countermelody, which either is left in the high register, or likewise transposed down an octave.

However, in the original construction of two voices, or of the subject and countersubject, two thirds or sixths may not be written consecutively, since they would become two octaves and fifths in the subsequent transposition of a tenth.

[261] Indication of How the Intervals are Changed
in Counterpoint at the Tenth

1.	2.	3.	4.	5.	6.	7.	8.	9.	10.
10.	9.	8.	7.	6.	5.	4.	3.	2.	1.

From these numbers one sees that the fifths become sixths, and that these in turn become fifths. The method of inventing this type is similar to the preceding. One seeks a melody which does not commence right at the beginning of the measure. Then one rewrites every tone an octave and a third lower. After this, one constructs a slow melodic line which harmonizes with both voices.[159] This forms the basis. Thus, from this instruction and the accompanying examples, one will also understand why we do not set this down in two parts.[160] It is done in this way only so that one can immediately see how the slow subject harmonizes with both versions of the rapid subject, without needing to know the rules of the ancients [Example 173].[161]

---

[158] Daube intends for invertible counterpoint to be clearly audible and to be used both in *galant* instrumental music and vocal church music. See nn. 159, 168, 171, and 172.

[159] Daube's composition of the more rapid countersubject in advance of the slower, plainer subject is a fairly radical departure from a tradition that originated with the *organa* of the thirteenth century and had recently been reinforced by Fux's species counterpoint method, *Gradus* (1725), Ger. trans., Mizler (1742). Daube's procedure, made possible in part by his simplified, predictable chordal progressions, allows greater freedom in composing the figurated countersubjects, thus making double counterpoint more attractive to those of *galant* taste. Compare pp. 221, 222, and 224.

[160] The following three-part layout is another standard tool of contrapuntal instruction. See n. 151.

[161] Daube consistently equates rules with "the ancients," freedom (the free style) with "the moderns," but feels that his contemporaries can benefit from older techniques by applying them in a modified, freer manner. In Ex. 173, the lowest voice has a bass clef in the original.

Ex. 173 Example of Counterpoint at the Tenth

The slow theme commences at the unison, but may also begin at the octave. If these three voices are examined, one discovers that contrary motion makes this counterpoint possible, since it is based on nothing but perfect chords, and therefore could probably very seldom be good without contrary motion. Of course, all three voices harmonize with one another even though no key is observed, but if one desires this to be done correctly, then one must modify the beginning at least slightly here, namely, by giving the third voice C instead of A.[162]

If one wants to set the slow theme in the bass and put the rapid countersubject above it at the tenth [see Example 174].

Ex. 174

[162] See n. 165.

Ex. 174 (*cont.*)

Here the construction of the upper voice will immediately be obvious to everyone, because it is merely the result of transposition. Both voices harmonize with the bass. The accompanying example demonstrates that bound tones can also be introduced in it [Example 175].

Ex. 175

Transposed to the tenth

From these examples the amateur already will have observed that this type of composition consists of nothing but two voices proceeding in thirds with each other, plus a slowly moving middle voice. These three voices subsequently might be transposed again, so that the slow voice is also placed a tenth lower or likewise transposed a third higher.

This counterpoint can very conveniently give rise to the foregoing type, at the octave, if the voice which has been transposed a tenth [264] is omitted. But counterpoint at the twelfth can be formed even better from it, if the voice which is set a tenth below is written down another third.[163]

Although this type demands no small judgement if it is to be introduced tastefully into a church piece or elsewhere, it is very easy to construct according to these instruc-

---

[163] The conversion of one type of invertible counterpoint to another by moving one of the lines the interval of a third, and the amplification of lines by parallel thirds or sixths permit harmonic diversity within a unified plan. These procedures were facilitated by the system of movable C clefs. As Fux stated, counterpoint at the twelfth "can be read variously in two, three, or even four parts" (Fux, *Gradus* (1725), Ger. trans., Mizler (1742), p. 149, Eng. trans. in Mann, *Fugue* p. 123). Other eighteenth-century theorists who deal with these techniques include Marpurg (*Abhandlung*, vol. I (1753), pp. 181–2, vol. II (1754), pp. 45–51) and Kirnberger (*Kunst*, vol. II/2 (1777), p. 132).

tions. If one examines this counterpoint minutely, one will find that, in essence, it is a succession of fifths, which is also true of the following species. But opposite or contrary motion makes the composition good. Although dissonances can also appear during contrary motion, they must be regarded merely as passing tones. When oblique or opposite motion is used, dissonances can result on the down beat of the measure, at least under the preceding condition. In adding and inventing the slow subject to the countersubject, one must make certain that it has an alternation of sixths, octaves, thirds, and fifths with the countersubject, especially on the first and third quarters of the measure.

We mentioned a short time ago that this type of counterpoint is based on a succession of fifths. To demonstrate this we want to cite another example, so that the amateur might be able to combine theory with practice in his study [Example 176].[164]

Ex. 176

One observes that the third voice amounts to nothing but the first voice written down a third and in the lower register. In the first measure the second and upper voices are a fifth apart. The second measure begins with a third; the third measure with an octave; the fourth measure again with an octave. At the beginning of the fifth measure one finds a fifth; in the sixth measure an octave; in the seventh measure a third. This is followed in the eighth measure by another octave and then another one in the ninth measure. The penultimate measure has a fifth which moves, in the last measure, to a third and then to the concluding octave. Now [Example 177] the third voice is rewritten an octave higher in the position of the first voice, and then transposed anew to a third below the

[164] Ex. 176: m. 5, second voice, *e'* in the original (noted in *Druckfehler*).

octave, namely to the tenth below. Now two voices have originated through the transposition of the first voice. The middle voice, or the slowly moving subject, remains unchanged here.

Ex. 177 With the Third Voice Rewritten in the First Voice

This at the tenth below

[267] Here, therefore, the slow subject again must harmonize with all three transpositions of the countersubject. As was said, the latter is first set down a tenth, but in this example this [transposition] is likewise placed an octave higher, and the transposition to the tenth below has been undertaken anew from here. If one takes these three transpositions together, they constitute a succession of perfect fifths. This might also disclose how such a counterpoint might be easily imitated. For example, one invents a melody, transposes it a fifth lower, and then writes both voices on one staff. To these two voices, which are a fifth apart, one writes a slow melody which, as the third voice, harmonizes with both. Afterward one writes this piece in the usual two voices as it is written out here, that is to say, these three voices are never heard, but rather only two of them, unless one still wanted to add a third voice which, however, must certainly not come into existence by means of transposition.

The third species of double counterpoint is counterpoint at the twelfth. The range of this type is the largest, because the two melodies encompass twelve steps. All dissonances and ties can be introduced in this kind of counterpoint. Only the fifth and the twelfth must not appear often, especially with so few voices, because their inversion results in the unison and the octave. Sixths should usually be tied; their inversion results in sevenths. The accompanying table shows how each interval changes when it is inverted.

12. 11. 10. 9. 8. 7. 6. 5. 4. 3. 2. 1.
1. 2. 3. 4. 5. 6. 7. 8. 9. 10. 11. 12.

Here one sees that the twelfth becomes an octave, the eleventh becomes a second, the tenth becomes a third, and so on.

Learning this kind of counterpoint is similar to learning the preceding kind. One writes down a melody, then transposes it a twelfth higher or lower, and, if it is workable, writes it on a staff. Next one constructs a slow melody that harmonizes with both voices, and then the counterpoint is finished. Both subjects, as was said, can be transposed an octave higher or lower. In short, both must be suitable to become the first or second voice through transposition [Example 178].

Ex. 178 Example of a Fugue Theme for Counterpoint at the Twelfth

If counterpoint at the twelfth is to be constructed from this bass melody, one must set it a fifth above the octave in the first voice, as [in Example 179].

Ex. 179 Transposed Up a Twelfth

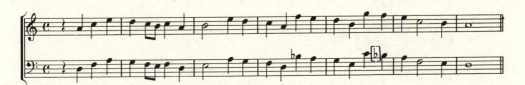

A slow melody is arranged between these two voices so that it harmonizes with both [Examples 180–81]. The three voices, that is, the slow and fast subjects, are usually written in score, although, as with the previous ones, only two parts are needed.

Ex. 180 At the Twelfth

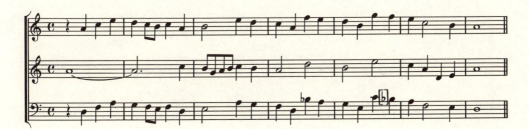

Ex. 181 In Another Way

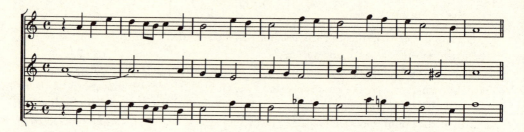

[270] Here everyone perceives of what this science consists. Even one who knows only the simple harmony of the common chords, can easily succeed in this otherwise artificial type of composition if he transposes the rapid subject in this way, and then constructs a slow melody that harmonizes with these two voices. By doing this one immediately discovers whether these three voices harmonize with each other and where they are resolved correctly. Here, however, as was said, the intention is not for these three voices to be constantly together like that, or to be playable.

The slow subject, too, can now be transposed to the twelfth [Example 182].

Ex. 182 Another Way

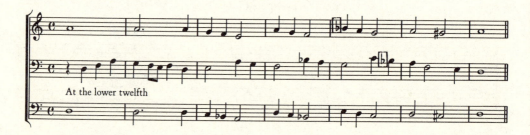

At the lower twelfth

Now the first voice, or the slow theme, can also be set an octave lower in the bass and again transposed up a twelfth into the upper voice, as [in Example 183].

Ex. 183 Yet Another Way

Here the rapid theme, first written a twelfth higher, has been set in the middle voice. If one wanted to place the rapid theme, originally set in the bass, one or two octaves higher in the upper voice, and then write it once more a twelfth lower [see Example 184].

Ex. 184 Another Way

This double counterpoint has been expressed in three voices throughout, so that it can be examined better, although, strictly speaking, it really exists in only two voices. The transposed voice is there only in order to indicate that one voice could sometimes be combined with the other theme in both its original and transposed versions. However, if one did want to sound three voices simultaneously, this might be done in the manner of double counterpoint at the tenth, [272] but in doing so, one or the other tone must be altered, or else the key would suffer.[165] Let us also present an example, prepared in this way, as explained. [Example 185.]

Ex. 185 The Foregoing Fugue Subject in Counterpoint at the Tenth

Transposed to the tenth

The harmony of this three-part example is still somewhat deficient. If one wanted to improve this, it might possibly be done in the following manner. [Example 186].

[165] Since double counterpoint at the tenth is based on oblique and contrary motion and perfect chords, all three voices may be sounded together. This practice, like conversion and amplification (see n. 163), touches on the modal connections of invertible counterpoint, since the inversion of two voices at an interval other than the octave often creates the effect of side-slipping to a different range and tonal center. (C major could sound more like A aeolian when the upper voice is transposed down a tenth.) Daube shows how to "correct" this situation in the following pair of examples. His "improvements" consist mainly of transforming the modal setting into a tonal idiom by means of "elevating" accidentals which strengthen the sense of key. Compare n. 167. Compare Kirnberger, *Kunst* vol. II/2 (1777), p. 73.

Ex. 186

From this multiple transposition of a single example one clearly sees how many modifications of harmony and melody are to be derived from one counterpoint. If the inversion of a subject and its countersubject are added, twice as many permutations can be drawn from it.[166]

To those who are completely unacquainted with the word[s] "melodic inversion", let us say that it occurs when the ascending steps and leaps which appear in the melody are repeated, inverted in such a way that the ascending intervals become descending intervals, and the reverse. To demonstrate, an upward leap of a fourth, fifth, etc. [274] subsequently occurs in the inversion as a downward leap of a fourth, fifth, etc. The note values remain the same. This inversion may be done in a different way, depending upon whether the intervals are close together or far apart. The preceding example, with the retention of the close intervals and the key, nevertheless offers one a choice of three different inversions [Example 187a–d]. Each type consists of contrary motion. But we must say that none of the three is inverted as strictly as possible. The retention of the key is responsible for this.[167]

Ex. 187

(a) The Previous Example

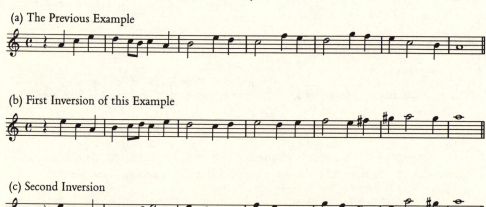

(b) First Inversion of this Example

(c) Second Inversion

---

[166] See pp. 227–8 and nn. 87 and 172.

[167] Free, tonal melodic inversion. Daube's modern, harmonic emphasis on preserving "the close intervals and the key" differs from the traditional intervallic approach of Fux: "occasionally, for a better melodic line, one uses a consonance not properly belonging to the triad . . ." (*Gradus* (1725), Ger. trans., Mizler (1742), p. 87, Eng. trans. in Mann, *Counterpoint*, p. 72).

Ex. 187 (cont.)

(d) Third Inversion

These three inversions, combined with the modified countersubject, make up the following double counterpoint [Examples 188–90].

Ex. 188 Inversion of the Melody of the Preceding Example with the Slow Countersubject

A twelfth lower

Ex. 189 Second Type of Inversion

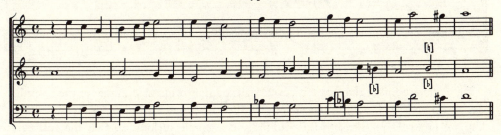

Ex. 190 Third Kind of Inversion

These many diverse modifications of a short melody were frequently of great benefit to the ancients. By means of them, every subject could be greatly changed, which was very useful in the church style. Therefore, if one also considered the additional possibility of rewriting such a short melody, now in double counterpoint at the octave, now at the tenth, and then at the twelfth, an initial melody of several measures could certainly be extended for as long as one might ever wish. And this was accomplished by art!

It is known that in former times the art of double counterpoint in general was the most important [technique] in all of composition. This could still be true, even if the melody were combined with art in such a way that the former reigned and the latter served.[168] In the future we will show what can be done with the melody itself by means of this same art. This will prove to be of great importance.

The counterpoint at the twelfth discussed here should rightly have been discussed first, since it can accommodate ties in a good melody. If one has practiced this kind, he also will be able to employ such a melody at the tenth, indeed, even at the octave. A short time ago, with the theme set in three voices, we have shown how it would apply at the tenth. On that page, 222, we are further reminded that the third voice should be heard an octave lower. The following example shows how to set the same melody at the octave [Example 191].

Ex. 191 Counterpoint at the Octave

This counterpoint at the octave is correct, although it originated in that at the twelfth. We intentionally chose only one melody and led it through all of these modifications. Also we preferred to take an easy example and a simple melody, so that the amateurs could grasp it more quickly. We hope to have explained the theory of counterpoint so that everyone who has only a moderate insight into composition might be able to understand it and profit by it. In any case, a little practice is of great value and will clarify whatever may still seem partly obscure.

By means of this resource a composer can introduce a most agreeable variety into arias, symphonies, etc. And in all large pieces [279] counterpoint may be prevalent in one or two melodic motives. These must not be long, however, so that the freedom of

---

[168] Daube proposes that double counterpoint, like canon, might be adapted to the modern, homophonic idiom by letting one main melody predominate, in contrast to the practice of "the ancients," who usually constructed two or more voices of nearly equal importance. Kirnberger says that even the two concerting parts of a duet must be invertible, so that the first voice, after presenting the main melody (*Hauptgesang*), can take the role of the accompanying voice (*begleitende Stimme*) (Sulzer, "Contrapunkt. (Musik.)," *Allgemeine Theorie*, vol. I (1771), p. 229). See Kirnberger in n. 171. Thus, although invertible counterpoint is "the most frequently used contrapuntal device" in the later eighteenth century, "the secondary parts are so simple that one simply does not think of it as being contrapuntal . . ." (Horsley in Kollmann, *Essay* (1799), p. xxix).

melody and harmony might always have supremacy. Even in magnificent, brilliant passages, double counterpoint at the octave can be introduced, and obtain a good effect [Example 192].[169]

Ex. 192

[169] As with canon (see n. 103), Daube suggests that short passages of "learned"-style double counterpoint interspersed in the prevailing style might provide the stylistic variety of rapidly alternating affects so congenial to the *galant* spirit.

Ex. 192 (cont.)

[182] The first four measures are actually carrying on double counterpoint at the octave. The melody of the upper voice is arranged so that the separate bass melody also harmonizes with it and subsequently, at the end of the first four measures, may move up into the upper voice while the initial melody of the upper voice may come down into the bass. The rapid movement of the inner voices produces an active harmony. At the end of this example [mm. 14–15] the two upper voices again have a short double counterpoint which occurs here as an episodic motif for a change from the brilliant and rushing styles. In this way double counterpoint can be used, and can show forth art and beauty. Even the very slow main subject can be employed if it is played by wind instruments.[170] A judgement built upon theory and practice can make use of everything, however insignificant it may appear to many people.[171] The alternation of the octave and third, and similarly of

---

[170] Compare Daube's use of sustained wind tones in Chapter 6, *passim*.

[171] Frequent defenses of double counterpoint and fugue in theoretical treatises suggest numerous critics, especially among dilettantes unaware of the contribution of these techniques to *galant* music. Quantz considers counterpoint at the octave essential for a beginning composer, because it is used in both artificial and *galant* pieces (*Versuch*, (1752), p. 12, Eng. trans., pp. 22–3). Kirnberger says that double counterpoint is indispensable to free-style compositions which involve concerting voices – from duets and trios to symphonies and concertos. (See n. 168.) As examples he cites works of Handel and K. H. Graun (Sulzer, "Contrapunkt. (Musik.)," *Allgemeine Theorie*, vol. I (1771), p. 230),

the third and the fifth, so common with the ancients, is presently used only by those who are acquainted with the variable effect of harmony.[172]

I2

DOUBLE FUGUE

This discussion is closely related to the preceding one. Here we will speak of the process of constructing a fugue according to the various double counterpoints, something which our forefathers held in great esteem. Experienced and skillful composers still value these pieces highly, because the greatest art of composition still rests in them.[173]

The double-fugue subject accordingly consists of two different melodies arranged so that they can constantly change places with one another throughout a piece.[174] The upper voice may sometimes be written an octave lower, and the lower voice, or the bass, an octave higher, in place of the upper voice. By means of this inversion, the two melodies are connected and joined together so that the ear always hears only one melody with regard to the upper voice.[175]

[283] Double fugues are divided into various types. One of them has much in common with the simple fugue. The only difference is that the countermelody which is written at the entrance of the second voice might also be inverted with it, or transposed down an octave. Subsequently, at one or another entrance of the initial melody, it may reappear, either above or below.[176]

---

composers whose works Daube admired and studied (*Beweis* (1782), p. 22 and *Erfindung* (1797/98), preface). Kirnberger claims that counterpoint and canon are criticized only by those who never had enough opportunity, ability, or patience to master them (*Kunst*, vol. II/3 (1779), p. 17), and states that counterpoint and compositional "purity," rather than detracting from beauty and expressiveness, are essential to those ends (ibid. vol. II/1 (1776), pp. 3–4, Eng. trans., pp. 283–4). Marpurg dedicates his *Abhandlung* (1753–4) to Telemann, whom he praises for proving that the *galant* style can be united with contrapuntal features, and insists that even composers of tasteful *galant* works must have a sound basis in double counterpoint (n.p.). For use of fugue in this era see Kirkendale, *Fuge, passim.*

[172] While Daube sees melodic extension as a primary advantage of double counterpoint in the works of the "ancients," he finds that even present-day compositions can benefit from the "many variations of harmony and melody . . . derived from one counterpoint." (See n. 186.) Other theorists also express an appreciation for the harmonic variety inherent in invertible counterpoint. Fux, for instance, explains that "the function of double counterpoint is to produce a different harmonic sound through inversion" (*Gradus* (1725) Ger. trans., Mizler (1742), p. 140, Eng. trans. in Mann, *Fugue*, p. 107). Compare Marpurg, *Abhandlung*, vol. I (1753), p. 169.

[173] See n. 171.

[174] Thus double-fugue subjects are in double counterpoint, just as the triple and quadruple fugues discussed later make use of triple and quadruple counterpoint respectively.

[175] Daube's emphasis on the continuity of a compound upper voice shows his homophonic orientation. Compare pp. 186, and 255–6.

[176] i.e., the invertible countersubject first enters with the answer, rather than with the subject. See n. 177. Compare Kollmann, *Essay* (1799), p. 49.

Ex. 193 Example of a Double Fugue Theme

[mm. 11–12, the lower voice is tied in the original]

Here [in Example 193] the opening of the fugue occurs in the usual manner. Not until the seventh measure [cf. m. 10] does one find the double counterpoint. There the second voice introduces a new melody, which is immediately taken up by the upper voice, whereby the inversion results, since the melody of the upper voice is now placed in the lower voice. This type can also be classified as simple fugue, whenever the simple fugue is intended to be [284] artificial.[177] In addition, there is the type in which the repetition [i.e., answer] enters in the middle of the initial melody etc., for which oblique motion serves admirably.[178]

---

[177] Kirnberger states that the double-fugue subject may first appear with the answer as a continuation of the leading voice, or may enter with the subject, as in Daube's "double fugue proper," (p. 233), or immediately after the subject (Sulzer, "Gegensatz. Contrasubject. (Musik.)," *Allgemeine Theorie*, vol. I (1771), pp. 443–4). Daube's and Kirnberger's remarks reflect ambivalence in classifying this most widely written type of fugue. Because it began with only one voice, it was not considered a true double fugue, but was scarcely differentiated from simple fugue, despite its invertible countersubject. Meanwhile there was a growing assumption that simple fugue would include an invertible countersubject introduced with the answer, as in Padre Martini's *Esemplare*, vol. II (1775), *passim*. Daube's statement that this type "can be classified also as [artificial] simple fugue" suggests an awareness of both definitions.

[178] Also compare Kollmann: "The Counterpoint may make its first appearance, either with the Principal Subject; or as a short transitory passage between it and the first Answer; or with the first Answer" (*Essay* (1799), p. 50).

Ex. 194 Another Example

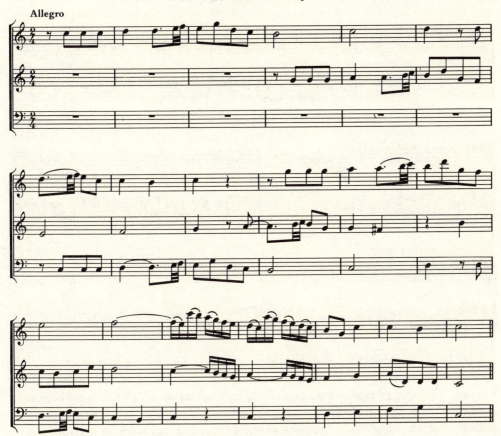

[In Example 194] the second voice begins before the first voice ends. The initial theme is arranged for this, however, so that long tones are being heard at the entrance of the second voice. The bass begins in the same way, except that the first voice again sounds a different motif with it. The peculiarity of this type is that all three voices are present before the end of the main theme, which is first concluded in the eighth measure by a cadence into the commencement of the following measure. This species of double fugue is artificial, and can also be made beautiful by means of a good melody.[179] We now turn to double fugue proper. Here two different melodies appear in quick succession at the beginning and alternate with one another in the manner described above, thus hastening toward the end amidst all sorts of entries, variations, etc.[180] A short time ago we stated that, for the sake of clarity, one melody should contain more slow than rapid intervals.[181]

[179] The belief that melody should retain a high priority in the strict style is consistent with Daube's *galant* aesthetic, in which melody was equated with nature. See n. 175 and pp. 156, 157, and 243.

[180] This type generally was accepted as double fugue. For "all sorts of entries, variation, etc.," see p. 240. Compare n. 172.

[181] Compare pp. 215–16. Daube repeatedly emphasizes clarity, as if persuading his readers that this *galant* objective is possible in double fugue. See n. 171. Differences in rhythm, time of entry, length, and instrumentation of subjects also are recommended. See n. 154 and pp. 244, 247, 249, 251, 254.

Ex. 195 Example of a Double Fugue with Two Subjects or Two Diverse Melodies

Here [in Example 195] the slow melody commences and the countersubject joins in with rapid tones at the end of the first measure. The inversion takes place in the fourth measure. The rapid passage is moved up a fifth, and the melody which was above becomes the lower voice. Both melodies go into the first-related key. Just as this example commences with the slow subject, so the next one should begin with the rapid subject [Example 196].[182]

Ex. 196 Another Example

[182] Daube considers the latter type less common. See p. 216.

Ex. 196 (*cont.*)

The main subject commences already in the second measure. The exchange occurs in the ninth measure, where the slow theme is found on top. For the conclusion of this type of double fugue, it is advisable to observe the following rules: [288]

(1) The two melodies must be invertible by means of counterpoint at the octave.

(2) Both melodies also must be capable of being transposed a third higher or lower without modulating out of the key. [183]

(3) The two voices must be able to follow one another rapidly, probably even within a single measure, which should occur especially during the continuation [of the fugue].[184]

(4) The repetition [i.e., answer] of each melody must be able to follow the corresponding subject at the fifth in such a way that the two voices harmonize well.

(5) Each main melody must be able to follow itself at the octave.[185]

(6) At least one melody, if not both, must precisely delineate the key, especially before a later entrance of the second melody.

We want to take up the first example here, and use it to try to demonstrate these rules [Example 197*a–v*].

---

[183] i.e., suitable for inversion at the tenth and twelfth.
[184] i.e., stretto involving two subjects.
[185] i.e., stretto of each subject with itself at the octave.

Ex. 197

(a)   Example According to the First Rule

(b)   Exchange of the Two Voices

Exchange

(c)   This Same Example According to the Second Rule

At the octave

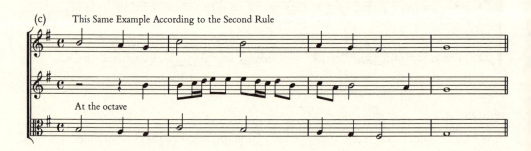

(d)   Exchange of the Two Voices, Written Down a Tenth

At the tenth

(e)   In a Different Manner

At the octave

Ex. 197a–v (*cont.*)

(f) Likewise

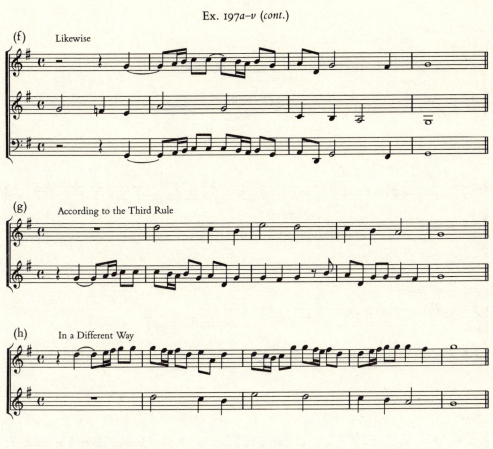

(g) According to the Third Rule

(h) In a Different Way

(i) Likewise

(j) Another Exchange of the Two Voices

(k)   According to the Fourth Rule

(l)   Another Procedure

(m)   Likewise

(n)   Yet Another Procedure

(o)   Likewise

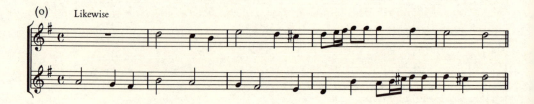

Ex. 197a–v (cont.)

Ex. 197a–v (cont.)

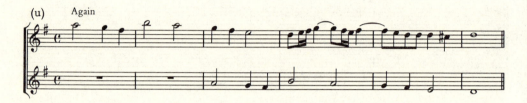

It is not necessary to give an example of the sixth rule because, in any event, the slow subject here strictly observes the key before the rapid countersubject enters. Now who should ever think that twenty-six variants could arise from one double-fugue theme, for which, moreover, no more than two keys are used? Every variant provides a different harmony for the ear. It is easy to judge, then, how long such a double fugue can last when short episodic melodies are also included as embellishments, and when, in addition, the fugue subject can be led into different keys.[186]

These six rules lend substance and beauty to the construction of all fugues. They are to be used to some extent for simple [297] fugues also. Yet we must say in this regard that not every theme is capable of yielding all of these modifications. It must be contrived especially for this [purpose]. In making the selection one should try to find a slow theme to which one could set a second voice, either a third higher or lower, without violating the key. After this, one should proceed with the countersubject in the same way. These two melodies, namely the slow and rapid themes, must also be capable of a good inver-

[186] For Daube, variety through contrapuntal manipulation is one of the main attractions of double fugue. See n. 172 and p. 263. Kirnberger also requires that the countersubject be invertible "in more than one counterpoint," in order to provide variety during each repetition of the theme (Sulzer, "Gegensatz. Contrasubject. (Musik.)," *Allgemeine Theorie*, vol. I (1771), pp. 443–4).

sion at the octave. When one has worked out such a double subject, it then is capable of all the previously shown variants. Although this has been touched upon already, we do want to go through this difficult material briefly once more.

Ex. 198

In this first attempt [Example 198a] it is not necessary to be particularly careful that the four voices, namely each theme accompanied in thirds, harmonize so perfectly. It is sufficient for each individual subject to be able to proceed in thirds or sixths. Here the entire slow subject accepts a third below [Example 198b], whereas the entire rapid subject prefers a third above. In this manner this example, as the foregoing one, can be rewritten as counterpoint at the tenth and twelfth [Examples 199–202].[187]

Ex. 199 Counterpoint at the Octave

---

[187] Ex. 200a: alto, note 1, c′ rather than a, probably a printing error, possibly to avoid interval of a seventh. These examples contain several irregularities due to the fifth at the entry of the rapid subject in Ex. 199a. Compare Ex. 201b.

Ex. 200 Counterpoint at the Tenth

(a)

(b)   Exchange of the Two Voices

Ex. 201 Counterpoint at the Twelfth

(a)

(b)   Another Way

Ex. 202 [Melodic] Inversion of the Foregoing Counterpoint at the Twelfth

(a)

(b)   [Melodic] Inversion of the Rapid Subject

[300] This double introduction may now be sufficient, although such a main article of artificial composition cannot be described too extensively. As far as the further arrangement of the middle and the end of the fugue is concerned, we will say that it certainly would be good to give some instruction for it. But to determine every entrance of the theme, to designate the keys into which modulations are made, and similarly to designate the rests, would mean, as we have said before, to impose limits on a composer's thoughts! In this way natural beauty is very often suppressed.[188] We will say only a little something about it. In two-part fugues one voice may rest for a while when the other voice has the main theme, that is, the theme with which the fugue began. In fugues in three, four, and more parts, the voice which has had the main subject at first can pause for a while to give the other voices room to sound the subject, countersubject, or repetition. It also happens that the voices come so close together that no inner voice could be [placed] between them. When the lowest voices have the theme, one, or sometimes two, of the upper voices accordingly must rest, so that the main melody would never be obscured or made unclear by the overly full texture.[189] Also, two voices can sometimes double one or another of the subjects, namely in thirds or sixths.[190]

The following concerns fugues which have three different melodies. Our forefathers were more fond of this type than we are.[191] Why? They valued art very highly and, in doing so, quite often neglected nature, or the invention and continuation of beautiful melody. The rules which perhaps were necessary to know in order to construct such a fugue consist of the following:

(1) The fifth should appear bound, or in passing.
(2) Dissonances must occur only as passing tones.
(3) The unison, third, octave, and sixth must be alternated continually, but none of these intervals may appear twice in succession.
(4) Contrary motion must be especially observed.

The ancients were even more strict about these rules, since they by no means tolerated the fifth, and used no dissonances at all. For the [301] construction of the bass to an upper voice they used nothing but thirds, octaves, and sixths, as we have already mentioned to some extent, on page 121. The third voice originated afterwards through the upward transposition of a third, of either the first voice or the bass. Also they alternated between

---

[188] Daube champions creative freedom even in strict-style genres. See pp. 186–7, 245, and 258.

[189] See n. 121.

[190] Here Daube indicates a direction taken in nineteenth-century compositions such as Mendelssohn's Prelude and Fugue I in E Minor, Op. 35 (1837) and Brahms' Variations and Fugue on a Theme by Handel, Op. 24 (1862). But while a parallel amplification perhaps contributed to the projection of the subject, it also lessened the "absolute independence of one voice from another" demanded by Marpurg (*Abhandlung*, vol. I (1753), p. 149, Eng. trans., in Mann, *Fugue*, p. 201).

[191] Multiple-subject fugues actually were studied by some dilettantes. Burney, after visiting Vienna in 1772, wrote that, "M. Gasman, *maestro di capella del corte, imperiale* . . . surprised me much by the number of fugues, and chorusses, which he shewed me of a very learned and singular construction, and which he had made as exercises and studies. Some of them were composed . . . upon two or three different *subjects*; and several of these, he said, the emperor had practised" (*Present State* (2/1775), vol. I, pp. 332–3, *Musical Tours*, ed. Scholes (1959), vol. II, p. 113).

the two voices, so that the third voice was transposed up a third, now from the one voice and then from the other. This derived voice was subsequently altered by means of sixteenth notes etc., to create a diversity among the melodies.

Ex. 203 Example of a Three-Part Subject of the Ancients

[302] Here [Example 203] the second voice originated through the transposition of the bass and the upper voice.[192] To differentiate it from the others, it then was written in eighth notes. The figures also show the origin of the second voice. Such a subject can be inverted twice. The first time, the second voice is put on top, the bass in the middle, and the former upper voice then is placed in the bass. The second time, the derived voice is set in the bass and the proper bass in the upper voice, which then is placed in the second voice. But in this case it is good if the new bass is set another fifth lower [Example 204].

Ex. 204

[303] This bass, written a twelfth lower, provides a fairly good bass voice, except that it [must] begin and end with F, and the second voice [must] commence with A. Counterpoint at the twelfth is of use here also. Notice that the movement of every voice is distinct from the other two. One likewise need not have the voices enter at the same time. If one voice commences on the downbeat, the second voice rests about an eighth or a quarter etc. in the first measure, and the third voice joins in at the end of the first measure. The voices must be of different lengths, as well. The theme which commences first

[192] Note that Ex. 203, ". . . of the Ancients," includes figured bass. Compare Ex. 215a and Ex. 221.

lasts until the other two have been concluded. The second [voice to enter] can be the shortest.[193] Yet everything will be left up to the imagination, experience, and judgement of the composer, since no strict limitations should, indeed could, be set.[194] The main consideration is that each theme should stand out clearly. It does not follow that all three melodies are heard at the beginning. One or two can appear in succession at the beginning, and the third melody added later, as if unexpectedly. This unexpected entrance can contribute to the pleasure of the listener.[195] Thus, a fugue might very well be provided with three subjects but, as was said, clarity must prevail throughout. The foregoing rules show how far we depart from the guiding principles of the ancients.

Ex. 205

This example [Example 205] contains fifths as well as passing dissonances, which formerly were serious mistakes. Counterpoint at the tenth can be very useful here. Even the bass theme may include fifths and passing dissonances without restriction. One could

[193] See nn. 154 and 181.

[194] Basically, Daube would impose his flexible regulatory procedures only to achieve the essence of fugue – imitation at the octave, fourth, or fifth; then, provided the themes are presented clearly and melodic continuity is achieved, "everything will be left up to the imagination . . . of the composer. . . ." Daube's comment recalls Beethoven's observation to Karl Holz sometime after 1817 that "it takes no great skill to write a fugue; I wrote dozens of them in my student days. But the imagination also claims its due, and in this day and age another, a really poetic element must enter into the old traditional form" (Lenz, *Beethoven*, vol. V (1860), p. 219, Eng. trans. in Kirkendale, *Fugue*, p. 134 and Thayer, *Beethoven*, vol. II, p. 389). Daube would grant the composer this "poetic license" years earlier, during a time when many theorists were attempting to codify, restrict, and preserve this "antique form," while many composers were carrying on the tradition of flexible fugal procedure from an earlier era. See n. 188.

[195] As in the free style, Daube advocates the element of surprise for the listener. In this context, however, Daube follows the custom of his italianate colleagues (see Horsley, *Fugue*, p. 355) in Stuttgart and Vienna in the initial, simultaneous presentation of the triple-fugue themes, and merely mentions the possibility of "unexpected," separate expositions later (p. 255). Reinken states that in a *contrafuga*, which he defines as a fugue with a countersubject, the themes are "not continually treated together, but also separately, one after the other, then at times together and against each other, which shows much greater mastery" (*Kompositionsregeln* (1670, in manuscript) in Sweelinck, *Werken*, vol. X, p. 54; see Mann, *Fugue*, p. 42). Compare Rameau: "All the entrances of the first fugue may be used without bringing in the other fugues. We then pass to the second, to the third, etc., mixing the preceding fugues with the new ones, although we may also introduce each fugue independently of the others and mix them only later. When we wish to have several fugues enter simultaneously, with one fugue in one part and another in another part, we must be on our guard against confusion, for one design will often overpower the other . . .' (Rameau, *Traité* (1722), p. 357, Eng. trans., p. 367). Marpurg, in addition to noting that the various fugue subjects may be treated separately, offers the reminder that the themes do not always have to be used in their entirety (*Abhandlung*, vol. I (1753), p. 131, Eng. trans. in Mann, *Fugue*, p. 191).

construct a fugue subject with three [304] different melodies, even without knowing these rules. To do so, one might perhaps consider only the inversion, in which it would very soon become evident whether there were still something to be changed here or there. This next example [Example 206][196] again differs from the above in that the first and third voices are based on counterpoint at the octave, but the second and third voices are based on counterpoint at the twelfth.

Ex. 206 Counterpoint at the Octave

The first subject is capable of being rewritten as counterpoint at the octave, because the two voices are close together.

Ex. 207 Counterpoint at the Twelfth

Ex. 208 Inversion of the Voices

A twelfth higher

---

[196] Ex. 206: the upper line is marked "2" in the original.

Here [Example 207] is the second subject which lends itself to counterpoint at the twelfth.[197] The same is also true of the third subject [Example 208]. Therefore, if one takes these three different melodies together, they can be inverted as often as desired and assume multifarious arrangements during the working out of the entire fugue [Examples 209–10]. The three simultaneous melodies will be clearly perceived by the ear, especially if different instruments are chosen for them.[198]

Ex. 209 All Three Melodies Together

Ex. 210 The Inversion

[m. 2, middle line, the *d″* is a dotted sixteenth note in the original; m. 3 had *a″* in the original]

An overly strict observation of the pertinent rules has been avoided intentionally. The entire [process of] invention, as was said, consists principally of writing a theme, and under it the very same theme transposed down a fifth. A bass which harmonizes with both voices is then written, as we have already indicated in the foregoing discussion. This bass must contain no ties, and dissonances should occur in passing. The third, octave, sixth, and unison must alternate well among one another. The transposed theme will demonstrate where the fifth may be introduced. The third melody may be arranged according to the other two. It must enter after a few rests. To expedite the invention of this third melody one selects only the beginning, then transposes the first melody down a third. These transposed tones, with a few subsequent modifications by means of doubling some tones and changing the note values etc., are easily brought to the point

[197] Ex. 207: middle line, beat 3, three eighth notes in the original.
[198] See p. 164 and n. 181.

that they can yield an entirely different melody. This is the manner in which a fugue theme with three different melodies is constructed. Just as this type consists of counterpoint at the octave and twelfth, so there is another species which contains counterpoint at the octave and the tenth. This has a considerable resemblance to the preceding type, since the third, octave, and sixth must be alternated here also, and two identical intervals may never follow in succession [Examples 211–14].

Ex. 211 First Example

Ex. 212 Second Example

Ex. 213 Third Example

Ex. 214 Fourth Example

In the first example one sees that the first and second melodies are in counterpoint at the octave. The second example already shows the inversion of these three melodies. The third melody is a tenth lower, whereas the second has been written a sixth higher (that is, the lower third raised [an octave]), but the first melody has remained in its regular position. The third example shows another inversion. The first melody has been rewritten a sixth higher and put into the second voice, whereas the second melody is a tenth lower [than it was originally], and the third has remained unchanged. In the fourth example one sees that the first melody was moved down a tenth [from the original], but the third melody was moved down only a third, while the second has been left unchanged. For the sake of those who are not yet practiced in such art pieces, we still want to repeat several things about the construction of this kind of three-part composition. One selects a short, simple melody and writes a bass for it, which contains no fifths nor dissonances, except in passing. Two thirds etc. may not occur in succession. At the same time one constantly tries to observe contrary motion. After this the melody is transposed a third higher, and from this transposition the highest or first melody must be formed. After this one discards a few of the initial tones from the first and second voices, or from the second and third voices, because not all three voices can begin at the same time [Example 215a–c].

Ex. 215

(a) The First Version with Two Voices

(b) One Voice Transposed Up a Third

(c) Omission of the Initial Tones

[310] After this preparation one tries to modify the uppermost voice. This is done by taking a tone from the second voice now and then, combining it with the first voice, and then filling the space between them with a passing tone. In this way the second melody is also somewhat changed, but here one is not concerned about a change by means of transposition up or down a third, or a combination of these, but rather one strives only to distinguish this melody a little better.[199] The bass may remain unchanged. After this adjustment, the three melodies might perhaps turn out like this [Example 216].

Ex. 216

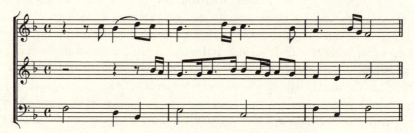

Here the first melody subsequently is made into the second voice, and the latter into the first voice. Because the second melody commences only briefly at the end of the first measure, the first melody can be modified appreciably. One will realize that the first example also began with this [melody]. After these preliminaries two different melodies can be transposed a third lower or a sixth higher at any time. We have said that contrary motion should be observed and also that the beginning of two melodies can be cut off, and the third perhaps shortened at the end. By means of this latter, more room will be made for the [other] two voices. At the end of each melody, one or two intervals may well be changed, especially in the transposition of a tenth.

The most artificial way to construct fugues consisting of three different melodies, is to derive both the others from one main melody. This is done when the second voice [to be written] introduces the intervals of the first voice in retrograde. These [311] tones, now rewritten into the second voice, must harmonize with the entrance and continuation of the first voice. The third voice [to be written], on the other hand, imitates the tones of the first voice in notes that move twice as slowly.[200] This therefore must furnish the slow motif and precisely agree with the other two melodies [Example 217].[201]

---

[199] See nn. 154 and 181.

[200] Deriving additional voices from the main subject is fairly common in late eighteenth-century fugues. Kirnberger states that countersubjects "must be taken from the main subject" (Sulzer, "Gegensatz. Contrasubject. (Musik.)," *Allgemeine Theorie*, vol. I (1771), p. 444). But such derivation – as in the episodes of "strict" fugues – generally entails motivic relationships, rather than strict canonic techniques applied to the entire theme. It would appear that Daube's particular "recipe" for the "most artificial" triple fugue is not part of traditional instruction, but represents a late eighteenth-century tendency to restrict and formalize the fugal procedure with artificial devices for intellectual satisfaction, sometimes to the point of being "gekünstelt" (i.e., overly artificial or unnatural). Marpurg uses the term "ricercare" (*recherchée*) for a strict fugue which makes extensive use of scholastic devices (*Abhandlung*, vol. I (1753), pp. 19–20; see Horsley, *Fugue*, p. 291), and although Daube insists on freedom in the continuation of a fugue, this term could be applied to the beginning of his artificial triple fugue and to some of his "fugues with four different melodies."

[201] Ex. 217: in the numbering of the melodies, "2" and "3" were reversed.

Ex. 217

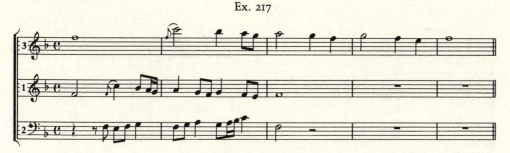

The accompaniment for the remainder of the slow melody is left to the freedom of the composer. Although this example is bad, we do believe that its construction might be difficult to imitate without the following rules:[202]

(1) A certain number of measures must be selected in advance and the middle marked off.
(2) The first half of the first measure must consist of the first chord.
(3) The last measure must contain the first chord. The middle division must likewise have one and the same chord.
(4) The first and last notes must be long so that, when the melody is written backwards, this long tone could be made short, and the remainder taken up by rests.

One writes a melody as far as the middle division, as prescribed, then constructs a harmonizing countermelody to it, and afterward adds the notes of this melody backwards onto the initial theme. Hereupon this entire melody is written backwards in the second voice and then the first two melodies are finished. The [312] third melody, as mentioned, is produced by augmentation of the note values. Because of this lengthening it happens that only half of the melody of the first voice is used [for the third voice]. If, unexpectedly, the last note of it is not represented by one of the two figures in the [proper] chord, it is changed accordingly.

This little-known fugue subject has the peculiarity that all dissonances take place in it, and also that only a single good melody needs to be contrived. The continuation of this fugue is similar to that of the other types.

Something still remains to be mentioned about fugues consisting of four different melodies. This type is not particularly different from the foregoing. For the most part, the same rules apply. There are two different species of these, in the first of which one has to observe only that the initial note must not be the fifth of the key because, in the inversion, it cannot furnish a root in the bass. We have already remarked that each melody should be differentiated from the others, partly by the earlier or later entrance, and partly by the completely dissimilar melody itself. Accordingly, one should simply write down four completely different melodies which harmonize well with one another, observing contrary motion of the voices, so that two voices could proceed in counterpoint at the octave, and the fifth would appear bound. It can also be remarked that one voice should consist of rapid tones, another of very slow tones, the third of notes intermixed with rests, and the fourth of slow and rapid tones [Examples 218–20].[203]

---

[202] Compare pp. 167–8 and 171–2.
[203] See nn. 154 and 181.

Ex. 218

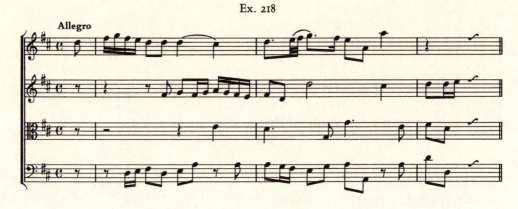

Ex. 219 First Inversion

Ex. 220 Second Exchange

[314] These two inversions will be enough to demonstrate that, even without those rules, one might be in a position to construct these fugue movements which exactly coincide in the inversion, [a technique] that, for the most part, had not yet been discovered by our forefathers.

The second type of four-part fugue is subject to many restrictions. At first a melody is written, and to this a bass voice is constructed which merely does not contain two thirds or sixths in succession, but rather, when the upper voice constitutes a third with the bass, a sixth, or an octave must follow; if a sixth precedes, a third and octave can follow. A fifth may not be tolerated here at all, except in passing. The same is to be understood of dissonances also; no bound tones may occur as dissonances. Therefore if two voices are contrived as prescribed, one can then add two more, since another voice, transposed up a third, can be written above each one, as we have said at various times before.[204] The voice which is written a third above the first voice can then very well leap to [either] the lower or higher octave [of an interval], and the voice written a third above the bass may do likewise [Examples 221–3].

Ex. 221 The First Melody

Ex. 222

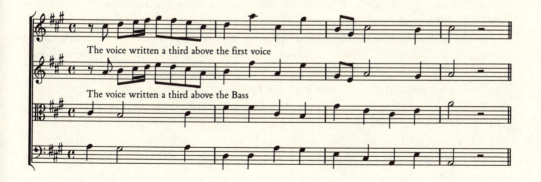

---

[204] Thus the subjects will be invertible in counterpoint at the tenth. See pp. 217–20.

Ex. 223 Cut Off and Varied

[316] From the first example it is clear how the bass should be constructed to a melody set in the second voice and that, in doing this, only the alternation of the third, octave, and sixth is taken into consideration. The second example already shows the four voices, and how the other two have originated merely from the upward transposition of a third. In the third example, however, one sees the modification of these voices. A few notes have been discarded from the beginning of the first voice, so that it now commences at the end of the first measure. In the second measure the space between the leaps has been filled with notes, and after that it has been varied only a little. The third voice also has been changed slightly. The beginning has been cut off, and the following tones have been divided and displaced with dotted rhythms. The bass, however, has remained unchanged. Clarity will inevitably result from this abridgement or abbreviation of a voice. All four different melodies are thereby made intelligible.[205] One knows now that no accompanying voices are present, but rather real melodies which are very different from one another. The ancients did not make use of this method (*Manier*). They knew little of the art of variation. Their modifications would consist of the following: when they let the first voice move along very slowly, the other had to be arranged with leaps against the first voice and the bass; the third voice was characterized by rapid tones, and the fourth would be interspersed with rests. Today, since everything in composition depends on clarity and melodiousness, and anything restless, whispering, or indistinct in the different voices is banished, there has been added the diversity of prosody, that is, the various note values, for the sole purpose of increasing the clarity.[206] The voice which commences first may not continue to the end of the other melodies, unless it is the bass which has the initial melody. The voices which have the ending, especially when there are only two of them, can be arranged in counterpoint at the octave, and may also contain dissonances.

[205] See nn. 154 and 181.
[206] Compare p. 266.

This kind of fugue might continue in the following way. At first one should try to present the various melodies clearly, then one would take the two melodies which are most suitable and pursue them for a while in the manner of a double fugue, and then join in unexpectedly with the other two.[207] When these have made their presence known, one might combine one of the former melodies with one of the latter two. After this [process of] variation, short secondary melodic motives could appear which are newly introduced [317] or derived from a main melodic motif. These short secondary motives serve to delay the main motif a little, in order to provide a melodic change for the listener, and also to furnish a good connection between one and another melody.[208] After this one may present three melodies [at one time], especially if the fourth is somewhat modified and precedes or follows. Thereupon one again would let two of them be particularly prominent. Then the same short secondary motives can appear in another key, followed, if one wishes, by three main motives again. Now the fugue moves toward the end. All four melodies can join in again. This can sometimes be done in the middle, too, in order to lengthen the fugue. The voices may now enter as they did at the beginning, or in another order. It is good if the main melodic motives are of one length, and are arranged so that they now can follow one another more rapidly.[209] The series of entries can also appear in other keys, since it may occur in the middle.[210] Likewise, one melody can be changed to some extent for the sake of the others. It may even be repeated in the manner of a simple fugue subject. All of this can take place toward the end. And although various inversions can result from counterpoint at the octave, tenth, and twelfth, yet the neighboring keys must not be neglected. Above everything else, one should concern oneself with a good melodic coherence. Without this nothing is accomplished in music. To whatever extent the melody might be divided among the voices, a good continuity certainly must prevail. Let us suggest the following means to attain this aim: when the four-part fugue is entirely constructed, one extracts a voice which contains no rest whatever; the other voices must contribute to its [formation]. For example, if the bass begins, one takes this beginning as far as the commencement of the first voice, and proceeds with the latter. If a few rests occur here, one determines which voice continues meanwhile, and then writes down the tones of this voice also until the first voice recommences. In this manner the whole melody which the ear perceives in hearing a piece is written down and then examined to see whether the piece is melodic throughout; whether the initial melody is well connected with what follows; whether the caesuras are an even number of measures apart; whether the modulations into other keys are found to be in agreement with nature; and also whether something strange and unexpected is present; and then, whether the entire melody is animated, that is to say, it also contains something pleasant, affecting, and lively, [318] or whether it is quite

---

[207] See n. 195.
[208] As with simple fugue, Daube's episodes may contain either new material (free fugue) or derived material (strict fugue). See nn. 139 and 144. For more on melodic continuity see the remainder of the paragraph and n. 175.
[209] i.e., stretto.
[210] See p. 207.

sleepy, inactive, and dragging. We are sure that no one will regret this examination.[211]
One will very soon discover what needs to be improved, and this improvement can
often be made by a small change of one or several tones. Short quarter or eighth rests
are not included with the intention that they should be filled in. When they are located
in the right place, they help to promote the good continuity of the melody. If the
melody is good, it will inevitably be made even better through the subsequent addition
of the other voices (*Harmonie*).

Now it is time to speak of another invention of antiquity, with regard to the most
artificial double fugues. The common type would be that in which one voice tries to
imitate the melody of the other in inversion. This type is divided into two parts, in the
first of which the melody of the second voice enters, inverted, to be sure, but not in the
same chords as the first voice [Example 224].[212]

Ex. 224

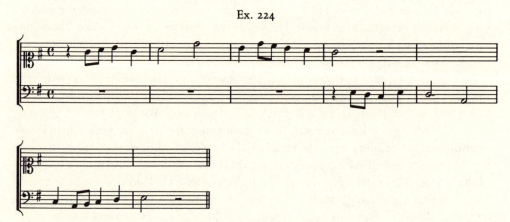

Here, of course, the size of the upward leaps in the first voice has been heeded by the
bass, so that the same size has been retained in the descending intervals, but the chords
of the first voice have not been retained in the second voice. This type is easy to construct. One merely observes where the tones of the initial voice proceed into the high or
low register, and keeps exactly the opposite in the second voice. Just as here the first
voice ascends a third by steps, [319] so the second voice descends the same number of
steps. In the first measure the first voice drops a third, in return for which the second
voice ascends a third. We have already said something about this above. The other type
is more natural. The inverted second voice retains all the chords from which the first
voice was taken [Example 225].[213]

---

[211] Of the five criteria listed by Daube, three pertain directly to melody and the *galant* idea that the ear is led by the uppermost voice, notwithstanding the presumed equality of all voices in the fugal style (see n. 115). The other two criteria
pertain to the use of closely related, "natural" keys customary in fugues of the period (see n. 140), and to symmetrical
phrase divisions, not formerly characteristic of fugue, but frequently applied to it as fugal imitation was incorporated
into other genres. See pp. 97–8 and 186–7 and nn. 117 and 143.

[212] Real melodic inversion without accidentals.

[213] Tonal melodic inversion with adjustments of numerical intervals as in fugue.

Ex. 225

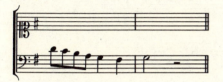

Only the F-sharp, at the conclusion of the bass in the sixth measure, does not agree here with the first voice, with respect to the similarity of the chords. In the third measure, the upper voice has a leap of a third, but the bass has a descent of only a second, because the [required] similarity of chords allowed no other arrangement. The half step at the conclusion of the first voice is also found in the bass at this point.

This is the proper type of inversion, which formerly was highly esteemed by the Italians.[214] For the construction of such uncommon double fugues, one should contrive a theme which is free of many large leaps and falls. The more stepwise tones and small leaps the melody contains, the more suitable it will be for this purpose. Then one simply takes care that these same steps and leaps are introduced inverted according to the foregoing description. When one voice ascends a third, fourth, or fifth, the second voice must fall a third, fourth, or fifth in return. Where the upper voice has whole or half steps, the second voice likewise must have [320] whole or half steps in the subsequent inversion. If one will observe this little rule, no difficulties will ensue. The crab-like double counterpoint also may be included in this type. It is formed when the second voice proceeds backwards from the end [Example 226].[215]

Ex. 226

[214] Daube's concept of fugue also shows the influence of Italian models in its simultaneous presentation of multiple fugue themes (see n. 195), and its use of contrasting episodic material (see nn. 139 and 208).

[215] See pp. 171–2.

Here one sees that the bass carries the melody of the first voice backwards, just as the melody of the upper voice begins with its ending. Instruction in this type seems to be superfluous. This example will suffice to demonstrate it clearly. However, it is even better if such a theme is arranged so that the bass can enter immediately after the first voice begins [Example 227].

Ex. 227

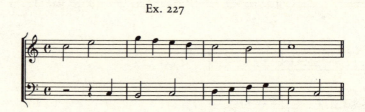

Such a theme can pass for two different melodies in the middle of a fugue, if one changes the long note [321] at the beginning of the bass into a short note, as here, and replaces what is missing with rests. In this way opportunity is provided for the two voices to enter successively. The conclusion of the upper voice in the penultimate example can also be C, and this same tone can be taken for the beginning of the bass. The rules pertaining to working out this type have been indicated above.

These unusual fugue subjects are prepared so that, for the most part, the second voice commences at the end of the first voice. Therefore if the second voice begins to invert the theme of the first voice after one measure of rest, another species is produced in which the two voices can commence either at the unison, at the octave, or the one at the octave and the other at the fifth, provided only that the inversion of the melody of the first voice is introduced well by the second voice [Example 228].

Ex. 228

In this example all the intervals in both voices are observed most strictly. The falls or leaps in the second voice are the same size as in the first voice. Even the chords have been taken into account as much as possible. Those fugue subjects in which the voices enter successively at the octave or at the unison are constructed in this same manner.

This and the two foregoing types are to be used whenever fugues are wanted. The melody of the initial motif [322] can be prepared as desired. One has every liberty.[216]

---

[216] See nn. 188 and 194.

We have indicated how to construct the countermelody for it. In working out these
two melodic motives one will find the mistakes to be improved upon. Counterpoint at
the octave is well suited to this also. All kinds of agreeable combinations, or short episodic melodies can be introduced here.

Another artificial type of double fugue was customary among the ancients. The second
voice would rest a quarter and then state the first tone of the upper voice and, after resting another quarter, would imitate the second tone, proceeding continually in this way
with the alternation of a tone from the upper voice and a rest. This type again comprised
different classes. The second voice would follow at the unison, at the octave, or at the
fourth, fifth, or sixth. One sees that, with this constraint, the upper voice could seldom
be very melodious, since one was obliged to arrange the continuation of its melody solely
according to the imitation of the second voice [Examples 229–31].[217]

Ex. 229

Ex. 230

Ex. 231

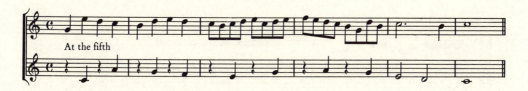

One sees that fifths and dissonances can also take place in this type. Because of the rest,
the fifth, as well as the unbound fourth which results from its inversion, may appear.
In the process of constructing all three examples, one writes only a quarter in [324]
the upper voice and then, after a quarter rest, puts this same tone into the second voice.

[217] The result is an augmentation canon combined with hocket technique. Ex. 230: the bass key signature has one flat in
the original.

After this one sets the second quarter note in the first voice and the theme is continued in this way until the end. The interval of imitation may be the octave, third, or another interval. If running passages should occur in the upper voice, they are arranged so that the second voice, after the quarter rest in each case, could continue with the tone of its preceding melody even during the passagework, as is shown in the third measure of the first and third examples. The second voice could also introduce the leaps and falls of the first voice in inversion, and the rests would still be incorporated [Example 232].

Ex. 232

The melodic line is borrowed from the first example above [Example 229], and yet it includes the inverted repetition.[218] We preferred to use it here so that one will see that different types or imitations can often be introduced with a fixed melody. In examining all of these species, one will certainly always find that the simplest melodies are far more capable of imitation and variation than the artificial ones. Noble simplicity is not excluded even from composition. Most pleasing melodies are based upon this [quality]. Likewise, most of the passions are represented by simple means.[219]

[325] The third unusual type of double fugue was that in which the second voice imitated the melody of the first voice twice as slowly or twice as fast. This type is further divided into two classes. In the first, the intervals are imitated as precisely as possible, whereas in the second, they are introduced in inversion. These imitations [i.e., answers] can occur at the octave, fifth, and fourth [Example 233a–c].

Ex. 233

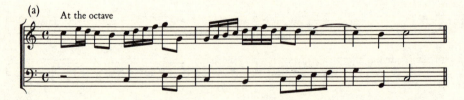

(a)   At the octave

---

[218] i.e., melodic inversion.

[219] Daube advocates simplicity as a quality of nature throughout his free-style discussions. Here it is a practical consideration as well as an aesthetic preference. Marpurg similarly notes that "the larger the number of voices in a fugue, the less florid the counterpoints should be. If one voice is written in a highly ornate style, the other would necessarily become a mere filling voice. Yet in the fugue, all voices should compete on the same level" (*Abhandlung*, vol. I (1753), p. 149, Eng. trans. in Mann, *Fugue*, p. 201). The fact that "noble simplicity is not excluded even from composition" refers to Daube's belief that the arts are united through their relationship to the qualities of nature. See n. 52.

Ex. 233a–c (cont.)

(b) At the fourth

(c) At the fifth

Here one sees the three imitations. To construct them one must especially contrive a theme composed of rapid intervals, half or three quarters of a measure [in length], which then is written down. Next, after a half or three quarters of a measure rest, it is written in the second voice in tones twice as long. Above these slow intervals one puts a rapid melody, of which a half measure again is given to the second voice, in tones twice as slow, and so one proceeds to write the voices alternately until the end. The close, or even the [last] half of the penultimate measure permits an exception, in view of the lower, slowly moving imitation, just as is found here. In the second and third examples the upper voice must be arranged so that its melody can be a fourth or fifth lower in the second voice, and still harmonize with the first voice. If the upper voice cannot remain in the same key because its melody is transposed in the second voice, the original key must none the less be observed again at the close. The second example demonstrates this. In the third [example] both voices remain together in one key until the end.

The second class of these double fugues is that in which the second voice introduces the melody of the first inverted and in long tones [Example 234].

Ex. 234

The initial melody is imitated inverted by the second voice until the third quarter of the fourth measure. All of the leaps, falls, and steps have been imitated most strictly in the inversion. The [process of] construction is similar to the foregoing, except that the half measure of the upper voice appears in its inversion in such a way that the size of the leaps in the first voice is retained most strictly in the second voice by means of falls which are exactly as large. In this example the beginning of the first voice shows such a leap up a third, which is imitated by the drop of a third.

The type in which two different melodic motives could be inverted simultaneously during the course of the fugue was also considered very artificial [Example 235a–b].[220] The following rules were given for the construction of this type:

(1) Fifths and syncopated dissonances must be avoided.
(2) Two successive sixths are permitted, but not two successive thirds.

Ex. 235

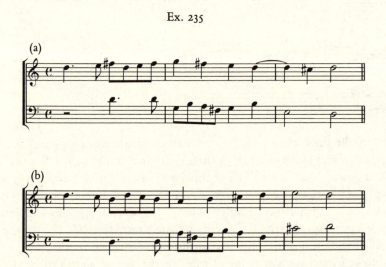

The third measure presents a tie despite the rule. If one wanted to construct such an example without these rules, one would write down one measure of a theme and to this at once the inversion. Then one would set the second voice to the proper beginning, as well as to the inversion of the upper voice, but so that the beginning of the second voice is then also written in inversion. One thus will soon see what must be changed in the inversion. This type also can be repeated or imitated at the fourth or fifth. In this case the repetition must be written first, followed by the inversion of both voices.[221] When the second voice undertakes the imitation at the fourth, and both voices subsequently are to be inverted, the upper voice must commence an octave above the initial tone of the second voice, while the second voice is given the initial tone of the first voice [Example 236a–b].

[220] Ex. 235a: the tie is missing in the original.
[221] Daube's procedures "without these rules" recall his instructions for canonic writing, Chapter 9.

Ex. 236

[329] However if the upper voice is to be inverted in its initial key, the second voice, which previously was a fourth lower, must descend another tone, and thus be set at the fifth and inverted.

Whoever enjoys working things out in this way might always want to construct these unusual fugue subjects. Even with this work he nevertheless would find a reason to wonder at the multifariousness and richness of harmony and melody. Many a beautiful melody, which he perhaps might not have found in any other way, would thereby fall into his hands, as it were. For, from where does the multifariousness of melody come? From the art of variation. What are all of the melodies which already are in the world, and are yet to come? Nothing other than simple variations, inversions, the decreasing and increasing of the note values of the twelve tones of an octave, and the higher or lower placement of them. But everything proceeds from the first, namely, from variation.[222] One might review page 143. The harmony also displays this richness. From where do so many different harmonies arise? From the retardation and anticipation of one or more intervals of the three main chords.[223] How do such different effects of the harmony in general originate? By the decreasing and increasing of the chord tones. The unison playing of all kinds of instruments makes a singular impression. How great and diverse an effect is produced by passages in thirds and sixths when performed on similar instruments of each type, then with dissimilar instruments of all sorts, or with the accompaniment of singing voices! The harmonic triad also has a special effect, and so likewise the inclusion of other intervals. Four-part harmony creates yet another impression. And how great is the full harmony that is heard from many different instruments together! If the three motions are considered, [it is found that] each one anew produces a separate

---

[222] Compare p. 6 of Daube's *Anleitung zur Erfindung der Melodie* (1797/98). See n. 87.
[223] See "Daube's harmonic system" in the Introduction, pp. 19–21.

effect.[224] We have just cited the first two of these here, namely the passages in sixths and thirds that come under parallel motion, and the inclusion of other intervals that produces contrary motion. Thus there remains oblique motion, which shows us its special, beautiful effect through art as well as nature. In the beginning of this work we have clearly described these three motions, as well as the foregoing, about the effect of the harmony.

[330] Here, in conclusion, we still must discuss the most artificial type of the unusual fugue subjects of our forefathers. In this type one could invert the counterpoint four times. If the [voice] exchange is added, eight variations are produced [Example 237a–h]. The following rules pertain to the construction of this type:

(1) The fifth must be entirely avoided.
(2) No ties nor dissonances must occur.
(3) Likewise, no single passing tone should be dissonant.

Ex. 237

[224] The topic of textural variety has run like a theme and variations throughout Daube's work. His repeated references to "effect" suggest the contemporaneous *Wirkungsästhetik*, which emphasized the effect of, rather than the theory behind, a work of literature, art, or music. (See Wünsch, "Wirkung und Rezeption," in *Reallexikon*, vol. IV, pp. 894–919.) This concept corroborates Daube's emphasis on "the ear," and recalls that the term "aesthetic" – the science of sense perception – had been introduced by A. G. Baumgarten in 1735 (Wellek, *Modern Criticism*, vol. III, p. 144).

Ex. 237a–h (cont.)

Here are eight different modifications. When a good theme is contrived, even this
artificial type can be used to advantage. In former times it was the most highly esteemed
art and masterwork. From this one sees how much the ancients endeavored to discover
through art that which they perhaps did not believe to be found in nature – we mean

melody. They tried to obtain the continuation of their melody in the ways described here.[225] Therefore, although such a piece was worked out by means of art, it surely could hardly have given the listeners as much pleasure, and was even less likely to produce the effect that one finds nowadays. However, one thing is certain: that if we combine the art of the old music with the grace and natural beauty of the present music, the two together can achieve a perfection to which must be counted principally the representation of the passions. We do not need to discard the old, but rather only to strive to improve it.[226] The fugue and the fixed melody (cantus firmus) were the main occupations of the ancient composers. We, on the other hand, have free imitation and transposition of the main and secondary motives of a melody. Their fugue consisted of nothing but art, in view of their theoretically proper entrances, as well as in the modification of the main melody itself. Ours admits of no constraint; it is fond of [both] nature and art. Their melody was simple, and furnished with few differing note values. Ours consists of many diverse note values, and the little leaps are filled out far more than they were formerly. Moreover, there are also the short ornaments, appoggiaturas, various kinds of trills, the *forte* and *piano*, the alternation of different instruments, etc. All of this makes our present music very distinct from that of the ancients. Poetry, above all, has contributed to this and, with the advent of opera, has fallen into the good hands of the opera composers. How much a good text assists in the invention of melody, indeed, how it even contributes to the felicitous continuation of a [333] good melody, is best known by experienced opera composers. The effect which poetry produced on music among the Greeks, which in turn was conducive to the former, still is achieved by both arts even today, and probably to a far higher degree. We find that with the improvement of opera and the increase of Singspiel, music has improved to the same degree, particularly the melody, in which poetry has always played the greatest part. This certainly was the guiding principle by which composers constructed their arias etc., and which in that way has contributed so much to the invention of melody. Indeed, even now it is poetry which very often offers to us the most beautiful thoughts, and in such a way that they seem to appear at just the right moment. Even texts that are designed for choirs, if they are ingeniously composed, can provide the best plan for the construction of a good symphony. However, if everything that has been said is to be done, the poetry itself must first be well written, full of harmony, and already of a melodious nature, for which many a poet does not have the inclination. For if the poet does not understand music, or at least does not have a good concept of this science, he certainly cannot help the composer.

In concluding this treatise we wish the sympathetic reader and friend of music to be satisfied with our work. We have done what we could. At least we can say that we spared no time nor effort, and avoided no wearisome work in order to seek out, to investigate and, through a considerable span of years, to test everything which we have explained in

---

[225] See p. 213 and nn. 172 and 186.

[226] One of Daube's guiding principles is the value and beauty of combining styles, although he holds the optimistic, Enlightenment view that the free style of the "moderns" is more "natural," and therefore superior to the rule-bound style of the "ancients." See the Introduction pp. 18–19 and 27–30. Compare pp. 69 and 243.

this book. We request that impartial readers might choose to compare our system with other musical writings and to examine them without prejudice. If this is done, we are sure that you will not condemn the publication of this work. Even though we might not have described everything clearly, a little reflection and practice exercise will still compensate for that deficiency. If perchance we have omitted something, it shall be supplied in the future.[227] We extend our wish even to [the possibility] that everything presented here may prove to be valuable and enjoyable, that the growth of music may be furthered thereby, and that a most agreeable relief from daily work may be provided by the purest pleasure in music.

[227] i.e., in a future volume of the *Dilettant* series. See the Introduction, pp. 10–17.

BIBLIOGRAPHY

Abert, Hermann. *Niccolò Jomelli als Opernkomponist*. Halle: Max Niemeyer, 1908

Adelung, Johann Christoph. *Grammatisch-Kritisches Wörterbuch der Hochdeutschen Mundart*. Leipzig: J. G. I. Breitkopf, Sohn und Compagnie, 1796

Adlung, Jacob. *Anleitung zu der musikalischen Gelehrtheit*. Erfurt: J. D. Jungnicol, 1758; facs. edn., Haus Joachim Moser. Kassel: Bärenreiter, 1953

Aldrich, Putnam. "Appoggiatura." In *The Harvard Dictionary of Music*, 2nd edn., ed. Willi Apel. Cambridge, MA: The Belknap Press of Harvard University Press, 1969. Pp. 43–6

Anderson, Emily. *Letters of Mozart and his Family*, 3rd edn. New York: W. W. Norton & Co., 1985

Aristotle. "On Education." In *Aristotle: Selections*. Tr. Philip Wheelwright. New York: The Odyssey Press, 1951. Pp. 285–7

Bach, Carl Philipp Emanuel. *Versuch über die wahre Art das Clavier zu spielen*, 2nd edn. Berlin: G. L. Winter, 1759. 1st edn. tr. and ed. William J. Mitchell as *Essay on the True Art of Playing Keyboard Instruments (1752)*. New York: W. W. Norton and Co., Inc., 1949

Batteux, Charles. *Les beaux arts reduits à un même principe*. Paris: Durand, 1746; rpt. New York and London: Johnson Reprint Corp., 1970

Bauer, W. A. and O. E. Deutsch, eds. *Mozart: Briefe und Aufzeichnungen*. Kassel: Bärenreiter, 1962–75

Becker, Carl Ferdinand. *Systematisch-chronologische Darstellung der musikalischen Literatur*. Leipzig: Verlag von Robert Friese, 1836–9; rpt. Amsterdam: Knuf, 1964

Becker, Carl L. *The Heavenly City of the Eighteenth-Century Philosophers*. New Haven: Yale University Press, 1932; rpt. 1963

Benary, Peter. *Die deutsche Kompositionslehre des 18. Jahrhunderts*. Leipzig: Breitkopf & Härtel, [1961]

Bononcini, Giovanni Maria. *Musico prattico*. Bologna: G. Monti, 1673; rpt. New York: Broude Brothers Limited, 1969

Breitkopf Thematic Catalogue, 1762–1787, ed. Barry S. Brook. Rpt. of *Catalogo delle Sinfonie*. New York: Dover Publications, Inc., 1966

Brossard, Sébastien de. *Dictionnaire de musique*. Paris: Ballard, 1703. Tr. Albion Gruber as *Dictionary of Music*. Henryville, PA: Institute of Mediaeval Music, c. 1982

Buelow, George. "Daube." In *The New Grove Dictionary of Music and Musicians*, ed. Stanley Sadie. London: Macmillan, 1980. Vol. V, p. 253

Burney, Charles. *Dr. Burney's Musical Tours in Europe*, ed. Percy A. Scholes. 2 vols. London: Oxford University Press, 1959

"Essay on Musical Criticism." In *A General History of Music from the Earliest Ages to the Present Time*. Vol. III (of 4). 2nd edn. London: printed for the author, 1789. Pp. vii–xi

"Essay on Musical Criticism." In *A General History of Music from the Earliest Ages to the Present Period*. Vol. II (of 2), ed. Frank Mercer. London, 1789; rpt. New York: Dover Publications, 1957. Pp. 7–11

The Present State of Music in Germany, the Netherlands, and the United Provinces. Vol. I. 2nd edn. London: printed for Becket, *et al.*, 1775

Tagebuch einer Musikalischen Reise durch Frankreich und Italien. Tr. E. D. Ebeling. Hamburg: Bode,
  1772; facs. edn., Richard Schaal. Kassel: Bärenreiter, 1959

Carse, Adam. *The History of Orchestration*. London: Kegan Paul, Trench, Trubner and Company,
  Ltd., 1925; rev. edn. New York: Dover Publications, Inc., 1964

The Orchestra in the XVIIIth Century. Cambridge: W. Heffer and Sons, Ltd., 1940

Chédeville, Esprit Philippe. *Sechs Galante Duos für zwei gleiche Melodieinstrumente, besonders
  Alt-Blockflöten*. *Hortus Musicus*, No. 199, ed. Arthur von Arx. Kassel, Basle, Tours, London:
  Bärenreiter, 1969

Cloeter, Hermine. *Johann Thomas Trattner, ein Grossunternehmer im Theresianischen Wien*. Graz:
  H. Böhlaus Nachf., 1952

Cockshoot, John V. *The Fugue in Beethoven's Piano Music*. London: Routledge and Kegan Paul,
  1959

Corte, Andrea della and G. M. Gatti. *Dizionario di musica*. Torino: G. B. Paravia e C., 1930

Dahlhaus, Carl. "Der Dilettant und der Banause in der Musikgeschichte." *Archiv für Musikwissenschaft* XXV (1968), 157–72

Daube, Johann Friedrich. *Anleitung zur Erfindung der Melodie und ihrer Fortsetzung*. Vienna: Täubel,
  1797/98

Beweis, daß die gottesdienstliche Musik. Vienna: Joh. Ferd. Edlen von Schönfeld, 1782

General-Baß in drey Accorden. Leipzig: J. B. Andrä, 1756; facs. edn. Eitelfriedrich Thom. Michael-
  stein [1984]. Tr. Barbara K. Wallace as "J. F. Daube's 'General-Baß in drey Accorden' (1756):
  A Translation and Commentary." Ph. D. diss., North Texas State University, 1983

Der Musikalische Dilettant: eine Abhandlung der Komposition. Vienna: von Trattner, 1773

"Sonata in F für Cembalo." *Oeuvres mélées contenant VI. sonates pour le clavecin de tant de plus
  célèbres compositeurs*. Pt. XI. Nürnberg: Haffner, 1763 [See Lang and Newmann for excerpts
  and discussion]

"Trio in D-Moll für Laute, Flöte (Violine) und Klavier," ed. Hans Neemann. Berlin-
  Lichterfelde: Chr. Friedrich Vieweg, 1927

"Trio a Liuto, Traverso e Basso in A minor." *Denkmäler der Tonkunst in Österreich*. Vol. LXXXVI
  (1967)

Deutsch, Otto Erich. "Haydns Musikbücherei." In *Musik und Verlag*. Kassel: Bärenreiter, 1968.
  Pp. 220–21

Directory of Music Research Libraries, ed. Rita Benton. Iowa City: University of Iowa Press, 1970

Dittersdorf, Carl Ditters von. *Autobiography*. Tr. Arthur D. Coleridge. London: Richard Bentley
  and Son, 1896; rpt. New York: Da Capo Press, 1970

Donington, Robert. *The Interpretation of Early Music*. London: Faber and Faber, 1963

Duckles, Vincent. "Johann Adam Hiller's 'Critical Prospectus for a Music Library'." In *Studies in
  Eighteenth-Century Music: A Tribute to Karl Geiringer on his Seventieth Birthday*, ed. H. C.
  Robbins Landon and R. E. Chapman. New York and London: Oxford University Press,
  1970. Pp. 177–85

Eitner, Robert. *Biographisch-Bibliographisches Quellen-Lexikon*. Vol. III. New York: Musurgia, 1947

Encyclopedia Britannica. "Musick." Vol. III. Edinburgh: Colin MacFarquhar, 1771

Fétis, François Joseph. *Biographie universelle des musiciens*. Paris: Librairie de Firmin-Didot et Cie.,
  1883

Fischer, Kurt von. "Arietta Variata." In *Studies in Eighteenth-Century Music: A Tribute to Karl
  Geiringer on his Seventieth Birthday*, ed. H. C. Robbins Landon and R. E. Chapman. New
  York and London: Oxford University Press, 1970. Pp. 224–35

Fischer, Wilhelm. "Zur Entwicklungsgeschichte des Wiener klassischen Stils." *Studien zur Musikwissenschaft* III. Leipzig: Breitkopf & Härtel; Vienna: Artaria & Co. (1915), 24–84

Forkel, Johann Nikolaus. *Allgemeine Litteratur der Musik*. Leipzig: Schwickertschen Verlag, 1792;
  rpt. Hildesheim: Georg Olms. 1962

Musikalischer Almanach für Deutschland auf das Jahr 1784. Leipzig: Schwickertschen Verlag, 1784

Framery, Nicolas Etienne and Pierre Louis Ginguené. *Encyclopédie méthodique, Musique*. Paris: Panckouche, 1791

Frankfurter Anzeigen. Vol. V, 1774, S. 518

Freystätter, Wilhelm. *Die Musikalischen Zeitschriften*. Amsterdam: Frits A. M. Knuf, 1963

Fricke, Gerhard. *Geschichte der deutschen Dichtung*. Hamburg and Lübeck: Matthiesen Verlag, 1961

Fux, Johann Joseph. *Gradus ad Parnassum*, Vienna, 1725; rpt. New York: Broude Bros., [1966]. Ger. tr. Loranz Mizler. Leipzig: Mizlerischen Bücherverlag, 1742; rpt. Hildesheim: Georg Olms, 1974. Partial Eng. tr. Alfred Mann as *Steps to Parnassus, the Study of Counterpoint*. New York: W. W. Norton and Co., 1943; rev. edn. as *The Study of Counterpoint*. New York: W. W. Norton and Co., Inc., 1965

Galeazzi, Francesco. *Elementi teorico-pratici di musica*. Vol. II. Rome: Puccinelli, 1796

Geiringer, Karl. "The Rise of Chamber Music." In *The Age of the Enlightenment, 1745–1790*. The Oxford History of Music. Vol. VII. London: Oxford University Press, 1973

Das gelehrte Österreich, ed. Ignaz de Luca. Vienna: von Ghelen, 1776–8

Das gelehrte Teutschland, ed. Georg Christoph Hamberger und Johann Georg Meusel. Vol. II. Lemgo, 1796; rpt. Hildesheim: Georg Olms, 1965

Gerber, Ernst Ludwig. "Eine freundliche Vorstellung über gearbeitete Instrumentalmusik, besonders über Symphonien." *Allgemeine musikalische Zeitung* XV (1813), cols. 457–63

Historisch-Biographisches Lexikon der Tonkünstler. 2 vols. Leipzig: Breitkopf, 1790–92, and *Neues Historisch-Biographisches Lexikon der Tonkünstler*. 4 vols, Leipzig: Kuhnel, 1812–14, ed. Othmar Wesseley. Graz: Akademische Druck u. Verlagsanstalt, 1966–77

Gericke, Hannelore. *Der Wiener Musikalienhandel von 1770–1778*. Graz and Cologne: Hermann Boehlaus Nachf., 1960

Hickman, Roger. "The Flowering of the Viennese String Quartet in the Late Eighteenth Centry." *The Music Review* L/3–4 (1989), 157–80

"Leopold Kozeluch and the Viennese *Quatuor Concertant*." *College Music Symposium* XXVI (1986), 42–52

Hadow, W. H. *The Viennese Period*. The Oxford History of Music. Vol. V. Oxford: Clarendon Press, 1904

Hanning, Barbara R. "Conversation and Musical Style in the Late Eighteenth-Century Parisian Salon." *Eighteenth-Century Studies* XXII/4 (1989), 512–28

Hanslick, Eduard. *Geschichte des Concertwesens in Wien*. Vienna: Wilhelm Braumüller, 1869; rpt. Westmead: Gregg International, 1971; New York: Georg Olms, 1979

Helm, Ernest Eugene. *Music at the Court of Frederick the Great*. Norman: University of Oklahoma Press, 1960

Hickman, Roger. "Leopold Kozeluch and the Viennese *Quatuor Concertant*." *College Music Symposium* XXVI (1986), 42–52

Hill, George R. "Haydn's Musical Clocks and their Implications for Late Eighteenth-Century Performance Practice." Senior Honors Project, Stanford University, 1965

Hiller, Johann Adam. *Wöchentliche Musikalische Nachrichten und Anmerkungen*. 4 vols. Leipzig: Verlag der Zeitungs-Expedition, 1766–70; rpt. Hildesheim and New York: Georg Olms, c. 1970

Horsley, Imogene. *Fugue: History and Practice*. New York: The Free Press, A Division of The Macmillan Company, 1966

Kahl, Willi. *Selbstbiographien Deutscher Musiker des XVIII. Jahrhunderts*. Cologne, 1948; rpt. Amsterdam: Frits Knuf, Staufen-Verlag, 1972

Kaiserlich Königliche allergnädigst-priviligirte Anzeigen, aus sämmtlich-kaiserlich-königlichen Erbländern. Vol. III, No. 48 (Dec 1) and No. 50 (Dec 15). Vienna, 1773

Kaiserlich Königliche allergnädigst-privilegirte Realzeitung der Wissenschaften, Künste und der Kommerzien. Vienna: Joseph Kurtzböck. Vol. II, No. 11 (11 March 1771), 177–8

Karbaum, Michael. "Das theoretische Werk Johann Friedrich Daubes: der Theoretiker J. F.

Daube: ein Beitrag zur Kompositionslehre des 18. Jahrhunderts." Diss., University of Vienna, 1968

Katalog des Augsburger Verlegers Lotter von 1753, ed. Adolf Layer. Vol. II of *Catalogus Musicus*. Kassel: Internationale Vereinigung der Musikbibliotheken; Internationale Gesellschaft für Musikwissenschaft, 1964

Kirchner, Joachim. *Die Grundlage des deutschen Zeitschriftenwesens . . . bis 1790*. 2 vols. Leipzig: Verlag Karl W. Hiersemann, 1928–31

Kirkendale, Warren. *Fuge und Fugato in der Kammermusik des Rokoko und der Klassik*. Tutzing: Hans Schneider, 1966

   Fugue and Fugato in Rococo and Classical Chamber Music, 2nd rev. edn. Tr. Margaret Bent and the author. Durham, N. C.: Duke University Press, 1979

Kirnberger, Johann Philipp. *Die Kunst des reinen Satzes in der Musik*. Berlin and Königsberg: Decker und Hartung. Vol. I, 1771; Vol. II, 1776–9; rpt. Hildesheim: Georg Olms, 1968. Tr. David Beach and Jurgen Thym as *The Art of Strict Musical Composition*. New Haven and London: Yale University Press, 1982

   Recueil d'airs de danse caractéristiques. Pt. I. Berlin: J. J. Hummel, [1777]

Koch, Heinrich Christoph. *Musikalisches Lexicon*. Frankfurt am Main: 1802; rpt. Hildesheim: Georg Olms, 1964

   Versuch einer Anleitung zur Composition. Pt. 3. Rudolstadt and Leipzig: Adam Friedrich Böhme, 1782, 1787, and 1793; rpt. Hildesheim: Georg Olms, 1969. Partial tr. Nancy Kovaleff Baker as *Introductory Essay on Composition*. Pt. 2, Sections 3 and 4. New Haven and London: Yale University Press, 1983

Kollmann, August Friedrich Christoph. *An Essay on Practical Musical Composition*. London: Selbstverlag, 1799; republished with a foreword by Imogene Horsley. New York: Da Capo Press, 1973

Landon, H. C. Robbins. *Haydn*. New York: Praeger Publishers, 1972

Lang, Paul Henry. *Music in Western Civilization*. New York: W. W. Norton, 1969

Lange, Martin. *Beiträge zur Entstehung der südwestdeutschen Klaviersonate im 18. Jahrhundert*. Giessen: Laukwitzer Anzeiger, 1930

LaRue, Jan. "Symphony, I. 18th century." *The New Grove Dictionary of Music and Musicians*, ed. Stanley Sadie. London: Macmillan, 1980. Vol. XVIII. Pp. 438–53

Le Huray, Peter and James Day, eds. *Music and Aesthetics in the Eighteenth and Early-Nineteenth Centuries*. Cambridge and New York: Cambridge University Press, 1981

Lemacher, Heinrich. *Handbuch der Hausmusik*. Graz: A. Pustet, 1948

Lenneberg, Hans. "Johann Mattheson on Affect and Rhetoric in Music." *Journal of Music Theory* II/1 (1958), 47–84, and II/2 (1958), 193–236

Lenz, Wilhelm von. *Beethoven. eine Kunststudie*. Vol. V. Hamburg: Hoffmann & Campe, 1860

Lessing, Gotthold Ephriam. *Sämtliche Schriften*. Vol. XIII. Leipzig: G. I. Göschen, 1897

Levy, Janet. "The Quatuor Concertant in the Latter Half of the Eighteenth Century." Ph. D. diss., Stanford University, 1971

Lippman, Edward A., ed. *Musical Aesthetics: A Historical Reader*. Vol. I. New York: Pendragon Press, 1986

Löhlein, Georg Simon. *Klavier-Schule, oder Kurze und gründliche Anweisung zur Melodie und Harmonie*. Leipzig and Züllichau: auf Kosten der Waisenhaus- und Frommanischen Buchhandlung, 1765

Lovejoy, Arthur O. "Plentitude and Sufficient Reason in Leibniz and Spinoza." In *The Great Chain of Being: A Study of the History of an Idea*. New York: Harper and Row, Publishers, 1936; rpt. 1960. Pp. 144–82

Mann, Alfred. *The Study of Fugue*, rev. edn. New York: W. W. Norton and Co., Inc., 1965

Marcello, Benedetto. "Il teatro alla moda," Tr. Reinhard G. Pauly. *The Musical Quarterly* XXXIV/3 (1948), 371–403, XXV/1 (1949), 85–105

Marpurg, Friedrich Wilhelm. *Abhandlung von der Fuge*. 2 vols. Berlin: A. Haude und J. C. Spener, 1753, 1754; rpt. New York and Hildesheim: Georg Olms, 1970

Historisch-kritische Beyträge zur Aufnahme der Musik. 5 vols. Berlin: G. A. Lang, 1754–78; rpt. Hildesheim: Georg Olms, 1970

Martini, Giambattista. *Esemplare o sia saggio fondamentale pratico di contrappunto.* 2 vols. Bologna: 1774–5; rpt. Ridgewood, NJ: Gregg Press, Inc., 1965

Mattheson, Johann. *Der vollkommene Capellmeister.* Hamburg: Christian Gerold, 1739; rpt. Kassel and Basle: Bärenreiter-Verlag, 1954. Tr. Ernest C. Harriss. Ann Arbor: UMI Research Press, 1981

McCredie, Andrew D. "Instrumentarium and Instrumentation in the North German Baroque Opera." Diss., University of Hamburg, 1964

Mennicke, Carl Heinrich. *Hasse und die Brüder Graun als Symphoniker.* Leipzig: Breitkopf & Härtel, 1906

Meusel, Johann Georg. *Lexicon der vom Jahr 1750 bis 1800 verstorbenen teutschen Schriftsteller.* Vol. II. Leipzig: 1803; rpt. Hildesheim: Georg Olms Verlagsbuchhandlung, 1967

Miesner, Heinrich. "Portraits aus dem Kreise Philipp Emanuel und Wilhelm Friedemann Bachs." In *Musik und Bild, Festschrift Max Seiffert zum siebzigsten Geburtstag.* Kassel: Bärenreiter Verlag, 1938. Pp. 101–16

Momigny, Jérôme-Joseph de. *Cours complet d'harmonie et de composition.* Paris: chez l'auteur, 1803–06

Morigi, Angelo. *Trattato di contrapunto fugato,* 4th edn., pubblicato da B. Asioli, Milan: Ricordi, c. 1807

Mozart, Leopold. *Versuch einer Gründlichen Violinschule,* 3rd edn. Augsburg: Lotter, 1789 [i.e. 1787]; rpt. Wiesbaden: Breitkopf & Härtel, 1983. Tr. Editha Knocker, with Preface by Alfred Einstein as *A Treatise on the Fundamental Principles of Violin Playing,* 2nd edn. London: Oxford University Press, 1951

Mozart, Wolfgang Amadeus. *Neue Ausgabe sämtlicher Werke* III/10 (1974). Kassel: Bärenreiter, [1955–]

Nalden, Charles. *Fugal Answer.* London: Oxford University Press, 1970

Neemann, Hans, ed. "Trio in D-Moll für Laute, Flöte (Violine) und Klavier." In "Alte Haus- und Kammermusik mit Laute." Berlin-Lichterfelde: Chr. Friedrich Vieweg, 1927

Newman, William S. *The Sonata in the Classic Era.* Chapel Hill: University of North Carolina Press, 1963

Petri, Johann Samuel. *Anleitung zur praktischen Musik,* 2nd edn. Leipzig: Breitkopf, 1782; rpt. Giebing über Prien am Chiemsee: E. Katzbichler, 1969

Plà, Juan Bautista. *Sechs Sonaten für zwei Oboen.* Mainz: Schott Edition 5898, 1969

Pohlmann, Ernst. *Laute, Theorbe, Chitarrone.* Lilienthal and Bremen: Edition Eres, 1975

Portheimische Zettelkatalog. Stadtsbibliothek Vienna. Entry 464

Portmann, Johann Gottlieb. *Leichtes Lehrbuch der Harmonie, Composition und des Generalbasses.* Darmstadt: J. J. Will, 1789

Powell, Newman W. "Early Keyboard Fingering and its Effect on Articulation." MA thesis, Stanford University, 1954

Prout, Ebenezer. *Fugue.* London: Augener, Ltd., 1891; rpt. New York: Greenwood Press, 1969

Quantz, Johann Joachim. *Sechs Duette für zwei Flöten,* op. 2, ed. Georg Müller. Wiesbaden: Breitkopf & Härtel, 1960

   Versuch einer Anweisung die Flöte traversière zu spielen. Berlin, 1752, with foreword and annotations by Arnold Schering. Leipzig: C. F. Kahnt Nachfolger, 1906. Tr. Edward R. Reilly as *On Playing the Flute,* 2nd edn. New York: Schirmer Books, 1985

Rameau, Jean-Philippe. *Démonstration du principe de l'harmonie.* Paris: Durand et Pisot, 1750

   Génération harmonique. Paris: Prault, 1737; facs. edn. in *The Complete Theoretical Writings of Jean-Philippe Rameau,* ed. Erwin R. Jacobi (n.p.: American Institute of Musicology, 1967–72), vol. III (1968). Pp. 1–150. Tr. Deborah Hayes as *Harmonic Generation.* Ann Arbor: University Microfilms, 1974

Nouveau système de musique théorique. Paris: Ballard, 1726

Traité de l'harmonie. Paris: Ballard, 1722; rpt. tr. and ed. Philip Gossett as *Treatise on Harmony.* New York: Dover Publications, Inc., 1971

Ratner, Leonard G. "*Ars combinatoria*: Chance and Choice in Eighteenth-Century Music." In *Studies in Eighteenth-Century Music: A Tribute to Karl Geiringer on his Seventieth Birthday,* ed. H. C. Robbins Landon and R. E. Chapman. New York and London: Oxford University Press, 1970. Pp. 343–63

Classic Music: Expression, Form, and Style. New York: Schirmer Books, 1980

"Eighteenth-Century Theories of Musical Period Structure." *The Musical Quarterly* XLII/4 (1956), 439–54

Harmony, Structure and Style. San Francisco: McGraw-Hill, 1962

Recueils imprimés xviiie siècle, Vol. II of *Répertoire International des sources musicales.* Munich and Duisburg: G. Henle Verlag, 1964

Reicha, Antoine. *Traité de haute composition musicale.* 2 vols. Paris: Zetter & cie, 1824–26

Traité de mélodie. Paris: Richault, 1814

Reichert, Georg. "Daube." *Musik in Geschichte und Gegenwart.* Vol. III, ed. Friedrich Blume. Kassel and Basle: Bärenreiter-Verlag, 1949

Reinken, Jan Adams. *Kompositionsregeln,* MS 1670, ed H. Gehrmann in vol. X of Jan Pieterszoon Sweelinck's *Werken.* Leipzig: Breitkopf & Härtel, 1901

Riemann, Hugo. *Geschichte der Musiktheorie im IX.–XIX. Jahrhundert.* Berlin: Max Hesses Verlag, 1898

Riemann Musik Lexikon, ed. Wilibald Gurlitt. Mainz: B. Schott's Söhne, 1889

Riepel, Joseph. *Anfangsgründe zur musikalischen Setzkunst.* I: *De rhythmopoeia, oder Von der Taktordnung.* Regensburg and Vienna: J. J. Lotter, 1752; II: *Grundregeln zur Tonordnung insgemein.* Frankfurt and Leipzig: Ulm, printed by Ch. U. Wagner, 1755; III: *Gründliche Erklärung der Tonordnung insbesondere, zugleich aber für die mehresten Organisten insgemein.* Frankfurt and Leipzig: n.p., 1757; IV: *Erläuterung der betrüglichen Tonordnung.* Augsburg: Johann Jakob Lotter, 1765; V: *Unentbehrliche Anmerkungen zum Kontrapunkt.* Regensburg: Jacob Christian Krippner, 1768

Baß-schlüssel, das ist, Anleitung für Anfänger und Liebhaber der Setzkunst. Regensburg: J. L. Montags Erben, 1786 [Probably planned as another *Capitel* of the *Anfangsgründe,* but published posthumously]

Rothschild, Germaine de. *Luigi Boccherini, his Life and Work.* Tr. Andreas Mayor. London: Oxford University Press, 1965

Rowen, Ruth Halle. *Early Chamber Music.* New York: Da Capo Press, 1974

Scheibe, Johann Adolph. *Der Critische Musicus,* 2nd edn. Leipzig: B. C. Breitkopf, 1745

"Die Theorie der Melodie und Harmonie." 1st pt. of *Über die Musikalische Composition.* Leipzig: Schwickert, 1773

Schubart, Christian Friedrich Daniel. *Ideen zu einer Aesthetik der Tonkunst.* Vienna: L. Schubart, 1806; rpt. Hildesheim: Georg Olms, 1969

Shirlaw, Matthew. *The Theory of Harmony,* 2nd edn. DeKalb, Illinois: Dr. Birchard Coar, 1955

Sittard, Josef. *Zur Geschichte der Musik und des Theaters am Württembergischen Hofe, 1458–1793.* Vol. II. Stuttgart: W. Kohlhammer, 1890; rpt. Hildesheim: Georg Olms, 1970

Smith, Preserved. *A History of Modern Culture,* Vol. II: *The Enlightenment, 1687–1776.* New York: Henry Holt and Co., 1934

Strunk, Oliver. *Source Readings in Music History.* New York: W. W. Norton and Co., Inc., 1950

Sulzer, Johann Georg. *Allgemeine Theorie der schönen Künste.* 2 vols. Leipzig: M. G. Weidemanns Erben und Reich, 1771 and 1774

Telemann, Georg Philipp. *Sechs kanonische Sonaten für zwei Violinen.* Peters Edition No. 4394

Thayer, Alexander Wheelock. *The Life of Ludwig van Beethoven,* ed. H. E. Krehbiel. 3 vols. New York: The Beethoven Association, Press of G. Schirmer, 1921

Thouret, Georg. *Friedrich der Grosse als Musik-Freund und Musiker.* Leipzig: Breitkopf & Härtel, 1898

Trattner, Johann Thomas von. *Catalogus der Joh. Thom. edlen v. Trattnern . . . verlegten Bücher.* Vienna, 1798

Türk, Daniel Gottlob. *Klavierschule, oder Anweisung zum Klavierspielen.* Leipzig and Halle: A. A. Heydeloff, 1789. Tr. Raymond H. Haggh as *School of Clavier Playing.* Lincoln and London: University of Nebraska Press, 1982

Twittenhoff, Wilhelm. *Die musiktheoretischen Schriften Joseph Riepels (1709–1782) als Beispiel einer anschaulicher Musiklehre.* Halle: Buchdruckerei des Waisenhauses G. m.b. H., 1934

Vogler, Georg Joseph. *Tonwissenschaft und Tonsetzkunst.* Mannheim: Kurfürstlichen Hofbuchdruckerei, 1776; rpt. Hildesheim and New York: Georg Olms, 1970

Wason, Robert W. *Viennese Harmonic Theory from Albrechtsberger to Schenker and Schoenberg.* Ann Arbor: UMI Research Press, 1982 and 1985

Wellek, René. *A History of Modern Criticism, 1750–1950.* Vol III. New Haven: Yale University Press, 1965

Wienerisches Diarium von Staats, vermischten und gelehrten Neuigkeiten. Vienna: Verlegt bey den von Ghelenschen Erben: Jan. 1773, Feb. 1774 and May 1775

"Wirkung." In *Wörterbuch der Literatur-Wissenschaft*, ed. Claus Träger. Leipzig: VEB Bibliographisches Institut, 1986

Wünsch, Marianne. "Wirkung und Rezeption." *Reallexikon der deutschen Literaturgeschichte*, ed. Klaus Kanzog and Achim Masser. 4 vols and index. Vol. IV. Berlin: Walter de Gruyter, 1984

Wurzbach, Constant von. *Biographisches Lexikon des Kaiserthums Österreich.* Vol. III. Vienna 1858; rpt. New York: Johnson Reprint Corporation, 1966

INDEX